LOW FODMAP COOKBOOK

400+ Easy and Delicious Recipes for your Digestive Health.
| 30-DAY MEAL PLAN and FOOD LIST Included

Suzanne Scarrett

suzannescarrett.com

Index

Acorn squash soup 106
Alfredo Peppered Shrimp 102
Almost Classic Hummus 146
Amaranth Breakfast 30
Antipasto on a Stick 47
Apple muffins 20
Apple Parfait 43
Apple, Berries, and Kale Smoothie 164
Asparagus couscous 78
Asparagus Pasta 137
Avocado and Sauerkraut 82
Avocado egg salad toast 37
Bacon-Jalapeño Egg Cups 31
Bagel, Salmon Cream Cheese 72
Baked Brie With Cranberry Chutney and Caramelized Pecans 79
Baked eggplant baba ganoush 138
Baked oatmeal cups 35
Baked Potato And Chicken Casserole 100
Baked rice with olives, feta and pomegranate 95
Baked Shrimp Mix 63
Baked Tortilla Chips 81
Balsamic Chicken 68
Balsamic Sesame Swordfish 58
Banana Almond Nice Cream 152
Banana Breakfast Pudding 44
Banana Coconut Nice Cream 149
Banana coconut oat breakfast cookies 15
Banana Cookie Dough Nice Cream 150
Banana Ice Cream 150
Banana Nut Boat 155
Banana oat waffles 41
Banana Smoothie 24
Banana strawberry popsicles 75
Banana Toast 31
Beef Bourguignon 98
Beef Stroganoff 99
Berries and Sea Moss Smoothie 163
Berry Banana Green Smoothie 162
Berry Compote 158
Berry Ginger Smoothie 37
Berry Smoothie 24
BLT omelet with blue cheese 40
Blueberry muffins 20
Blueberry Smoothie 162
Blueberry Sorbet 147
Breakfast Squash Bread 42
Breakfast Wrap 24
Broccoli Fritters 53
Broiled Spiced Orange 150
Browned-butter coconut pancakes 40
Buttercream Lactose-free Icing 152
Buttermilk oat pancakes 18
Candied Ginger Frosting 156
Candied Pumpkin Seeds 80
Caramel Sauce 149
Carrot and fennel soup 97
Carrot Cake Bites 81
Carrot Dip 146
Carrot Parsnip Chips 154
Carrot spread 77
Carrot Tomato Soup 83
Cheese-And-Herb Polenta Wedges With Watercress Salad 130
Cheesy Chicken Fritters 50
Cherry Almond Bake 45
Cherry tomato bruschetta 136
Chia almond butter pudding 76
Chia Breakfast Pudding With Cantaloupe 43
Chia Pudding 151
Chia Strawberry Popsicles 147
Chicken Alfredo Pasta Bake 51
Chicken and Butter Sauce 104
Chicken and Olives Salsa 66
Chicken Avocado and Raspberry Salad 85
Chicken ratatouille 87
Chicken Shawarma 68
Chicken Tacos 104
Chicken Tikka Skewers 130
Chicken wings platter 77
Chickpea Curry 108

Chickpea Salad Pitas 142
Chili Chicken Mix 67
Chili Coconut Crusted Fish 56
Chili Salmon With Cilantro Salad 57
Chive and Onion-Infused Dip 131
Chocolate Coconut Fudge Sauce 135
Chocolate coconut granola 15
Chocolate Dipping Sauce 134
Chocolate matcha balls 75
Chocolate mousse 78
Chocolate pancakes 15
Chocolate Truffles 153
Chocolate Zucchini Bread 124
Chocolate–peanut Butter Balls 154
Cilantro lime rice 96
Cinnamon Almond Crepes 24
Cinnamon Carrot Milkshake 163
Citrusy Salsa 146
Clams with Tomato Sauce 103
Coated Pecans 80
Coconut Chicken Rice Noodle 62
Coconut Cinnamon Popcorn 151
Coconut tofu curry 93
Coconut Whipped Cream 148
Coleslaw Salad 117
Corn Porridge With Maple and Raisins 23
Cornbread muffins 17
Couscous-avocado salad 113
Crab and Miso Soup 47
Cranberry Festive Water 161
Cranberry Orange Smoothie 25
Cranberry Sauce 134
Creamy Butternut Porridge 82
Creamy sweet potatoes and collards 111
Creamy yogurt banana bowls 77
Crispy Falafel 51
Croutons 118
Crunchy roasted chickpeas 71
Cucumber Salad 118
Cucumber Sesame Salad 85
Cucumbers with feta, mint, and sumac 136
Curry and Roasted Cauliflower 124
Dark Chocolate Dip 153
Dark Chocolate Glaze 156
Dark chocolate mousse 76
Dark Chocolate–covered Pretzels 154
Delicious Coconut Macaroons 21
Dijon Fish Fillets 65
Dragon fruit smoothie bowl 36
Duck and Orange Warm Salad 67
Dukkah-Crusted Snapper 57
Easy Cauliflower Rice 22
Easy Lemon Chicken 54
Easy salad wraps 79
Easy spaghetti squash 139
Easy Trail Mix 149
Easy zucchini patties 107
Egg Scramble 21
Egg Wraps 28
Eggplant Caviar 137
Eggs in Squash Rings 86
Falafel bites 116
Farro Cucumber-Mint Salad 111
Feta & spinach pita bake 142
Feta, Pumpkin, And Chive Fritters 129
Fish Wallpaper with Green Bean Salad 32
Flourless Banana Cinnamon Pancakes 29
Flourless Vegan Banana Peanut Butter Pancakes 29
Fluffy Blueberry Pancakes 121
Fluffy pancakes 39
Four cheese baked penne with greens and tomatoes 94
Freekeh, chickpea, and herb salad 117
French Oven Beef 99
French toast 25
Fried Codfish with Almonds 102
Fruit And Cheese Crostini 156
Fruit and Millet Breakfast 42
Fruit and Yogurt Parfait 22

Fruit Cobbler 158
Ginger and Spring Egg Drop Soup 83
Ginger Carrot Soup 120
Gingersnap granola 19
Glazed Bananas in Phyllo Nut Cups 72
Glazed Edamame 118
Golden Turmeric Milk 37
Greek Baklava 72
Greek Chicken Bites 103
Greek Pasta Salad 61
Greek Pork 105
Greek Tuna Salad Bites 74
Green Apple Salad with Garbanzo 34
Green beans, pine nuts 135
Green Hibiscus Smoothie 25
Green kiwi smoothie 38
Green Olive Tapenade 138
Grilled swordfish with tomato olive salsa 92
Ham and cheese strata 16
Harissa With Vegetable Noodles 110
Hash brown potatoes 41
Healthy & quick energy bites 77
Healthy Banana bread 19
Healthy Broccoli Muffins 22
Healthy coconut blueberry balls 71
Hearty Minestrone 125
Hearty Oatmeal 26
Herb-Stuffed Pork Loin Roast 55
Homemade Gravy 135
Immune Boosting Smoothie 26
Italian Breakfast Hash 44
Key Lime Pie 158
Kiwi Yogurt Freezer Bars 149
Lamb Casserole 99
Lamb curry 94
Lemon Butter Shrimp Over Vegetable Noodles 60
Lemon Chicken 68
Lemon Chicken Mix 68
Lemon poppy seed waffles 18
Lemon-Oregano Chicken Drumsticks 58
Lemony Feta and Sweet Potato Mash 84
Lettuce Tacos with Chicken to the Shepherd 33
Low Fodmap Carrot Cake Energy Balls 123
Low fodmap chili mac 88
Low fodmap cioppino 97
Low FODMAP Granola Bars With Peanut Prune Puree 123
Low Fodmap Hawaiian Toasties 59
Low FODMAP scampi 87
Low Fodmap Stuffing 55
Low Fodmap Tortillas 122
Low Fodmap Vegetable Stock 123
Low-Fodmap Brownies 144
Low-Fodmap Butterscotch 145
Low-Fodmap Carrot Juice 160
Low-Fodmap Cheese Bread 127
Low-Fodmap Cookies 145
Low-Fodmap Cucumber Bites 128
Low-Fodmap Cupcake 145
Low-Fodmap Green Smoothie 160
Low-Fodmap Lemon Bar 144
Low-Fodmap Lemonade 161
Low-Fodmap Salmon Cakes 129
Low-Fodmap Spring Rolls 128
Low-Fodmap Tomato Bruschetta 127
Low-Fodmap Tomato Juice 161
Low-Fodmap Turmeric, Ginger Lemon Juice 160
LowFodmap Carrot & Corn Fritters 59
Mango and Banana Smoothie 163
Maple Mustard Chicken With Rosemary 100
Maple pumpkin spice granola with pecans 17
Maple-Ginger Oatmeal 23
Margherita slices 79
Marinated Tuna Steak 65
Melon And Berry Compote 29
Melon And Yogurt Parfait 30
Mexican Breakfast Toast 43
Mexican Lime Chicken 47
Milky Oat 23
Minestrone 50
Mini frittatas 38
Minty Melon Mélange 149

Morning Sweet Bread 43
Moroccan Chicken 101
Mushroom Bacon 22
Mushroom omelet 18
Mustard Maple Sauce 133
One Pan Chicken Cacciatore 101
Orange Banana Alkaline Smoothie 164
Orange chicken and broccoli bowl 88
Orange Ginger Festive Water 161
Overnight eggnog French toast 16
Overnight oats and chia 39
Pad Thai Noodles 48
Pad Thai With Shrimps 62
Paleo Fudge 156
Pan-Fried Salmon With Salad 108
Pan-Fried Trout 73
Papaya Breakfast Boat 45
Paprika Calamari With Garden Salad 56
Parmesan barley risotto 140
Parmesan Coated Wings 48
Parmesan crusted flounder 94
Parmesan Potato Wedges 154
Pasta with basil, tomato & zucchini 106
Pasta With Salmon And Dill 60
Peach Compote 159
Peanut Butter and Banana Overnight Oats 26
Peanut Butter Bowl 29
Peanut Butter Green Smoothie 162
Pear Jam 157
Pecan Salmon Fillets 64
Penne with tahini sauce 140
Peppermint Patties 148
Pesto Eggs Rice Bowl 28
Pesto Pasta Salad 118
Pina Colada Bites 48
Pineapple-coconut Smoothie 28
Pineapple, Yogurt On Rice Cakes 152
Pistachio arugula salad 78
Poached eggs with lemon hollandaise sauce 39
Pork and Chestnuts Mix 105
Pork Rind Salmon Cakes 69
Pot beef stew 86
Potato eggplant curry 90
Potato Salad 121
Prosciutto-wrapped Cantaloupe 152
Pumpkin and Roast Pepper Hummus 132
Pumpkin Dip 132
Pumpkin Peanut Pudding 82
Pumpkin pie oatmeal 36
Quick Curry Casserole 101
Quick vegetable kebabs 116
Quinoa Salad 119
Quinoa Tofu Scramble 31
Quinoa with almonds and cranberries 115
Raspberry and Chard Smoothie 163
Raspberry Curd 157
Raw Pad Thai (With Zucchini Noodles) 125
Red Cabbage Sauerkraut 133
Refreshing strawberry popsicles 76
Rice Pudding 82
Roast beef hash 91
Roasted almonds 75
Roasted Broccoli 53
Roasted brussels sprouts and halloumi salad 112
Roasted Carrots 122
Roasted cherry tomato Caprese 139
Roasted eggplant salad 140
Roasted green beans 75
Roasted harissa carrots 136
Roasted Maple Carrots 53
Roasted Pepper Pasta 60
Roasted Pumpkin Seeds 151
Roasted red pepper hummus 137
Roasted vegetable mélange 113
Roasted veggies 140
Roasted Zucchini 119
Romaine wedge salad 112
Rosemary Beef Stew 52
Rosemary Pork Chops 69
Salmon and Broccoli 64
Salmon and Cabbage Hash 45

Salmon And Spinach 61
Salmon Apple Salad Sandwich 73
Salmon Balls 103
Salmon Cakes and Lemony Herb Aioli 84
Salmon with basil-caper pesto 88
Salted Caramel Fondue 150
Salty Cheese Fritters 141
Sausage Cheese Balls 80
Sautéed Zucchini 120
Savory Breakfast Bowl 41
Savory Chicken and Rice Muffins 49
Savory pistachio balls 75
Scrambled Eggs 30
Scrambled Tofu 27
Sheet Pan Egg in the Hole 35
Sheet Pan Steak Fajitas 34
Sheet Pan Tuscan Chicken 34
Sherry and Butter Prawns 102
Shrimp and Beans Salad 64
Shrimp and Lemon Sauce 63
Shrimp Pasta 65
Shrimp with Beans 52
Simple Zucchini Muffins 22
Smoked salmo and spinach frittata cups 36
Smoked Salmon & Cheese on Bread 73
Smoked Salmon Toast 141
Smoky Barbecue Sauce 133
Smoky Red Pepper Dressing 133
Spaghetti Bolognese 61
Spanakopita spinach pie 96
Spiced Tofu Bites 131
Spicy Chicken Drumsticks 56
Spinach Pasta 120
Steak And Potatoes Sheet Pan Meal 98
Steak With Olives and Mushrooms 105
Sticky pork ribs 89
Strawberry bread 21
Strawberry Gummies 147
Strawberry Ice Cream 148
Strawberry Sorbet 147
Strawberry Tart Filling 157
Stuffed Chicken Breasts 74
Stuffed Peaches 158
Stuffed red peppers with quinoa and zucchini 96
Summer Berry Smoothie 30
Summer Medley Parfait 46
Summer Popsicle 155
Sunflower Seed Butter 132
Sweet & Tangy Green Beans 54
Sweet And Savory Popcorn 151
Sweet and Sour Vegetable Noodles 111
Sweet Chili Sauce 134
Sweet Life Bowl 126
Sweet Potato Balls 108
Sweet potato chickpea buddha bowl 106
Sweet Potato Pudding 153
Sweet Potato Toast 27
Tapenade 81
Tartar Sauce 135

Tasty Blueberry Waffles 37
Tasty Ranch Potatoes 121
Tasty zucchini chips 71
Tender Lamb 69
Thai curry tofu and green beans 91
The Mediterranean baked chickpeas 116
Tomato and basil frittata 32
Tortellini in red pepper sauce 117
Traditional Hummus 132
Tropical Fruit Salad 28
Tropical Smoothie 162
Tuesday Tacos 49
Tuna Bowl With Kale 66
Tuna Noodle Casserole 63
Tuna With Vegetable Mix 65
Tuna, Lemongrass, And Basil Risotto Patties 130
Turkey burgers 89
Turkey Burgers with Spinach 83
Turkey Burgers with Spinach and Feta 49
Turkey Sausage Patties 27
Turkey shepherd's pie 92
Turkey Verde With Brown Rice 104
Turmeric Baked Chicken Breast 67
Turmeric Pineapple Smoothie 162
Vanilla Frosting 155
Vegetable Chips 120
Vegetable Noodle Miso Soup 85
Vegetable Noodles With Bolognese 109
Vegetable Noodles With Chicken 110
Vegetable Pasta 109
Vegetable soup Moroccan style 114
Veggie ramen miso soup 114
Veggie Variety 109
Walnut and Red Pepper Spread 138
Warm & soft-baked pears 76
Warm Lemon Tapioca Pudding 152
Water Melon Cucumber Smoothie 164
Whipped Cream 155
Whole roast fish 90
Worcestershire Pork Chops 69
Yummy cauliflower fritters 114
Zucchini crisp 107
Zucchini fries 115
Zucchini pasta 142
Zucchini pasta with mango-kiwi sauce 115

Suzanne Scarrett

Hi, I'm Suzanne. Thank you for purchasing my book.

I invite you immediately to visit my website, which I manage every day:

www.suzannescarrett.com

Every day I receive dozens of emails and many more personal requests for help.

I am genuinely happy and proud of everything my team and I can do and deliver to our customers.

You will find several recipes with images and articles about nutrition and health. Furthermore, I am at your complete disposal to receive any advice or request you want to write privately.

If you wish, you can also subscribe for free to my mailing list. I do not send spam, and your contact remains private.

To subscribe, scan the QR code with your smartphone.

Finally, you will also find a section to contact me privately if you wish.

All that remains is to wish you much joy and serenity by reading this book.

Thank you for purchasing my book.

Suzanne Scarrett

Introduction

Low FODMAP diets are designed to target the foods that can trigger irritable bowel syndrome and other gastrointestinal symptoms by reducing fiber intake.

These regimens are important for people with digestive disorders like IBS, Crohn's disease, ulcerative colitis, and diverticulitis. They were originally designed by Australian researchers who discovered that certain sugars in food aggravated the symptoms of these diseases. They reduced these foods from their own diets and then began recommending them to patients in need of relief from their chronic stomach problems.

Low FODMAP is low on dietary fiber. The most often recommended diet is used by the Monash health club, which encourages clients to eat a high intake of vegetables, fruits, eggs, and lean proteins (meat, fish, and chicken) to avoid constipation and other bowel symptoms. It also adheres to the low-fructan Diet Action Group (DAG) program in which all fructose-containing foods are avoided.

The World Health Organization has been studying the effects of FODMAPs on digestive disorders, including IBS, within its research on functional gastrointestinal disorders. It reported that easy-to-digest foods have a larger place in IBS diet plans than previously thought.

The low FODMAP diet encourages eating more foods with high water content. This includes lots of fresh fruits and vegetables. Aim for five to nine portions of fruit and vegetables a day, plus three servings each of legumes, nuts, and seeds.

The diet does not specify what types of protein should be eaten, other than to avoid processed meats such as preserved ham or bacon. For those who don't eat meat or fish, eggs are a good protein source. Legumes include lentils, chickpeas, and baked beans, while nuts include almonds, peanuts, and walnuts. Seeds include pumpkin, sunflower, and sesame.

When following a low FODMAP diet, people eat more often and smaller meals. Although many of the recipes in this book are high in fiber, this is not required.

You can check whether or not a food is low FODMAP by looking at the ingredient list on an ingredient label - if ingredients are listed, and they contain one or more of the following: apples, apricots, bananas, berries, cherries, citrus fruit (lemons and limes), grapes, guavas, honeydew melon (seeded varieties only), kiwifruit, mangoes, and papayas. If a packaged food contains any of these ingredients, then it must be low FODMAP.

The Monash Health Club also recommends using a side effect checklist to help you monitor your progress. This includes things such as: waking up feeling rested and not bloated, experiencing fewer symptoms during the day, using fewer antidiarrheal medications, and needing fewer laxatives once you've completed the diet for at least one month.

Another low FODMAP way of monitoring the diet is by checking the pH of your urine. When following a completely low FODMAP diet, it is important to drink enough water and to have enough fluids throughout the day to avoid constipation. This can be checked by measuring your urine pH.

The diet was developed by researchers at Monash University in Australia, who began working on the diet in 2002. The current version of the low FODMAP diet is low on fiber and high in water-rich foods such as vegetables and fruits. These foods include fructose and fructans, which are fructose-containing carbohydrates that are poorly absorbed and produce chronic gastrointestinal symptoms when consumed in large quantities.

Low FODMAP diets have been modified to meet the needs of people with different digestive disorders such as IBS. This includes patients with IBS-C and IBS-D.

What is FODMAP diet and IBS

FODMAP is an acronym that stands for:

FERMENTABLE

Bacteria in the large intestine ferment these poorly absorbed carbohydrates (bowel).

OLIGOSACCHARIDES

Saccharide means sugar, and oligo means little. So they are individual sugars that have been linked to form a chain.

The two main oligosaccharides that are FODMAPs are:

Fructans are fructose sugars that have been linked together to form a chain (with glucose at the very end).

Galactooligosaccharides (GOS) are oligosaccharides made up of galactose sugars bonded together at the end with fructose and glucose.

DISACCHARIDES

Saccharide means sugar, and di means two. So they are two separate sugars that have been combined to form a double sugar.

Lactose, a FODMAP disaccharide composed of an individual glucose sugar connected to an individual galactose sugar, is the most significant FODMAP disaccharide.

MONOSACCHARIDES

Saccharide means sugar, and mono signifies one. So they are sugars in their own right.

Excess fructose is a key FODMAP monosaccharide. Fructose does not have to be avoided entirely. On the low fodmap diet, only foods that contain more fructose than glucose (also known as "excess fructose") should be avoided.

An item is acceptable for the low fodmap diet if it contains more glucose than fructose or if glucose and fructose are present in equal ("balanced") proportions.

If a food (for example, a piece of fruit) contains more glucose than fructose or equal amounts of fructose and glucose, it is suitable to eat; however, only one piece of suitable fruit should be consumed at a time. This doesn't mean you can only have one piece of fruit per day! You can have several but spread them out so that you only have one per sitting.

AND POLYOLS

A polyol is a sugar molecule with an alcohol side chain attached. Polyols are also known as sugar alcohols but don't worry; they won't get you drunk!

Sorbitol and mannitol are the two polyols found most frequently in foods.

Irritable Bowel Syndrome

Irritable bowel syndrome (IBS) is a common gastrointestinal disorder that affects around 15% of the population. Males and ladies of various ages are affected. Excess flatulence, stomach bloating, distension, pain, or discomfort, and changed bowel habits are all symptoms (diarrhea, constipation, or a combination of both). The intensity of these symptoms varies from day to day and week to week. Because IBS is diagnosed based on the pattern of symptoms, it's critical to rule out other disorders with similar symptoms, such as celiac disease and inflammatory bowel disease (IBD), which can potentially be mistaken for IBS. Before starting a low-FODMAP or gluten-free diet, everyone with IBS symptoms should be evaluated for these illnesses, so if you haven't already, talk to your doctor about getting tested. However, keep in mind that IBS and other digestive diseases can coexist.

FODMAPs cause IBS

FODMAPs all have the same characteristics:

1. They have a low absorption rate in the small intestine. This implies that many of these molecules skip past the small intestine without being absorbed instead of traveling straight to the colon. This is due to their inability to be broken down or their delayed absorption. Our capacity to digest and absorb various FODMAPs varies from person to person: Fructose absorption varies from person to person; some people do not produce enough lactase (the enzyme needed to break down lactose), and the capacity to absorb polyols (which are the wrong shape to pass easily through the small intestinal lining) also varies. Fructans and galactooligosaccharides (GOS) are poorly absorbed in everyone since none of us can digest them.

2. They are little molecules that are eaten in high doses. The body tries to "dilute" tiny, concentrated molecules by pumping water into the gastrointestinal system when they are poorly absorbed. Extra fluid in the gastrointestinal system can produce diarrhea and interfere with the gut's muscular activity.

3. They're "quick food" for the bacteria that exist in the big intestine naturally. Billions of bacteria live in the large intestine (and the bottom section of the small intestine). If chemicals aren't absorbed in the small intestine, they make their way to the large intestine. These food molecules are seen as rapid food by the bacteria that reside there, and they are swiftly broken down, releasing hydrogen, carbon dioxide, and methane gases. The length of the chain determines how rapidly the molecules are fermented: In comparison to fiber, which comprises considerably longer chain molecules known as polysaccharides, oligosaccharides, and simple sugars ferment relatively quickly. In most meals, many forms of FODMAPs are present. Their effects are cumulative since they all produce distension in the same way until they reach the lower small intestine and colon. This indicates that the degree of intestinal distension can be determined by the overall quantity of FODMAPs taken rather than the amount of anyone FODMAP. Suppose someone who has trouble digesting lactose and absorbing fructose consumes a meal with some lactose. In that case, fructans, polyols, GOS, and fructose, the effect on the intestine will be $1 + 1 + 1 + 1 + 1 = 5$ times larger than if they ate the same quantity of simply one of that FODMAPs. As a result, we must take all FODMAPs into account while changing our diet.

How the diet works

Implementing Low-FODMAP Diet

If you've been diagnosed with IBS, or if you've had bloating and abdominal discomfort without a change in bowel habits, or if you and/or your doctor believe you should follow the low fodmap diet for another reason, your first step should be to contact a registered dietitian who specializes in gastrointestinal nutrition. That isn't to argue that following a low fodmap diet is impossible, but it will necessitate major dietary and lifestyle modifications. You'll need to understand your illness, which foods are appropriate, and what will happen if you don't stick to the diet. To keep your symptoms under control, we recommend sticking to the low fodmap diet for at least two months and avoiding any FODMAPs. Whether your symptoms have improved after this period, slowly reintroduce one FODMAP group at a time to determine if you can handle it. This is easiest to accomplish with the assistance of a qualified dietitian, who will examine your symptoms and recommend the best course of action, but for additional information on how to do it yourself and meal plans, go here.

At first, you may find certain components of the low fodmap diet to be overwhelming. Each morning, you'll have to ask yourself the following questions: What will I be doing today? Is it necessary for me to bring food? Should I eat something before I leave? Will there be something I can eat there? If you have to follow a specific diet, it can begin to control your thinking, and some individuals are better at dealing with this than others. Seek therapy or other assistance if you're having problems adapting. Here are some more considerations to keep in mind while creating a low fodmap diet to your specific needs:

Consider all the FODMAP groups. They all have the potential to cause bowel distension and other IBS symptoms.

No one can absorb fructans, GOS, or polyols well. This means you should always avoid them when first implementing the low fodmap diet.

Only some people have lactose or fructose malabsorption. A breath hydrogen test will tell you whether or not you need to limit lactose or excess fructose in your diet.

Some FODMAPs cause more trouble in some people than others. This depends on the proportions of each FODMAP in their diet, how well or poorly they absorb fructose and lactose, and how sensitive they are to each FODMAP, which could be related to which bacteria they have in their bowel. You'll learn which FODMAPs give you the most trouble through a combination of clinical tests and trials in your diet.

How the diet can help you

Primarily, the benefit of a Low FODMAP diet is to alleviate the symptoms of IBS. However, there are other incidental benefits of following this diet. Some of these include the following:

- Often, people lose weight on the Low FODMAP diet, as it eliminates a great deal of starchy and sugary foods, two main culprits in weight gain. It also reduces the bloating that is one of the main symptoms of IBS, alleviating discomfort and helping you feel slimmer in your clothes in general.

- It can also be helpful in managing other conditions in which consumption of sugar is discouraged, such as Type 2 diabetes. This can improve overall health outcomes, leading to reduced risk of heart disease and stroke.

- Some studies have shown that a Low FODMAP diet can also be beneficial for more serious gastrointestinal disorders such as Crohn's disease.

- It can free you of the discomfort that impairs your quality of life. Many people who suffer with IBS are reluctant to engage in many everyday activities, never knowing when an attack might require an urgent bathroom break. The Low FODMAP diet can give you back that freedom and confidence.

- A Low FODMAP diet has also been shown to reduce histamines, linked to allergic reactions. People who follow a Low FODMAP diet have often discovered allergic sensitivities to certain foods, which they can then avoid in future.

- Finally, following the Low FODMAP diet can help those with IBS improve their mood and increase their energy levels, as their general quality of life continues to get better. As symptoms improve or dissipate altogether, reports of anxiety and depression significantly decrease.

Symptoms of IBS

The symptoms of IBS are wide-ranging, as mentioned above, but in order for these symptoms to be considered the chronic condition of IBS, they must present over long periods of time. Just about everyone experiences some of these symptoms on occasion, if they become regular issues or constant problems, however, then IBS is the likely culprit. Again, do consult a physician when trying to determine a diagnosis. Symptoms can include the following:

Abdominal pain, such as cramping associated with a bowel movement.

- Diarrhea that occurs regularly.

- Constipation that occurs regularly.
- Often, both diarrhea and constipation are regular issues.
- Changes in appearance or frequency of bowel movements.
- Increased gas.

Bloating: this last symptom is the one of the most frequently reported among many sufferers of IBS and can be greatly improved through dietary changes for most.

If you have any of the following symptoms, especially if they persist, you should consult your physician immediately:

- Rectal bleeding
- Difficulty swallowing
- Diarrhea during the night
- Unexplained vomiting
- Anemia from iron deficiency
- Unexpected or unexplained weight loss
- Persistent pain without relief from passing gas or bowel movement

Causes of IBS

While it is probably unclear as to what exactly causes IBS, there is agreement that some particular factors seem to play a role. In addition, there are triggers—distinct from causes—that can make IBS flare up. Understanding these underlying causes and potential triggers of IBS can help us make the necessary lifestyle changes to confront and manage this uncomfortable condition. They include the following:

- **Intestinal contractions** seem to play a role in most IBS cases. If the muscles in the large intestine contract too hard or too long, this can cause gas and bloating, sometimes diarrhea. If the muscles contract too weakly or infrequently, this can slow the passage of food through the digestive system and can cause hard stools that may be painful to pass.
- **The nervous system** also appears to be a factor in IBS. The nerves of the digestive system are sensitive, and if they are damaged or somehow not communicating effectively with the brain, this can signal the body to overreact to normal digestive functioning. People who have had surgeries that affect the intestines or who have taken medications that impact the digestive system (such as opioids) can be at risk for developing IBS and other related disorders, such as SIBO and gastroparesis.
- There is some indication that **severe infections** can lead to IBS, as well. If you have experienced gastroenteritis, for example, you could be at risk for developing IBS. In addition, excessive bacterial growth in the intestines (as seen in SIBO) can also occur in or lead to IBS.
- The **microbiomes** that are housed in the gut can also be a cause of IBS symptoms. Some research has shown that the gut microbes in those with IBS differ from those who have healthy digestive systems. Many proponents of probiotics suggest that they can help with this imbalance in the gut microbiome, though there have, as of yet, been no definitive studies proving this.
- IBS can also be triggered by **stress**. Some studies have shown a correlation between lots of stress in early childhood and the development of IBS later in life, as well. Either way, stress seems to be a significant factor in triggering IBS symptoms.

- **Poor sleep** can also be a factor that leads to increased experience of symptoms. Stress and poor sleep, of course, often go hand in hand.
- If you have IBS symptoms, you might also want to be tested for allergies: **food allergies** can sometimes be an underlying cause of IBS or a triggering factor for symptoms.
- Finally, many people have discovered that a **diet high in "FODMAP" foods** (defined in detail below) can trigger or worsen the symptoms of IBS. This is most likely why you are reading this book today!

Be sure to procure a diagnosis with your doctor before determining that you have IBS. While there isn't any one definitive test to determine whether or not you have IBS, your doctor will be well-equipped to take your medical history, current complaints, and recommend any further tests, such as a colonoscopy or endoscopy. Some symptoms of IBS can actually be related to other, more serious health conditions, so it is important to follow up with your physician.

Low FODMAP Diet Food List

There are various methods in which you can arrange foods by level of FODMAPs, either by type of food (vegetable, fruit, meat) or by category of FODMAP (lactose, fructose, glucose). Both of these methods have advantages and disadvantages. In the first case, simply listing foods is simple and straightforward; you know what you can eat, and what you should avoid, especially in the restriction stage of the diet. However, this kind of list doesn't necessarily indicate what other foods belong in that category, making the process of reintroduction longer. Remember that when you reintroduce a food, if it causes symptoms, then you should avoid it and other foods within that category. Thus, in the second case, you can clearly see what foods are related, making the process of reintroduction quicker. Ultimately, however, you will be the best judge of what you can and cannot eat in order to manage your IBS symptoms. There is no overarching list of foods that work for each individual. What follows here are general lists of foods that should be allowed, allowed only in small portions, and avoided entirely in the restriction stage of the diet. Foods to be avoided, then later tested for reintroduction, are listed both by category of FODMAP and type of food. These food lists are not exhaustive, but they can help you get started right away. For some more detailed charts, check out IBS Diets which is managed by physicians and dieticians or Lauren Lund's list, a registered dietician who consults with Monash University.

Allowed: Low FODMAP Foods
Generally speaking, you should build your diet around Low FODMAP foods such as these:

- Eggs
- Meat, other than sausages or other cured meats which often contain sugars
- Certain cheeses, including cheddar and feta
- Non-dairy milks, such as almond
- Whole grains, like rice, oats, and quinoa
- Vegetables, including potatoes, eggplant, cucumber, and zucchini
- Fruits, including strawberries, blueberries, grapes, and oranges

Allowed in Small Portions: Moderate FODMAP Foods
These foods list can be eaten in limited amounts, though you might want to consider avoiding them altogether during the restriction stage of the diet:

- Avocados and tomatoes
- Broccoli and cabbage (cruciferous vegetables)
- Fruits in general have lots of fructose, so stick with those listed above and cantaloupe or melon
- Sweet potatoes

It must also be noted that, in most cases, it is more important to regulate the portion size of moderate FODMAP foods rather than avoid altogether. In addition, there is some disagreement over which moderate foods should be allowed, especially in the restriction stage of the diet.

Avoid: High FODMAP Foods

These foods should be strictly avoided during the restriction stage of the Low FODMAP diet, and reintroduced slowly to determine if they trigger symptoms:

- Foods high in lactose, including dairy-based milk, yogurt, ice cream, and cottage cheese
- Foods high in fructose, including asparagus, sugar snap peas, apples, pears, and honey
- Foods high in fructans, including onions, garlic, artichokes, wheat, beans, and lentils
- Foods high in polyols, including mushrooms, cauliflower, blackberries, and cherries. This group also includes artificial sweeteners such as sorbitol, mannitol, and xylitol. These sweeteners have been known to bother the digestive systems of people who do not even have IBS.

Basic recipes

1. Banana coconut oat breakfast cookies

Preparation time: 10 minutes | **Cooking time:** 20 minutes | **Serving:** 5
Ingredients:

- Old-fashioned oats – one cup   All-purpose flour – half cup, low fodmap
- Dried banana chips – 1 ½ cup, chopped Unsweetened broad coconut chips or flakes – half cup
- Chia seeds – two tbsp   Ground flax seeds – two tbsp
- Cinnamon – one tsp   Baking powder – half tsp
- Salt – ¼ tsp   Very ripe banana – one, mashed
- Maple syrup – ¼ cup   Vegetable oil – ¼ cup
- Vanilla extract – one tsp

Directions:
1. Preheat the oven to 325 degrees Fahrenheit.
2. Line a half-sheet baking pan lined with parchment paper and keeps it aside.
3. Add salt, baking powder, cinnamon, flax seeds, chia seeds, coconut, banana chips, flour, and oats into the mixing bowl. Whisk until combined. Make a well in the middle of the mixture.
4. Whisk the vanilla, oil, maple syrup, and mashed banana into the bowl.
5. Place over dry mixture and fold it very well. Place ¼ cup of mixture (ten cookies) onto the pan. Bake for fifteen to twenty minutes.
6. Let cool the pan on the rack.

Nutrition: Calories; 178kcal, carbohydrates; 21g, protein; 2g, fat; 10g

2. Chocolate coconut granola

Preparation time: 5 minutes | **Cooking time:** 30 minutes | **Serving:** 8
Ingredients:

- Old-fashioned rolled oats – four cups Quinoa flakes – one cup
- Salt – ¼ tsp   Vegetable oil – 2/3 cup
- 1/3 cup   Maple syrup – 1/3 cup
- Vanilla extract – one tsp   Unsweetened coconut flakes/chips – ¾ cup, shredded
- Cacao nibs – half cup

Directions:
1. Preheat the oven to 325 degrees Fahrenheit.
2. Rimmed baking sheet pan and keep it aside.
3. Stir all ingredients with a wooden spoon and combine them well.
4. Place it into the pan and bake for fifteen minutes.
5. Then, toss granola with a big spatula and bake for fifteen minutes more.
6. Let cool the pan onto the rack.

Nutrition: Calories; 585kcal, Carbohydrates; 79g, Protein; 14g, Fat; 24g

3. Chocolate pancakes

Preparation time: 10 minutes | **Cooking time:** 10 minutes | **Serving:** 4
Ingredients:

- All-purpose flour – 1 ¼ cups, low Fodmap   Cocoa or Black Cocoa – 1/3 cup
- Glucose syrup – 1/3 cup
- Baking powder – 1 ½ tsp
- Salt – half tsp   Lactose-free milk – 1 1/3 cups

- Unsalted butter – four tbsp, melted
- Eggs – two, big
- Vanilla extract – one tsp   Instant espresso powder – half tsp, optional

Directions:

1. Add salt, baking powder, glucose syrup, cocoa, and flour into the mixing bowl. Whisk until combined well. Make a well in the middle of the mixture.
2. Whisk espresso powder, vanilla, eggs, butter, and milk in another bowl.
3. Place wet mixture over dry mixture and whisk until smooth.
4. Next, heat the non-stick pan and coat with nonstick cooking spray.
5. Place three tbsp of butter and cook over medium flame for one minute.
6. When golden brown, flip over and cook for one minute more.
7. Top with pure maple syrup, salted caramel sauce, or lactose-free ice cream.

Nutrition: Calories; 111kcal, carbohydrates; 16g, protein; 2g, fat; 4g

4. Ham and cheese strata

Preparation time: 15 minutes | **Cooking time:** 40 minutes | **Serving:** 16

Ingredients:

- Eggs – ten, big
- Lactose-free milk or half-and-half – two cups
- Dijon mustard – two tsp
- Dried thyme – one half tsp
- Kosher salt and ground black pepper – optional
- French bread – four cups, cubed, low fodmap, gluten-free
- Ham – eight ounces, diced
- Shredded cheese – eight ounces, cheddar, gruyere, monterey jack
- Cherry tomatoes – half dry pint, halved

Directions:

1. Whisk the eggs, half-and-half or milk into the bowl.
2. Add mustard and thyme and whisk it well. Sprinkle with pepper and salt.

3. Then, fold in bread cubes. Let sit until the oven is preheated.
4. Preheat the oven to 350 degrees Fahrenheit. Let coat the inner side of the casserole dish with non-stick spray.
5. Then, fold tomatoes, cheeses, and ham into the strata mixture and place it into the pan. Place it into the oven and bake for thirty-five to forty-five minutes.
6. Let cool the pan onto the rack for five minutes.
7. Serve and enjoy!

Nutrition: Calories; 163kcal, carbohydrates; 7g, protein; 12g, fat; 10g

5. Overnight eggnog French toast

Preparation time: 5 minutes | **Cooking time:** 40 minutes | **Serving:** 3

Ingredients:

1. White bread – 1 ½ pounds, low fodmap, gluten-free, sliced   Eggs – eight, big
2. Lactose - 3,5/2 – 2 ¾ cups
3. Agave syrup ¾ cup
4. Whiskey – two tbsp
5. Vanilla extract – one tbsp
6. Freshly ground nutmeg – one ts x
7. Cinnamon – half tsp
8. Optional   Maple syrup

Directions:

1. Firstly, coat the inner side of the oven-safe dish with non-stick cooking spray. Place the slices of bread in a slightly overlapping fashion.
2. Whisk eggs into the bowl until combined well. Add Agave syrup and half-and-half and whisk it well.
3. Add whiskey, half tsp nutmeg, and vanilla and whisk it well.
4. Place mixture over the bread. Cover the dish with plastic wrap. Place it into the refrigerator overnight.
5. Sprinkle bread with cinnamon and nutmeg.
6. Preheat the oven to 350 degrees Fahrenheit.
7. Bake it for forty to fifty minutes until

golden brown. Remove from the oven. Sprinkle with Agave syrup-

8. Top with maple syrup.

Nutrition: Calories; 232kcal, carbohydrates; 28g, protein; 6g, fat; 11g

6. Maple pumpkin spice granola with pecans

Preparation time: 5 minutes | **Cooking time:** 40 minutes | **Serving:** 22

Ingredients:

- Old-fashioned rolled oats – three cups gluten-free
- Pecan – ¾ cup, halves
- Cinnamon – two tsp
- Ginger – one tsp
- Nutmeg – ¼ tsp
- Salt – 1/8 tsp
- Pinch cloves
- Pure pumpkin purée – half cup
- Maple syrup – 1/3 cup
- Vegetable oil – 1/3 cup
- Glucose syrup – ¼ cup
- Vanilla – one tsp
- Dried cranberries – half cup, optional

Directions:

1. Preheat the oven to 325 degrees Fahrenheit.
2. Rimmed baking sheet and keep it aside.
3. Add cloves, salt, nutmeg, ginger, cinnamon, oats, and pecans into the mixing bowl and combine well.
4. Whisk the vanilla, glucose syrup, oil, maple syrup, pumpkin puree in another bowl and mix well.
5. Stir the wet mixture and dry mixture with a wooden spoon until combined well.
6. Place it into the oven and bake for twenty minutes.
7. Toss granola around with a spatula and bake for twenty minutes more.
8. Let cool the pan on the rack.
9. Serve and enjoy!

Nutrition: Calories; 121kcal, Carbohydrates; 13g, Protein; 2g, Fat; 7g

7. Cornbread muffins

Preparation time: 10 minutes | **Cooking time:** 20 minutes | **Serving:** 12

Ingredients:

- Lactose-free whole milk – 1 ½ cups
- Lemon juice – one tbsp + one tsp
- Yellow cornmeal – 1 ¾ cups, fine stone-ground
- All-purpose flour – one cup, low fodmap, gluten-free
- Corn syrup – 1/3 cup
- Baking powder – one tbsp + one tsp
- Salt – one tsp
- Unsalted butter – four tbsp, melted
- Neutral flavored oil – ¼ cup canola or vegetable
- Eggs – two, big

Directions:

1. Preheat the oven to 400 degrees Fahrenheit.
2. Let coat twelve muffins well with non-stick cooking spray. Keep it aside.
3. Add lemon juice and milk into the bowl. Stir well. Let sit for five minutes.
4. Whisk the salt, baking powder, corn syrup, flour, and cornmeal into the mixing bowl. Make a well in the middle of the mixture and keep it aside.
5. After that, whisk the eggs, vegetable oil, and melted butter into the milk until combined well. Place this wet mixture into the well of the dry mixture and whisk it well.
6. Divide the mixture into the pan and bake for fourteen to eighteen minutes. Let cool the pan for two minutes on the rack.
7. Serve and enjoy!

Nutrition: Calories; 242kcal, carbohydrates; 32g, protein; 4g, fat; 11g

8. Mushroom omelet

Preparation time: 5 minutes | **Cooking time:** 10 minutes | **Serving:** 1

Ingredients:
- Eggs – two, big
- Water – one tsp
- Kosher salt and ground black pepper– to taste
- Unsalted butter – two tbsp
- Cleaned oyster mushrooms – one cup, chopped

Directions:
1. Whisk the water and eggs into the mixing bowl. Sprinkle with pepper and salt. Keep it aside.
2. Add half of the butter into the skillet and cook over medium flame until bubbly.
3. Then, add mushrooms and cook for few minutes until softened.
4. Sprinkle with pepper and salt. Scrape into the bowl. Wipe out the skillet and add butter to it and melt over medium flame until bubbly.
5. Place egg mixture and cook over medium flame until set.
6. Place reserved mushrooms over half of the omelet. Fold one half of the omelet over another half of omelet.
7. Transfer omelet to the serving plate.
8. Garnish with remaining mushrooms.

Nutrition: Calories; 397kcal, Carbohydrates; 5g, Protein; 16g, Fat; 33g

9. Lemon poppy seed waffles

Preparation time: 5 minutes | **Cooking time:** 10 minutes | **Serving:** 6

Ingredients:
- All-purpose flour – two cups, low fodmap, gluten-free
- Corn syrup – two tbsp
- Baking powder – one tbsp + one tsp
- Poppy seeds – one tbsp + one tsp
- Lemon zest – one tbsp
- Salt – one tsp
- Lactose-free whole milk – 1 ½ cups
- Unsalted butter – half cup, cut into pieces
- Eggs – two, big

Directions:
1. Preheat the waffle iron. Preheat the oven to 200 degrees Fahrenheit.
2. Whisk the salt, lemon zest, poppy seeds, baking powder, corn syrup, and flour into the mixing bowl. Combine it well. Make a well in the middle of the mixture and keep it aside.
3. Add butter and milk into the saucepan and heat it over a low-medium flame. Whisk it well.
4. Place it into the mixing bowl. Let cool it.
5. Place butter and milk into the microwave until butter is melted.
6. Let cool it. Whisk eggs into the milk or butter mixture until combined well. Place it into the dry mixture and whisk it well until combined.
7. Let coat waffle maker with non-stick cooking spray.
8. Place batter into the waffle maker and cook for four minutes until golden brown or crispy.
9. Keep waffles warm in the oven at 200 degrees Fahrenheit.
10. Top with maple syrup.

Nutrition: Calories; 395kcal, carbohydrates; 48g, protein; 7g, fat; 19g

10. Buttermilk oat pancakes

Preparation time: 5 minutes | **Cooking time:** 10 minutes | **Serving:** 4
Ingredients:
- Lactose free milk – one cup
- Lemon juice – one tbsp
- Egg – one, big
- Vegetable oil or melted unsalted butter – two tbsp
- All-purpose flour – six tbsp, low fodmap, gluten-free
- Old-fashioned oats – one cup
- Glucose syrup – one tbsp

- Baking powder – half tsp
- Baking soda – half tsp
- Salt – half tsp

Directions:
1. Add lemon juice and milk into the measuring cup. Let rest for five minutes.
2. During this, whisk the oil and egg into the mixing bowl. Add milk to it and whisk it well.
3. Add salt, baking soda, baking powder, glucose syrup, oats, and flour into the blender or food processor and blend until smooth.
4. Place dry mixture over the wet mixture and whisk it well until combined well.
5. Heat the non-stick pan and coat with non-stick cooking spray.
6. Place ¼ cup of batter into the pan and cook over medium flame for one to two minutes.
7. Flip over and cook for one minute until golden brown.
8. Top with maple syrup and roasted strawberries.

Nutrition: Calories; 387kcal, carbohydrates; 56g, protein; 12g, fat; 13g

11. Healthy Banana bread
Preparation time: 10 minutes | **Cooking Time:** 1 hour | **Serving:** 14
Ingredients:
- All-purpose flour – 1 ½ cups, low fodmap, gluten-free
- Baking soda – one tsp
- Salt – half tsp
- Vegetable oil – 1/3 cup
- Corn syrup – 2/4 cup
- Eggs – two, big
- Fork-mashed ripe banana – 1 ½ cups
- Vanilla extract – one tsp
- Toasted walnut or pecan halves – one cup, chopped

Directions:
1. Preheat the oven to 350 degrees Fahrenheit.
2. Let coat the loaf pan with non-stick cooking spray.
3. Whisk the salt, baking soda, and flour into the bowl and keep it aside.
4. Whisk the corn syrup and oil in the medium bowl until combined well.
5. Whisk eggs until incorporated. Add vanilla and banana and whisk it well.
6. Place wet ingredients over dry ingredients and whisk it well.
7. Fold in chocolate morsels or walnuts.
8. Place batter into the loaf pan and bake for fifty minutes to one hour.
9. When done, cool the pan on the rack for ten minutes.
10. Serve and enjoy!

Nutrition: Calories; 441kcal, carbohydrates; 76g, protein; 11g, fat; 14g

12. Gingersnap granola
Preparation time: 5 minutes | **Cooking time:** 30 minutes | **Serving:** 24
Ingredients:
- Old-fashioned rolled oats – three cups
- Quinoa flakes – one cup
- Neutral flavored vegetable oil – 2/3 cup, safflower, canola
- Maple syrup – 1/3 cup
- Agave syrup – 1/3 cup
- Gingerroot – three tbsp, grated, peeled
- Dried ground ginger – one tbsp
- Coriander – ¼ tsp
- Cinnamon – ¼ tsp
- Salt – ¼ tsp
- Almonds – half cup, sliced, blanched

Directions:
1. Preheat the oven to 325 degrees Fahrenheit. Rimmed half-sheet pan.
2. Mix the salt, cinnamon, coriander, ginger, gingerroot, agave syrup, maple syrup, oil, oats, and quinoa flakes into the mixing bowl. Combined well.
3. Fold in sliced almonds. Place granola onto the rimmed baking sheet.

4. Place it into the oven and bake for fifteen minutes.
5. Stir it well and again bake for twelve to fifteen minutes more until golden brown.
6. Let cool the pan on the rack.
7. Serve and enjoy!

Nutrition: Calories; 227kcal, carbohydrates; 32g, protein; 5g, fat; 9g

13. Apple muffins

Preparation time: 5 minutes | **Cooking time:** 20 minutes | **Serving:** 12
Ingredients:
Topping:
- Glucose syrup– three tbsp
- All-purpose flour – two tbsp, low fodmap, gluten-free
- Unsalted butter – two tbsp, softened
- Cinnamon – half tsp
- Pinch of salt

Muffins:
- Lactose-free whole milk – one cup
- Lemon juice – one tbsp
- Neutral flavored vegetable oil – 1/3 cup
- Glucose syrup – half cup
- Egg – one, big   Vanilla extract – one tsp
- All-purpose flour – 2 ¼ cups, low fodmap, gluten-free
- Baking powder – one tsp
- Baking soda – one tsp   Salt – half tsp
- Cinnamon – ¾ tsp
- Cloves – ¼ tsp
- Nutmeg – ¼ tsp
- Pink Lady or Granny Smith apple – one, cored and diced

Directions:
1. Preheat the oven to 350 degrees Fahrenheit.
2. Coat the inner side of the twelve muffin wells with non-stick cooking spray. Keep it aside.

For the topping:
1. Stir all topping ingredients into the bowl and combine it well. Keep it aside.

2. For the muffins:
3. Mix the lemon juice and milk into the bowl. Let sit for five minutes.
4. Whisk the vanilla, egg, glucose syrup, and oil into the bowl until smooth.
5. Next, whisk the spices, salt, soda, baking powder, and flour in another bowl. Make a well in the middle of the mixture. Place wet mixture in it. Then, fold in chopped apples.
6. Place mixture into the pan. Top with topping over muffins.
7. Place it into the oven and bake for fifteen to twenty minutes.
8. Let cool it for five minutes.
9. Serve and enjoy!

Nutrition: Calories; 236kcal, carbohydrates; 37g, protein; 3g, fat; 9g

14. Blueberry muffins

Preparation time: 10 minutes | **Cooking time:** 25 minutes | **Serving:** 12
Ingredients:
- All-purpose flour – two cups, low fodmap, gluten-free
- Baking powder – two tsp
- Salt – half tsp   Unsalted butter – half cup, softened and cut into pieces
- Corn syrup – one cup + two tbsp
- Vanilla extract – two tsp
- Eggs – two, big
- Lactose-free whole milk – half cup
- Fresh blueberries – 2 ¼ cups

Directions:
1. Preheat the oven to 400 degrees Fahrenheit.
2. Let coat twelve muffin wells with non-stick cooking spray. Keep it aside.
3. Whisk the salt, baking powder, and flour in the medium bowl. Keep it aside.
4. Next, beat butter using an electric mixer on medium-high speed for two to three minutes until creamy.
5. Then, add one cup of corn syrup and beat for two minutes.

6. Next, add vanilla and eggs and beat them well.
7. Add flour mixture in three additions.
8. Break 2/3 cup of blueberries with a potato masher, or you can use a fork.
9. Fold in muffin batter. Place batter into the muffin pans and sprinkle with two tbsp corn syrup.
10. Place it into the oven and bake for twenty to twenty-five minutes.
11. Let cool it on the rack for five minutes.
12. Serve and enjoy!

Nutrition: Calories; 271kcal, carbohydrates; 44g, protein; 2g, fat; 9g

15. Strawberry bread

Preparation time: 10 minutes | **Cooking time:** 45 minutes | **Serving:** 12

Ingredients:

- Frozen unsweetened strawberries – five ounces, thawed
- Neutral flavored vegetable oil – 2/3 cup
- Eggs – two, big, beaten
- Cinnamon – 1 ½ tsp
- Vanilla extract – one tsp
- All-purpose flour – 1 ½ cups, gluten-free, low fodmap
- Glucose syrup – one cup
- Baking soda – half tsp
- Salt – half tsp
- Toasted walnut or pecan halves – one cup, chopped

Directions:

1. Preheat the oven to 350 degrees Fahrenheit. Let coat the inner side of the loaf pan with nonstick cooking spray. Then, it is lined with parchment paper.
2. After that, mash the strawberries with a fork into the mixing bowl.
3. Whisk vanilla extract, cinnamon, oil, and beaten eggs until mixed well.
4. Whisk the nuts, salt, baking soda, glucose syrup, and flour in the big bowl.
5. Add wet strawberry mixture to the dry ingredients and combine well.

6. Place batter into the pan and bake for forty to forty-five minutes.
7. Let cool the rack for ten minutes.

Nutrition: Calories; 332kcal, carbohydrates; 37g, protein; 4g, fat; 19g

16. Egg Scramble

Preparation time: 10 minutes | **Cooking time:** 20 minutes | **Servings:** 4

Ingredients:

- 4 organic pasture-raised eggs, whisked
- ¼ C. chives
- 4 tbsp. grass-fed ghee
- Pinch Celtic Sea salt

Directions

1. Start by heating the ghee in a pan over low heat and add the chives. Cover the pan and cook for about 20 minutes.
2. Add the eggs and scramble until cooked. Mix in well whilst stirring.
3. Serve with a pinch of salt and enjoy.

Nutrition: Calories: 298 kcal, Fat: 12 g Fiber: 2g Carbs: 20 g Protein: 5 g

17. Delicious Coconut Macaroons

Preparation time: 5 minutes | **Cooking time:** 30 minutes | **Servings:** 6

Ingredients

- 1 tbsp. raw cocoa powder
- 3 dates, pitted
- 2 tsp. vanilla extract
- ¼ C. raisins
- 6 egg whites
- 2 C. coconut, unsweetened and shredded
- ⅛ tsp. sea salt

Directions

1. Preheat the oven at 350°F/176°C.
2. Combine all ingredients together in the bowl.
3. Line the baking tray with parchment paper.
4. Place 1 tbsp. of dough on the baking tray. Press down to flatten.
5. Bake in preheated oven for 15 minutes or until golden.
6. Serve and enjoy.

Nutrition: Calories: 200 kcal, Fat: 8 g, Fiber: 4g, Carbs: 8 g, Protein: 3 g.

18. Healthy Broccoli Muffins

Preparation time: 5 minutes | **Cooking time:** 30 minutes | **Servings:** 6

Ingredients

- 12 eggs, whisked
- Coconut oil
- 1 C. broccoli, chopped
- ¼ C. of chives
- Pepper
- Sea salt

Directions

1. Grease muffin tray with coconut oil.
2. Divide evenly broccoli and chives in the muffin tray.
3. Now divide evenly eggs in the muffin tray.
4. Season with pepper and salt.
5. Bake at 400°F/204°C for 15 minutes.

Nutrition: Calories: 283 kcal, Fat: 8 g, Fiber: 1g, Carbs: 3 g, Protein: 9 g

19. Simple Zucchini Muffins

Preparation time: 5 minutes | **Cooking time:** 40 minutes | **Servings:** 5

Ingredients

- Coconut oil
- 1 C. zucchini, shredded
- 3 eggs
- 1 C. almond flour
- ¼ tsp. sea salt

Directions

1. Grease muffin tray with coconut oil.
2. Add all ingredients into the blender, and blend until mix.
3. Pour into grease muffin tray and bake at 350°F/176°C for 25 minutes.
4. Serve warm and enjoy.

Nutrition: Calories: 354 kcal, Fat: 14 g, Fiber: 2 g, Carbs: 16 g, Protein: 26 g,

20. Easy Cauliflower Rice

Preparation time: 5 minutes | **Cooking time:** 20 minutes | **Servings:** 5

Ingredients

- 1 lb. cauliflower, cut into florets
- 2 tbsp. coconut oil
- Pepper
- Salt

Directions

1. Add cauliflower florets into the food processor and process to a rice-like texture.
2. Melt oil in the pan over medium heat.
3. Add cauliflower to the pan and sauté for 6 minutes.
4. Season with pepper and salt.
5. Serve and enjoy.

Nutrition: Calories: 83 kcal, Fat: 8 g, Fiber: 1 g, Carbs: 3 g, Protein: 9 g

21. Mushroom Bacon

Preparation time: 10 minutes | **Cooking time:** 20 minutes | **Servings:** 3

Ingredients

- 1 tbsp. oil
- 1 packet Portobello mushroom
- ½ C. maple syrup
- 1 tbsp. liquid smoke
- Pinch salt
- Pinch pepper

Directions

1. In a bowl mix marinate the mushroom slices, mix with liquid smoke, maple syrup salt, and pepper.
2. Cut the mushrooms into strips and marinate for 12–15 minutes.
3. In a skillet, cook mushrooms for 3–5 minutes or until browned.
4. Remove, add lettuce, sliced tomato, and serve.

Nutrition: Calories: 200 kcal, Fat: 8 g, Fiber: 2g, Carbs: 8 g, Protein: 6 g

22. Fruit and Yogurt Parfait

Preparation time: 10 minutes | **Cooking time:** 0 minutes | **Servings:** 2

Ingredients

- 2 C. yogurt, lactose-free plain, non-fat
- 3 tbsp. pure maple syrup
- ¼ tsp. ginger, ground
- ½ banana, peeled and sliced
- ¼ C. pecans, chopped

Directions

1. In a small bowl, whisk together the yogurt, syrup, and ginger.
2. Spoon ½ C. of the yogurt mixture into each of the 2 parfait glasses.
3. Top each with ½ of the banana slices.
4. Top each with another ½ C. yogurt mixture.
5. Sprinkle each with 2 tbsp. pecans. Serve.

Nutrition: Calories: 354 kcal, Protein: 14 g, Fat: 14 g, Carbs: 46 g

23. Maple-Ginger Oatmeal

Preparation time: 5 minutes | **Cooking time:** 0 minutes | **Servings:** 2

Ingredients

- 1½ C. water
- Pinch salt
- 1 C. oats, old-fashioned, rolled
- ¼ C. pure maple syrup
- ½ tsp. ginger, ground

Directions

1. In a small pot, bring the water and salt to a boil over medium-high heat.
2. Stir in oats, syrup, and ginger.
3. Reduce the heat to medium-low.
4. Cook, frequently stirring for 5 minutes.
5. Serve.

Nutrition: Calories: 258 kcal, Protein: 7 g, Fat: 3 g, Carbs: 53 g

24. Corn Porridge With Maple and Raisins

Preparation time: 5 minutes | **Cooking time:** 0 minutes | **Servings:** 2

Ingredients

- ¾ C. cornmeal
- 2¼ C. water, divided
- Pinch salt
- 1 tbsp. pure maple syrup
- 3 tbsp. raisins

Directions

1. In a small bowl, whisk together the cornmeal and ¾ C. of water.
2. In a small pot, bring the remaining 1½ C. of water and the salt to a boil over medium-high heat.
3. Whisk in the cornmeal slurry. Cook, stirring for 10–12 minutes, until thick.
4. Stir in the maple syrup, and raisins.
5. Then serve hot.

Nutrition: Calories: 288 kcal, Protein: 6 g, Fat: 3 g, Carbs: 60 g

25. Milky Oat

Preparation time: 8 minutes | **Cooking time:** 0 minutes | **Servings:** 2

Ingredients

- 1 C. oats
- ½ C. coconut milk, low-fat
- ½ C. water
- 1 tsp. liquid stevia

Directions

1. Mix up together the coconut milk and water in the saucepan.
2. Add oats and stir.
3. Close the lid and cook the oats over medium heat for 10 minutes.
4. When the oats are cooked, let them chill for 5–10 minutes.
5. Then add liquid stevia and stir it.
6. After this, transfer the milky oat to the bowls and serve!

Nutrition: Calories: 293 kcal, Fat: 17 g, Carbs: 31 g, Protein: 6.8 g

Breakfast

26. Banana Smoothie

Preparation Time: 5 minutes | **Cooking Time:** 5 minutes | **Servings:** 2

Ingredients:

- 2 medium bananas, peeled and sliced
- ¼ Tsp. ground nutmeg
- 1 cup almond milk, unsweetened
- ½ cup gluten-free rolled oats
- 1 Tsp. pure vanilla extract, sugar-free
- ¼ Tsp. ground cinnamon
- 1 Tsp. pure maple syrup
- ¼ cup canned coconut milk, chilled

Directions:

1. Open a can of coconut milk and empty out the liquid in a lidded container to use in a different recipe.
2. Use a food blender to pulse maple syrup, nutmeg, cinnamon, vanilla extract, solid coconut milk, oats, almond milk, and bananas for approximately 60 seconds or until it is a smooth consistency.
3. Divide between 2 glasses and enjoy immediately!

Nutrition: Protein: 15g, Carbohydrates: 53g, Fat: 5g, Sodium: 81g, Fiber: 7g, Calories: 274

27. Berry Smoothie

Preparation Time: 5 minutes | **Cooking Time:** 5 minutes | **Servings:** 2

Ingredients:

- 1 cup blueberries, Frozen
- 2 cups almond milk, unsweetened
- 2 medium bananas
- ⅛ Tsp. ground cinnamon
- 1 cup strawberries, Frozen

Directions:

1. Pulse blueberries, almond milk, bananas, and strawberries in a food blender for approximately 60 seconds or until a smooth consistency.
2. Distribute to 2 glasses and dust with cinnamon.
3. Enjoy immediately!

Nutrition: Protein: 10g, Carbohydrates: 55g, Fat: 6g, Sodium: 117g, Fiber: 6g, Calories: 293

28. Breakfast Wrap

Preparation Time: 5 minutes | **Cooking Time:** 5 minutes | **Servings:** 4

Ingredients:

- 4 corn tortillas
- 8 slices cheddar cheese
- 2 cups spinach leaves
- ½ cup avocado

Directions:

1. Remove the shell from avocado and mash in a glass dish.
2. Rinse spinach leaves and shake to remove excess water.
3. Arrange tortillas on a flat surface.
4. Evenly divide and layer avocado, spinach leaves, and cheddar cheese on each.
5. Rotate to enclose, starting at the base.
6. Enjoy immediately.

Nutrition: Protein: 9g, Carbs: 15g, Fat: 13g, Sodium: 156g, Fiber: 3g, Calories: 205

29. Cinnamon Almond Crepes

Preparation Time: 10 minutes | **Cooking Time:** 20 minutes | **Servings:** 4

Ingredients:

- ½ cup almond flour
- 2 medium bananas

- ¼ Tsp. pure vanilla extract, sugar-free
- 1 cup almond milk, separated
- ¼ Tsp. ground cinnamon
- tbsp. extra virgin olive oil, separated

Directions:
1. Empty 2 teaspoons of olive oil into a skillet and allow it to warm up.
2. In the meantime, blend almond milk, bananas, vanilla extract, cinnamon, and almond flour in a glass dish with an electric beater for 45 seconds.
3. Transfer a ladle of batter to the pan and swirl it around to distribute it evenly around.
4. Heat for 30 seconds or until edges turn darker, then turn to the other side.
5. Warm for an additional 30 seconds, then transfer to a serving platter. Enclose with tin foil.
6. Empty another 2 teaspoons in the skillet and repeat steps 3 through 6 until you have completed 8 crepes.
7. Enjoy immediately with your favorite fruits or compote.

Nutrition: Protein: 3g, Carbohydrates: 17g, Fat: 11g, Sodium: 29g, Fiber: 2g, Calories: 165

30. Cranberry Orange Smoothie

Preparation Time: 10 minutes | **Cooking Time:** 5 minutes | **Servings:** 2
Ingredients:
- 1⅛ cups orange juice, freshly squeezed
- 1 cup cranberries, raw
- ¼ cup almond milk, unsweetened
- 1 medium banana
- 1 tbsp. lemon juice
- 1 Tsp. pure maple syrup
- 1 cup of ice cubes

Directions:
1. Use a glass dish to squeeze orange juice and remove the seeds.
2. Transfer to a food blender and pulse cranberries, almond milk, banana, lemon juice, maple syrup, and ice until it reaches your desired consistency.

3. Divide between two glasses and enjoy immediately!

Nutrition: Protein: 3g, Carbohydrates: 38g, Fat: 1g, Sodium: 18g, Fiber: 4g, Calories: 164

31. French toast

Preparation Time: 10 minutes | **Cooking Time:** 25 minutes | **Servings:** 4
Ingredients:
- 1 cup almond milk, unsweetened
- 1⅓ cup tofu, firm and plain
- 2 Tsp. pure vanilla extract, sugar-free
- 4 slices gluten-free bread of your choice
- 4 Tsp. extra virgin olive oil, separated
- 2 tbsp. pure maple syrup

Directions:
1. Use a food blender to pulse vanilla extract, almond milk, and tofu until a smooth consistency.
2. Add 2 teaspoons of olive oil into a large skillet and warm.
3. Transfer the wet mix to a shallow dish and immerse the bread in it for 60 seconds on each side. Transfer to a plate until ready to brown.
4. Cook 2 slices at once for 3 minutes on each side, then transfer to a serving platter.
5. Repeat for remaining slices of bread until complete.
6. Top with maple syrup and enjoy while warm.

Nutrition: Protein: 11g, Carb: 26g, Fat: 10g, Sodium: 184g, Fiber: 1g, Calories: 230

32. Green Hibiscus Smoothie

Preparation Time: 15 minutes | **Cooking Time:** 10 minutes | **Servings:** 2
Ingredients:
- 1 hibiscus tea bag
- ½ inch ginger root, peeled
- ½ cup of water
- 1 cup zucchini, cubed
- ½ cup raspberries, Frozen
- ½ cup of coconut milk, liquid

Directions:

1. Empty water into a mug and nuke in the microwave for 1 minute.
2. Insert the tea bag and allow it too to steep for 5 minutes.
3. In the meantime, scrub zucchini and chop into small cubes. Transfer to a food blender.
4. Wash raspberries and shake to remove excess water. Transfer to the food blender. Remove
5. Remove tea bag from the water and empty it into the blender.
6. Combine ginger and coconut milk in the blender and pulse for approximately 30 seconds or until smooth.
7. Transfer to two glasses and enjoy immediately!

Nutrition: Protein: 2g, Carbohydrates: 8g, Fat: 12g, Sodium: 11g, Fiber: 3g, Calories: 142

33. Hearty Oatmeal

Preparation Time: 5 minutes | **Cooking Time:** 10 minutes | **Servings:** 4
Ingredients:
- 4 cups of water
- ½ Tsp. iodized salt
- 2 cups gluten-free rolled oats
- ½ Tsp. ground cloves
- 1 Tsp. ground cinnamon
- 4 tbsp. chia seeds
- ½ Tsp. ground nutmeg
- 4 tbsp. pure maple syrup

Directions:

1. Empty salt and water into a saucepan and warm on the highest heat setting until it starts to bubble.
2. Combine oats into hot water and heat for 5 minutes while occasionally tossing.
3. Blend ground cloves, chia seeds, ground cinnamon, ground nutmeg, and maple syrup, then warm for another 5 minutes.
4. Serve immediately and enjoy!

Nutrition: Protein: 8g, Carbohydrates: 45g, Fat: 3g, Sodium: 300g, Fiber: 8g, Calories: 171

34. Immune Boosting Smoothie

Preparation Time: 5 minutes | **Cooking Time:** 10 minutes | **Servings:** 2

Ingredients:
- 2 cups spinach
- 1-inch ginger root, peeled
- 2 kale leaves
- 2 medium rib celery
- ⅛ Tsp. iodized salt
- 2 medium cucumbers
- 2 tbsp. lime juice
- 2 cups ice

Directions:

1. Thoroughly rinse spinach, celery, and kale, then shake to remove any extra water. Remove the tough ends of the kale and discard.
2. Scrub cucumbers well and chop into small sections.
3. Use a food blender to pulse salt, lime juice, ginger, cucumbers, celery, kale, and spinach until a smooth consistency.
4. Combine ice and continue to pulse until it reaches your desired consistency.
5. Distribute to two glasses and enjoy it immediately!

Nutrition: Protein: 3g, Carbohydrates: 9g, Fat: 1g, Sodium: 221g, Fiber: 3g, Calories: 49ù

35. Peanut Butter and Banana Overnight Oats

Preparation Time: 10 minutes | **Cooking Time:** 5 minutes + overnight | **Servings:** 4
Ingredients:
- 2 cups gluten-free rolled oats
- 4 Tsp. chia seeds
- 2 medium bananas, mashed
- 4 tbsp. peanut butter, natural and no sugar added
- 2 cups almond milk, unsweetened
- 1 Tsp. ground cinnamon

Directions:

1. Blend cinnamon, almond milk, peanut

butter, bananas, chia seeds, and oats in a glass dish.
2. Toss to combine fully and cover with a layer of plastic wrap.
3. Transfer to the refrigerator and serve the next morning immediately if you desire it cold. If you prefer hot, nuke in the microwave for 60 seconds before enjoying.

Nutrition: Protein: 19g, Carbs: 60g, Fat: 14g, Sodium: 158g, Fiber: 13g, Calories: 359

36. Scrambled Tofu

Preparation Time: 10 minutes | **Cooking Time:** 10 minutes | **Servings:** 4
Ingredients:
- 1 Lb. pre-pressed tofu, firm
- 1 cup of water
- 4 Tsp. gluten-free soy sauce*
- 1 Tsp. ground turmeric
- 2 cup carrots, chopped finely

Directions:
1. Use a glass dish to blend turmeric, soy sauce, and water until integrated.
2. Scrub carrots and chop into small sections. Transfer to the dish.
3. Break apart tofu into smaller sections into the dish, then toss to combine fully.
4. Wover the medium setting of heat.
5. Distribute the mixture into the pan and occasionally toss while it heats for 5 minutes.
6. Remove w/ a slotted spoon and serve immediately. Enjoy!

Nutrition: Protein: 19g, Carbs: 11g, Fat: 13g, Sodium: 137g, Fiber: 4g, Calories: 224

37. Sweet Potato Toast

Preparation Time: 20 minutes | **Cooking Time:** 25 minutes | **Servings:** 4
Ingredients:
- 2 large, sweet potatoes
- 2 tbsp. pure maple syrup

Directions:

1. Set your oven to 400°F. Layer a flat sheet with baking paper.
2. Section sweet potatoes in halves lengthwise, then slice each half into thin pieces.
3. Transfer to the prepped sheet and heat for 20 minutes.
4. Drizzle with maple syrup and enjoy!

Nutrition: Protein: 2g, Carbohydrates: 25g, Fat: 0g, Sodium: 34g, Fiber: 3g, Calories: 107

38. Turkey Sausage Patties

Preparation Time: 20 minutes | **Cooking Time:** 35 minutes | **Servings:** 4
Ingredients:
- ½ Lb. ground turkey
- ¼ Tsp. iodized salt
- ½ Tsp. sage seasoning
- 1 tbsp. extra virgin olive oil
- ½ Tsp. rosemary seasoning
- ⅛ Tsp. black pepper
- ½ tbsp. pure maple syrup

Directions:
1. Use a glass dish to combine ground turkey, salt, sage, rosemary, black pepper, and maple syrup until incorporated.
2. Heat olive oil in a large skillet on your stove's medium heat setting.
3. Form 4 evenly sized patties and arrange in the pan, then cook in batches, if necessary, as you want to leave some space in between to cook evenly.
4. Heat for approximately 6 minutes, then flips to the other side. Continue to brown for an additional 6 minutes or until cooked fully.
5. Transfer patties to a plate lined with kitchen paper to remove any excess grease.
6. Enjoy immediately!

Nutrition: Protein: 11g, Carbohydrates: 2g, Fat: 8g, Sodium: 179g, Fiber: 0g, Calories: 121

39. Egg Wraps

Preparation Time: 5 minutes | **Cooking Time:** 5 Minutes | **Servings:** 4

Ingredients:

- Oil to grease the pan (from the approved food list: avocado, olive, or sunflower)
- 4-8 eggs
- Pinch of salt
- Pepper

Directions:

7. Grease a non-stick pan with oil then place over medium heat to warm.
8. Whisk the egg in a bowl and pour it into the pan, ensuring it is spread evenly. Add in salt and pepper to taste.
9. Cook for 30-60 seconds on each side; gently flip when the edges on the first side are cooked.
10. Place on a plate to cool and repeat with the remainder of the eggs.

Nutrition: 414 Cal, 33g Fat, 2g Carbs, 25g Protein

40. Tropical Fruit Salad

Preparation Time: 5 minutes | **Cooking Time:** 0 Minutes | **Servings:**4

Ingredients:

- 2 bananas, sliced
- 1 papaya, peeled, seeded, and cut into bite-size cubes
- 1 cup pineapple chunks, fresh or canned, drained
- 2 tablespoons unsweetened shredded coconut

Directions:

1. A medium bowl, gently stir together the bananas, papaya, pineapple chunks, and coconut.

Nutrition: Calories: 116, Total Fat: 1g, Carbohydrates: 28g, Sodium: 8mg, Protein: 1

41. Pineapple-coconut Smoothie

Preparation Time: 5 minutes | **Cooking Time:** 0 Minutes | **Servings:** 2

Ingredients:

- 2 cups crushed pineapple, fresh or canned in water and drained
- 1 cup canned full-fat coconut milk
- 1 cup unsweetened almond milk
- 1 cup crushed ice
- 2 tablespoons chia seeds or flaxseed

Directions:

1. A blender, combine the pineapple, coconut milk, almond milk, ice, and chia seeds. Blend until smooth.

Nutrition: Calories: 415, Total Fat: 33g, Carbs: 31g, Sodium: 112mg, Protein: 5g.

42. Pesto Eggs Rice Bowl

Preparation Time: 5 minutes | **Cooking Time:** 0 Minutes | **Servings:**1

Ingredients:

- 1/2 cup cooked brown rice
- 1/8 cup Pesto Sauce (see Chapter 13)
- 1 hardboiled large egg
- 1/8 medium avocado
- 1 tablespoon grated Parmesan cheese

Directions:

5. Place cooked rice in a soup bowl.
6. Pour pesto over rice and stir until rice is evenly covered.
7. Cut hardboiled egg in half.
8. Place on top of rice and pesto. Place avocado on top.

9. Sprinkle with Parmesan cheese. Enjoy!

Nutrition: Calories: 275, Fat: 13g, Protein: 14g, Sodium: 297mg, Carbohydrates: 26.

43. Flourless Banana Cinnamon Pancakes

Preparation Time: 5 minutes | **Cooking Time:** 6 Minutes | **Servings:** 1

Ingredients:

- 1 large egg
- 1/2 ripe medium banana
- 1 teaspoon chia seeds
- 1 teaspoon ground cinnamon
- 1 tablespoon coconut oil

Directions:

1. In a glass measuring cup, mix together egg, banana, chia seeds, and cinnamon. Be sure to mash bananas very well or use a blender to mix ingredients until smooth on low speed.
2. Heat oil in a medium skillet over medium heat. Pour a couple of batches of batter onto skillet and cook pancakes until bubbly on top and golden on bottom, about 4 minutes. Flip and cook about 2 more minutes.

Nutrition: Calories: 265, Fat: 20g, Protein: 8g, Sodium: 72mg, Carbohydrates: 17.

44. Flourless Vegan Banana Peanut Butter Pancakes

Preparation Time: 5 minutes | **Cooking Time:** 6 Minutes | **Servings:** 1

Ingredients:

- 2 flax eggs (see Chapter 16)
- 1/2 ripe medium banana
- 1 teaspoon chia seeds
- 1 tablespoon peanut butter
- 1 tablespoon coconut oil

Directions:

1. In a glass measuring cup, mix together flax eggs, banana, chia seeds, and peanut butter.
2. Be sure to mash bananas well or use a blender to mix ingredients until smooth on low speed.
3. Heat oil in a medium skillet over medium heat.
4. Pour a couple of batches of batter onto the skillet and cook pancakes until bubbly on top and golden on bottom, about 4 minutes.
5. Flip and cook about 2 more minutes.

Nutrition: Calories: 425, Fat: 33g, Protein: 18g, Sodium: 215mg, Carbohydrates: 18.

45. Peanut Butter Bowl

Preparation Time: 5 minutes | **Cooking Time:** 5 Minutes | **Servings:** 2

Ingredients:

- 2 bananas, chopped and frozen
- 1 ½ cups Greek yogurt
- 2 tbsp peanut butter
- ¼ cup chopped nuts

Directions:

1. In a blender, mix the bananas, yogurt, and peanut butter.
2. When the mixture is a smooth consistency, pour it into a bowl and top with chopped nuts.
3. Simple!

Nutrition: 519g Cal, 35g Fat, 5.5g Carbs, 15.5 g Protein.

46. Melon And Berry Compote

Preparation Time: 5 minutes | **Cooking Time:** 0 Minutes | **Servings:** 2

Ingredients:

- 2 cups chopped cantaloupe
- 2 cups fresh blueberries

- ¼ cup unsweetened coconut flakes
- 2 tablespoons flaxseed

Directions:
2. A medium bowl, gently stir together the cantaloupe, blueberries, coconut flakes, and flaxseed.

Nutrition: Calories: 196, Total Fat: 5g, Carbs: 36g, Sodium: 29mg, Protein: 4.

47. Scrambled Eggs

Preparation Time: 5 minutes | **Cooking Time:** 5 Minutes | **Servings:** 4

Ingredients:
- 10 large eggs
- ¾ cup (180 ml) lactose-free milk
- Salt and freshly ground black pepper
- 3 tablespoons (45 g) salted butter
- Toasted gluten-free, soy-free bread, for serving

Directions:
1. Crack the eggs into a large bowl, add the milk, and whisk until combined. Season with salt and pepper.
2. Melt the butter in a medium frying pan over low heat. Pour in the egg mixture.
3. Use a wooden spoon to gently push the egg mixture from the edge into the middle of the pan to prevent sticking.
4. Cook for 4 to 5 minutes, continuing to stir gently, until nearly cooked—the eggs should still be creamy and slightly runny.
5. Serve immediately with toasted gluten-free bread.

Nutrition: 282 Calories, 17 g protein, 22 g total fat, 4 g carbohydrates, 560 mg sodium.

48. Summer Berry Smoothie

Preparation Time: 5 minutes | **Cooking Time:** 6 Minutes | **Servings:** 4

Ingredients:

- 1 large banana, unripe
- ¼ cup blueberries

- 1 ¼ cups lactose-free milk, even vegetable milk (no oat milk for gluten-free)
- 1 cup Greek yogurt
- Ice

Directions:
1. Place ingredients in a blender and mix until smooth.

Nutrition: 406g Cal, 3.3 g Fat, 10.7 g Carbs, 5.8 g Protein.

49. Melon And Yogurt Parfait

Preparation Time: 5 minutes | **Cooking Time:** 0 Minutes | **Servings:** 2

Ingredients:

- 2 cups chopped honeydew melon, divided
- 2 cups plain, unsweetened, lactose-free yogurt
- ¼ cup macadamia nuts, chopped

Directions:
1. In each of two medium parfait glasses or bowls, place ½ cup honeydew melon.
2. Layer a ½ cup yogurt on top of the melon.
3. Top each with 2 tablespoons macadamia nuts.
4. Repeat with the remaining ingredients.

Nutrition: Calories: 356, Total Fat:16g, Carbs: 35g, Sodium: 203mg, Protein: 16.

50. Amaranth Breakfast

Preparation Time: 5 minutes | **Cooking Time:** 20 Minutes | **Servings:** 4

Ingredients:
- 1 cup amaranth seeds
- 3 cups water
- 2 teaspoons ground cinnamon
- 1 tablespoon pure vanilla extract
- 1/4 cup shelled pecans, lightly chopped

Directions:

1. Heat a heavy-bottomed saucepan over medium heat and add amaranth. Toast amaranth, stirring occasionally for 5 minutes until fragrant.
2. Pour in 3 cups water and bring to a boil. Lower heat and add cinnamon and vanilla. Cover, then simmer for 20 minutes, stirring occasionally.
3. While amaranth is simmering, place pecans under broiler for 4 minutes to toast.
4. When amaranth has finished cooking, give it a good stir and remove from heat. Serve in bowls topped with the pecans.

Nutrition: Calories: 230, Fat: 5g, Protein: 6g, Sodium: 5mg, Carbohydrates: 41.

51. Banana Toast

Preparation Time: 5 minutes | **Cooking Time:** 5 Minutes | **Servings** 2

Ingredients:

- 4 gluten-free sandwich bread slices
- 1 ripe banana
- ½ teaspoon ground cinnamon

Directions:

1. Toast the bread to your desired doneness.
2. In a small bowl, mash the banana with the cinnamon and spread it on the toast.

Nutrition: Calories: 102, Total Fat: <1g, Carbs: 23g, Sodium: 123mg, Protein: 2.

52. Quinoa Tofu Scramble

Preparation Time: 5 Minutes | **Cooking Time:** 15 Minutes | **Servings:** 4

Ingredients

- ½ tsp. iodized salt, separated
- 8 oz. pre-pressed tofu, firm
- ½ tsp. turmeric powder
- 2 cups spinach

- ¼ tsp. black pepper

Direction:

2. Ensure the quinoa is properly rinsed under cold water.
3. Transfer to a deep pot and blend ¼ teaspoon of salt with water.
4. Heat on the highest setting until the fluid is starting to bubble, then turn the burner temperature down.
5. Warm for an additional 12 minutes or until fluid is fully reduced.
6. Rinse spinach well and shake to remove excess moisture.
7. Set aside.
8. Break tofu into small sections and put it into the pan.
9. Combine the leftover ¼ teaspoon of salt, turmeric, and black pepper until fully incorporated.
10. Warm the mixture on the stove for approximately 3 minutes while continuously tossing.
11. Toss in spinach and continue to stir continuously for an additional 2 minutes.
12. Layer quinoa and tofu scramble into each serving dish.
13. Serve immediately and enjoy!

Nutrition: Protein: 9g, Carbohydrates: 3g, Fat: 8g, Sodium: 311g, Fiber: 2g, Calories: 117.

53. Bacon-Jalapeño Egg Cups

Preparation Time: 5 minutes | **Cooking Time:** 25 minutes | **Servings:** 6

Ingredients:

For the Bacon
- 6 bacon slices
- 1 tablespoon butter

For the Eggs

- 2 jalapeño peppers
- 4 large eggs
- Pink Himalayan salt
- Freshly ground black pepper
- ¼ cup shredded Mexican blend cheese

- 2 ounces cream cheese, at room temperature

Directions:

To make the Bacon:

1. Bacon egg cups are the perfect keto breakfast, snack, or even side dish.
2. The crispy bacon on the outside, mixed with the creamy egg middle and spicy jalapeño, will start your day with a kick.
3. The cream cheese mixed with bits of jalapeño pepper provides just the right amount of heat.
4. Preheat the oven to 375°F.
5. While the oven is warming up, heat a large skillet over medium-high heat. Add the bacon slices and cook partially, about 4 minutes.
6. Transfer the bacon to a paper towel−lined plate. Coat six cups of a standard muffin tin with the butter.
7. Place a partially cooked bacon strip in each cup to line the sides.

To make the Eggs:

1. Cut one jalapeño lengthwise, seed it, and mince it.
2. Cut the remaining jalapeño into rings, discarding the seeds.
3. Set aside.
4. In a medium bowl, beat the eggs with a hand mixer until well beaten.
5. Add the cream cheese and diced jalapeño, season with pink Himalayan salt and pepper, and beat again to combine.
6. Pour the egg mixture into the prepared muffin tin, filling each cup about two-thirds of the way up so they have room to rise.
7. Top each cup with some of the shredded cheese and a ring of jalapeño, and bake for 20 minutes.

Cool for 10 minutes, and serve hot.

SUBSTITUTION TIP: If you don't have jalapeños available, or you don't like spicy food, you can use bell peppers or another vegetable with a little crunch, like asparagus.

Nutrition: Calories: 159 kcal, Total Fat: 13g, Saturated Fat: 0g, Cholesterol: 0mg, Sodium: 0 mg, Carbs: 1g, Fiber: 0g, Sugar: 0g, Protein: 9g

54. Fish Wallpaper with Green Bean Salad

Preparation time: 5 minutes | **Cooking Time:** 15 minutes | **Servings:** 4

Ingredients

- 2 cups of tomato
- 1/2 cup of lemon juice
- 1 piece of roasted habanero chili
- 1 teaspoon salt
- 4 pieces of fish
- 2 teaspoons of olive oil
- 4 pinches of salt
- 4 pieces of yellow lemon cut into slices
- 2 Tablespoon of chives
- 4 pieces of serrano chili
- 4 tablespoons fresh coriander
- 1/4 cup epazote cut into strips
- 1 cup of green bean
- 4 teaspoons of olive oil
- 4 pinches of salt

Directions:

1. Preheat the oven to 360 °F.
2. Add the tomato, yellow lemon juice, habanero pepper and salt to the blender.
3. Blends perfectly well.
4. Spread an aluminum foil with waxed paper on top add the fish and garnish with the olive oil, add the salt, the sauce, the slices of lemon, the chives, the Chile, the coriander, and the epazote.
5. Close and bake around 20 minutes.
6. Inside a pot with boiling water and add salt, cook the green beans 5 minutes until they are cooked: drain and reserve
7. Serve the fish, add green beans, season with olive oil and add salt to it.

Nutrition: Calories 96, Carbohydrates 18.4g,

Proteins 5.9g, Lipids 0.6g, Dietary fiber 7.2g, Sugars4.7g.

55. Tomato and basil frittata

Preparation time: 10 Minutes | **Cooking Time:** 25 Minutes | **Servings:** 4

Ingredients:

- 10 large eggs
- 5 slices of bacon, sliced into small pieces
- ¼ C. of chives
- 113 g. baby spinach leaves
- 2 small ripe tomatoes cut into thin slices
- 15 ml. whole or homemade mustard
- Fresh basil leaves to taste (to garnish)
- 15 ml. Paleo or butter cooking fat
- Sea salt with freshly ground black pepper to add taste

Directions:

1. Preheat the oven to 360°F.
2. Beat the eggs and mustard in a bowl and season to taste.
3. Heat the cooking fat in an oven-proof frying pan over medium heat.
4. Cook the bacon and add the chives (approximately 5 to 6 minutes).
5. Add the spinach into the pan and cook for another minute or until the spinach is wilted. Pour the egg mixture into the pan.
6. Cook until it hardens a little and places the tomatoes on top.
7. Once the edges well cook the frittata, but still dripping in the center, put the pan into the oven till the frittata takes a nice golden color.
8. Garnish with some basil leaves on top and serve.

Nutrition: Carbs 11g, Dietary Fiber 1g, Protein 8g

56. Lettuce Tacos with Chicken to the Shepherd

Preparation time: 1 h 20 minutes | **Cooking time:** 35 minutes | **Servings:** 6

Ingredients

- 50 grams of achiote for the marinade
- 1/4 cup of apple vinegar for the marinade
- 3 pieces of guajillo Chile clean, deveined and seedless, hydrated for the marinade
- 2 pieces of wide chili clean, deveined and seedless, hydrated for the marinade
- 1/2 cup pineapple juice for marinade
- 1 tablespoon salt marinade
- 1 tablespoon fat pepper for marinade
- 2 pieces of clove for the marinade
- 1 tablespoon oregano for the marinade
- 1 piece of roasted guaje tomato, for the marinade
- 1 tablespoon cumin for the marinade
- 1 piece of boneless and skinless chicken breast, cut into small cubes
- 1 tablespoon of olive or flax oil
- Enough of French Lettuce Eva
- 1/2 piece of pineapple cut into half moons
- 1/2 cup chopped coriander
- 2 Tablespoon of chives
- To the taste of tree chili sauce to accompany
- To the taste of lemon to accompany

Directions:

1. For the marinade:
2. Blend the achiote, vinegar, chilies, chives, juice, salt, pepper, cloves, oregano, tomato, and cumin until a homogeneous mixture is obtained.
3. Put the chicken and the marinade inside a bowl with the shepherd marinade for 1 hour in refrigeration.
4. Heat a pan over medium heat with the oil and cook the chicken you marinated until it is cooked.
5. Reserve covered.
6. Heat a grill over high heat, roast the pineapple until golden brown, remove and cut into cubes, reserve.
7. On a table place sheets of French Lettuce Eva add the chicken to the shepherd and serve with the roasted pineapple, cilantro,

chives, served with a little sauce and lemons.

Nutrition : Calories 92.2, Carbs 22.3g, Proteins 1.6g, Lipids 0.9g, Dietary fiber 2.9g, Sugars, 6.6g, Cholesterol 0mg.

57. Green Apple Salad with Garbanzo

Preparation time: 10 minutes | **Cooking time:** 2 min | **Servings:** 1
Ingredients:

- 2 cups chopped Eva Lettuce
- 1 cup chopped arugula
- 1 cup of green apple cut into thin slices
- 1/4 cup of toasted chickpea
- 2 teaspoons of olive oil
- 1/4 cup strawberry
- 1 pinch of salt
- 1 pinch of pepper
- 3 tablespoons of raspberry vinegar

Directions

1. In a bowl add the lettuce, the arugula, add the green apple, with the chickpea.
2. Mix perfectly well.
3. Reservation.
4. Add the olive oil with the strawberry, salt, pepper and raspberry vinegar to the blender.
5. Blends perfectly well. Serve the salad on a plate and add the strawberry vinaigrette to garnish.
6. Enjoy

Nutrition: Calories 878, Carbs 122g, Proteins 36.2g, Lipids 34.1g, Dietary fiber 36.5g, Cholesterol 0ml.

58. Sheet Pan Steak Fajitas

Preparation Time: 10 Minutes | **Cooking Time:** 25 Minutes | **Servings:** 4
Ingredients:

- 2 teaspoons chili powder
- 2 teaspoons ground cumin
- 1 teaspoon smoked paprika
- Salt and black pepper, to taste

- 680 grams sirloin steak, cut into thin strips
- 1 green bell pepper, cut into strips
- 1 orange bell pepper, cut into strips
- 3 tablespoons olive oil
- 2 tablespoons freshly squeezed lime juice
- 6 (8-inch) flour, corn tortillas or carb balance, warmed

Directions:

1. Preheat oven to 425 °F.
2. Lightly oil a baking sheet or coat with nonstick spray.
3. In a small bowl, combine chili powder, cumin, paprika, 2 teaspoons salt and 2 teaspoons pepper.
4. Place steak and bell peppers in a single layer onto the prepared baking sheet. Stir in olive oil and chili powder mixture; gently toss to combine.
5. Place into oven and bake for 25 minutes, or until the steak is completely cooked through and the vegetables are crisp-tender.
6. Stir in lime juice. Serve immediately with tortillas.

Nutrition: Calories 440, Fat 33g, Carbs 5g, Fiber 1g, Sugar 1g, Protein 31g, Vitamin C 78mg, Iron 3.7mg.

59. Sheet Pan Tuscan Chicken

Preparation Time: 10 Minutes | **Cooking Time:** 25 Minutes | **Servings:** 4
Ingredients:

- 4 wholes Boneless, Chicken Thighs
- 6 whole Roma Tomatoes, quartered
- 1-pound Green Beans
- 1 cup Olive Oil
- 1/3 cup Balsamic Vinegar
- 1 teaspoon Dried Parsley Flakes
- 1 teaspoon Salt
- 1 teaspoon Black Pepper
- 2 Tablespoons Parsley

Directions:

To a bowl or pitcher, add the olive oil and balsamic vinegar, along with the parsley, salt, and pepper.

Whisk it until it's well blended. Place the chicken in a large zipper bag and pour in half the dressing.

Seal the bag and set it aside.

Cut the tomatoes in quarters.

Trim the ends off the green beans, and place the veggies in a large zipper bag.

Pour in the rest of the dressing, then seal the bag and set them aside.

Preheat the oven to 425 °F Arrange the chicken and veggies on a sheet pan, Pour a little of the marinade on top of the chicken. Roast in the oven for 25 minutes, shaking the pan once during that time.

Variations

With a few minutes left of cook time, lay slices of fresh mozzarella on each chicken breast. Return them to the oven until melted. Sprinkle ½ cup shredded Parmesan all over the pan as soon as you remove it from the oven. Let it sit a few minutes before serving.

Nutrition: Calories 441, Fat 22g, Saturated Fat 5g, Cholesterol 119mg, Sodium 986 mg, Potassium 1044mg, Carbs 15g, Fiber 3g, Sugar 8g, Protein 43g, Calcium 215mg, iron 2.5 mg.

60. Sheet Pan Egg in the Hole

Preparation Time: 10 Minutes | **Cooking Time:** 20 Minutes | **Servings:** 6
Ingredients:

- 12 slices bacon
- 6 slices bread
- Butter, at room temperature
- 6 large eggs
- 6 tablespoons Mozzarella cheese
- Salt and freshly black pepper, to taste
- Red pepper flakes, to taste
- 2 tablespoons chopped fresh chives

Directions

- Preheat oven to 400 °F.
- Place bacon in a single layer onto a baking sheet.

- Place into oven and bake until par-cooked, about for 5-7 minutes.
- Transfer to a paper towel-lined plate. Lightly oil a baking sheet or coat with nonstick spray.
- Cut a 3-inch hole in the center of each bread slice. Butter one side of the bread slices.
- Place the bread onto the prepared baking sheet, buttered side down.
- Add bacon slices and eggs, gently cracking the eggs into each hole and keeping the yolk intact.
- Sprinkle with Parmesan and red pepper flakes; season with salt and pepper, to taste.
- If your bacon is too thick, cut it in half so the egg can sink into the hole.
- Place into oven and bake until the egg whites have set about 12-15 minutes.
- Serve immediately, garnished with chives, if desired.

Nutrition: Calories 292, Total Fat 19.0g, Saturated Fat 9.5g, Cholesterol 223.0mg, Sodium 700.0mg, Total Carbohydrate 13.0g, Dietary Fiber 1.0g, Protein 15.0g,

61. Baked oatmeal cups

Preparation time: 10 minutes | **Cooking time:** 20 minutes | **Serving:** 12
Ingredients:

- Almond milk – one cup, unsweetened
- Banana – half cup, mashed
- Avocado oil – ¼ cup
- Pure maple syrup – ¼ cup
- Egg – one
- Pure vanilla extract – one tsp
- Rolled oats – 1 ½ cups
- Baking flour – one cup
- Ground cinnamon – one tsp
- Salt – ¼ tsp
- Pecan – 12 halves

For topping: peanut butter and maple syrup

Directions:

1. Preheat the oven to 350 degrees Fahrenheit.
2. Let coat a muffin tin with non-stick cooking spray.
3. Whisk the vanilla, egg, maple syrup, oil, mashed banana, and almond milk into the big bowl. Then, add salt, cinnamon, rolled oats, and gluten-free flour. Stir well.
4. Divide the batter into the muffin tin.
5. Top with pecan halves.
6. Place it into the oven and bake for twenty to twenty-two minutes until golden brown.
7. Let cool it.
8. Top with maple syrup and peanut butter.

Nutrition: Calories; 314, Carbs; 47.3g, protein; 5.4g, fat; 10.4g

62. Dragon fruit smoothie bowl

Preparation time: 5 minutes | **Cooking time:** 0 minutes | **Serving:** 1

Ingredients:
- Dragon fruit – one cup, frozen, cubes
- Pineapple – ½ cup, frozen
- Protein powder – 2 tbsp, low fodmap
- Almond milk – ½ cup
- For topping:
- Kiwi – half, peeled and sliced
- Coconut – one tbsp, shredded

Directions:
1. Add almond milk, protein powder, pineapple, and dragon fruit into the food processor or blender and blend until you get a thick smoothie.
2. Pour smoothie into the bowl.
3. Top with sliced or diced kiwi and shredded coconut.

Nutrition: Calories; 295kcal, Carbs; 39.5g, protein; 24g, fat; 3.4g

63. Pumpkin pie oatmeal

Preparation time: 5 minutes | **Cooking time:** 5 minutes | **Serving:** 4

Ingredients:
- Rolled oats – two cups
- Unsweetened almond milk – two cups
- Pure pumpkin puree – half cup
- Vanilla extract – half tsp
- Pumpkin pie spice – one tsp
- Pure maple syrup – 1/3 cup
- Pecan – 20 halves, chopped

Directions:
1. Firstly, add milk and oats into the saucepan and place them over medium-high flame. Then, bring to a boil.
2. Lower the speed of the flame and simmer until you get desired thickness. Stir often.
3. Add pure maple syrup, pumpkin pie spice, pumpkin puree, and vanilla extract and stir and cook it well.
4. Serve and top with pecan halves.

Nutrition: Calories; 354kcal, Carbs; 53.7g, protein; 9.8g, fat; 9.5g

64. Smoked salmo and spinach frittata cups

Preparation time: 5 minutes | **Cooking time:** 25 minutes | **Serving:** 4

Ingredients:
- Eggs – 10
- Lemon zest – half tsp
- Lemon juice – one tbsp
- Fresh dill – one tbsp, minced
- Spinach – one cup, chopped
- Smoked salmon – 4 ounces, prepared with low fodmap ingredients, cut into bite-sized pieces

Directions:
1. Preheat the oven to 350 degrees Fahrenheit.
2. Let coat the muffin tin with non-stick cooking spray.
3. Add dill, lemon juice, lemon zest, and eggs into the bowl.
4. Spread spinach and salmon into the muffin tin cups.

5. Add egg mixture and place them into the oven and bake for 18 to 22 minutes.
6. Remove cups from the oven.
7. Let cool it.
8. Serve and enjoy!

Nutrition: Calories; 215kcal, carbohydrates; 1.5g, protein; 21.1g, fat; 13.2g

65. Avocado egg salad toast

Preparation time: 10 minutes | **Cooking time:** 0 minutes | **Serving:** 4
Ingredients:
Ripe avocado –one
Hard-boiled eggs – four, diced
Fresh lemon juice – 1 tbsp
Parsley – one tbsp, chopped
Kosher salt – half tsp
Black pepper – ¼ tsp
- Sourdough bread – four slices, white, toasted, gluten-free

Directions:
1. Slice avocado in half and remove the pit.
2. Scoop flesh from the skin and add it into the bowl.
3. Divide the mixture onto each slice of toasted bread.
4. Garnish with fresh parsley leaves.
Nutrition: Calories; 328kcal, carbohydrates; 5g, protein; 4g, fat; 3g

66. Berry Ginger Smoothie

Preparation time: 5 minutes | **Cooking time:** 0 minutes | **Serving:** 2
Ingredients:
- Strawberries – ¾ cup, frozen
- Raspberries – ¾ cup, frozen
- Banana – half, peeled
- Orange – one, peeled
- Ginger – 1-inch piece, peeled
- Almond milk – one cup

Directions:
1. Add all of the ingredients into the food processor and blender and blend until thick and smooth.
2. Add more almond milk if needed.

3. Pour smoothie into the tall glass.
4. Serve and enjoy!
Nutrition: Calories; 136kcal, carbohydrates; 30g, protein; 3g, fat; 2g

67. Tasty Blueberry Waffles

Preparation time: 15 minutes | **Cooking time:** 20 minutes | **Serving:** 8-10
Ingredients:
- Chickpea flour – 1 ¾ cup
- Baking powder – 1 tbsp
- Salt – half tsp
- Cinnamon – half tsp
- Eggs – 2, separate the yolks from the whites
- Non-dairy milk – ¾ cup
- Butter – 84g, melted
- Vanilla extract – one tsp
- Lemon zest – one tsp
- Blueberries, ¾ cup

Directions:
1. Prepare the waffle. Let choose the temperature and adjust it to medium-high. Let grease the plates.
2. Whisk the cinnamon, salt, baking powder, and flour into the bowl and keep it aside. Add egg whites into the mixing bowl. Mix with a stand mixer until soft peaks form. Keep it aside.
3. Whisk egg yolks, vanilla extract, and melted butter into the bowl. Combine until smooth batter forms.
4. Add whipped egg whites into the batter and combine it well.
5. Add blueberries and lemon zest and mix it well.
6. When ready to cook, stir well.
7. Pour batter into the waffle iron. Close the lid. Let cook until crispy.
8. Transfer the waffles to the cooling rack.
9. Garnish with pure maple syrup and blueberries.
Nutrition: Calories; 213kcal, carbohydrates; 17g, protein; 8g, fat; 12g

68. Golden Turmeric Milk

Preparation time: 5 minutes | **Cooking time:** 5 minutes | **Serving:** 2

Ingredients:

- Dairy-free milk – 2 cups, such as coconut, almond
- Turmeric powder – 1 tsp, chopped
- Ginger powder – ¼ tsp
- Ground cinnamon – ½ tsp
- Black pepper – ¼ tsp
- Maple syrup – 1 tsp

Directions:

1. Add all ingredients except the maple syrup into the blender and blend until smooth.
2. Pour non-dairy milk mixture into the saucepan with maple syrup and black pepper and cook for three to five minutes over medium flame.
3. Pour milk into the cup.
4. Serve!

Nutrition: Calories; 61kcal, carbohydrates; 6g, protein; 1g, fiber; 1g

69. Green kiwi smoothie

Preparation time: 5 minutes | **Serving:** 2

Ingredients:

- Green grapes – one cup, seedless
- Kiwi – one, peeled and cut into chunks
- Water – two tbsp
- English cucumber – 20cm, cut into chunks
- Baby spinach – two cups, chopped stemmed, washed and dried
- Ice cubes – 1 ½ to 2 cups

Directions:

1. Firstly, add green grapes, kiwi, water, English cucumber, baby spinach, and ice cubes into the blender.
2. Blend on high speed until smooth.
3. Add a small amount of ice cubes and blend until frosty.
4. Add more ice cubes if desired.
5. Serve and enjoy!
6. You can prepare this without ice cubes.

7. When you are ready to drink it, then add ice cubes and shake it well.

Nutrition: Calories; 132kcal, Carbohydrates; 33g, Protein; 3g, Fat; 1g

70. Mini frittatas

Preparation time: 10 minutes | **Cooking time:** 45 minutes | **Serving:** 6

Ingredients:

- Olive oil – two tbsp
- Scallions – one cup, chopped, green parts
- Yukon Gold potatoes – six ounces, diced, peeled
- Zucchini – half , medium-sized, trimmed, diced
- Red bell pepper – half, medium-sized, trimmed, cored and diced
- Baby arugula or baby kale or baby spinach – 1 ½ cups
- Kosher salt and black pepper(ground) – to taste
- Eggs – eight, big-sized
- Cheese – four ounces, cheddar, Monterey jack or feta, shredded or crumbled
- Herbs – like, dill, thyme or tarragon, optional

Some of options:

- Bacon – cooked, crisp
- Black olives
- Cherry tomatoes – raw
- Broccoli florets – raw or cooked
- Oyster mushrooms – sautéed

Directions:

1. Preheat the oven to 375 degrees Fahrenheit.
2. Let coat the inner side of twelve muffin tins with non-stick cooking spray.
3. Keep it aside on the rimmed baking sheet.
4. Add oil into the skillet and heat over medium-low flame.
5. Then, add potatoes and scallion greens and cook until tender, for eight minutes.
6. Add bell pepper and zucchini and cook until crispy and tender.

7. Add kale or arugula and spinach and cook until wilted.
8. Sprinkle with pepper and salt.
9. After that, whisk eggs into the mixing bowl. Add herbs and then fold in cooked vegetables. Next, split the mixture into the ramekins.
10. Top with your favorite options; cheese, vegetables, and bacon. Combine it well.
11. Poke the options down into the mixture with your hands or spoon.
12. Place it into the oven and bake for fifteen to twenty minutes until set.
13. Serve hot!

Nutrition: Calories; 270kcal, carbohydrates; 11g, protein; 17g, fat; 18g

71. Fluffy pancakes

Preparation time: 5 minutes | **Cooking time:** 15 minutes | **Serving:** 8
Ingredients:
- All-purpose flour – two cups, low fodmap, gluten-free
- Glucose syrup – ¼ cup
- Baking powder – one tbsp + one tsp, gluten-free
- Salt – half tsp
- Baking soda – ¼ tsp
- Whole lactose free milk – 1 ¾ cups
- Unsalted butter – ¼ cup, melted
- Egg – one, big-sized
- Vanilla extract – one teaspoon

Directions:
1. Whisk baking soda, salt, baking powder, glucose syrup, and flour into the mixing bowl until combined. Next, make a well in the middle of the mixture.
2. Whisk the wet ingredients in another bowl.
3. Add wet ingredients to dry ingredients until smooth. But do not overbeat.
4. Heat the non-stick pan and coat with non-stick spray.
5. Place ¼ cup batter into the pan and cook over medium flame for one to two minutes.

6. Flip over and cook for one minute until golden brown.
7. Top with maple syrup.

Nutrition: Calories; 253kcal, carbohydrates; 41g, protein; 5g, fat; 8g

72. Poached eggs with lemon hollandaise sauce

Preparation time: 10 minutes | **Cooking time:** 10 minutes | **Serving:** 2
Ingredients:
- Eggs:
- White vinegar – one tablespoon
- Eggs – four
- Buttered toast – to serve, gluten-free, low fodmap
- Mixed lettuce leaves – A handful, to serve
- Salt and pepper – ground
- Lemon hollandaise sauce:
- Lemon juice – 1 ½ tbsp
- Egg yolks – two
- Corn syrup – 1/8 tsp
- Rock salt – pinch
- Black pepper – to taste
- Butter – two tbsp, dairy-free

Directions:
1. Add 1 ¼ inch of water and vinegar into the frying pan. Let boil it.
2. Break the egg into a small sieve and then place it into the bowl.
3. Stir the water until swirls and place the whole egg into the frying pan.
4. Do it with the remaining egg. Cook for two minutes.
5. Then, scoop out and put onto the paper towel to drain it.

To prepare hollandaise sauce:
1. Whisk the black pepper, salt, corn syrup, lemon juice, and egg yolks into the bowl until smooth.
2. Melt the butter into the microwave and then add it into the mixture and whisk it well.
3. Next, heat the hollandaise sauce into the microwave for fifteen seconds and whisk

it well. Then, heat in ten seconds bursts. Whisk until thick.

4. Place a poached egg on the buttered toast. Top with mixed lettuce leaves and drizzle with hollandaise sauce.
5. Sprinkle with pepper and salt.
6. <u>Nutrition:</u> Calories; 289kcal, Carbohydrates; 2g, Protein; 14g, Fat; 24g

73. Overnight oats and chia

Preparation time: 10 minutes | **Chill time:** 8 hours | **Serving:** 6
Ingredients:
- Unsweetened almond milk – 1 1/3 cups
- Old-fashioned rolled oats – one cup
- Chia seeds – three tbsp
- Maple syrup - one to two tbsp, optional

<u>Directions:</u>
1. Add all ingredients into the airtight container and make sure that everything is mixed well. Then, place it into the refrigerator overnight.
2. When ready to serve, top with low fodmap topping.
3. Serve and enjoy!

<u>Nutrition:</u> Calories; 194kcal, carbohydrates; 31g, protein; 6g, fat; 4g

74. BLT omelet with blue cheese

Preparation time: 5 minutes | **Cooking time:** 5 minutes | **Serving:** 2
Ingredients:
- Eggs – four, big-sized
- Water – two tsp
- Kosher salt and ground black pepper – to taste
- Cherry or grape tomatoes – eight, halved
- Crisp bacon – four piece, cooked, crumbled or chopped into bite-sized pieces
- Crumbled blue cheese – two ounces, you can use feta cheese also
- Baby lettuces – A handful
- Unsalted butter – one tbsp

<u>Directions:</u>
1. Whisk the egg into the mixing bowl. Then, add water and sprinkle with pepper and salt. Add cheese, lettuce, bacon, and tomatoes and whisk all together until combine well.
2. Add butter into the skillet and melt it over medium flame until bubbly.
3. Place omelet mixture in it and cook over medium flame.
4. Cook until omelet has a tiny bit of moisture left, but it is not too wet or not over dry.
5. After that, fold one half of omelet onto the other half and place it onto the serving plate.
6. Serve and enjoy!

<u>Nutrition:</u> Calories; 301kcal, carbohydrates; 2g, protein; 18g, fat; 23g

75. Browned-butter coconut pancakes

Preparation time: 5 minutes | **Cooking time:** 10 minutes | **Serving:** 4
Ingredients:
- Unsalted butter – five tbsp, cut into pieces
- All-purpose flour – 1 ¼ cups, low fodmap gluten-free
- Unsweetened coconut – ¼ cup, grated or shredded
- Baking powder – one tbsp + one tsp
- Salt – half tsp
- Whole milk – 1 to 1 ½ cups, lactose-free
- Eggs – two, big-sized
- Almond extract – 1/8 tsp
- Maple Syrup – to taste

<u>Directions:</u>
1. Add butter into the saucepan and melt over medium-low flame.
2. Cook until brown but do not burn it. Let cool it to lukewarm.
3. During this, whisk the salt, baking powder, coconut, and flour into the

mixing bowl and combine it well. Next, make a well in the middle of the mixture and keep it aside.

4. Whisk the almond extract, melted browned butter, egg, and a small amount of milk in another bowl and combine well.
5. Place mixture into the well of the dry mixture and whisk it well.
6. Add more milk if the mixture is thick.
7. Next, heat the non-stick pan and coat it with non-stick cooking spray. Place ¼ cup of batter into the pan and cook over medium flame until bubbles appear, for one to two minutes.
8. Flip over and cook for one minute more until golden brown.
9. Top with pure maple syrup.

Nutrition: Calories; 375kcal, carbohydrates; 40g, protein; 6g, fat; 21g

76. Banana oat waffles

Preparation time: 5 minutes | **Cooking time:** 15 minutes | **Serving:** 6

Ingredients:

- All-purpose flour – one cup, low fodmap gluten-free
- Old-fashioned rolled oats – one cup
- Glucose syrup– three tbs
- Baking powder – one tbsp
- Pinch of salt
- Baking soda – half tsp
- Cinnamon – ¼ tsp
- Nutmeg – 1/8 tsp, grated
- Lactose-free buttermilk or lactose-free whole milk – 1 ½ cups,
- Eggs – two, big-sized
- Vanilla extract – half tsp
- Unsalted butter – ¼ cup, melted
- Ripe banana – one, peeled and sliced thinly, medium-sized

Directions:
1. Preheat the waffle iron. Preheat the oven to 200 degrees Fahrenheit.

2. Whisk the nutmeg, cinnamon, salt, baking soda, baking powder, oats, glucose syrup, and flour into the bowl. Keep it aside.
3. Whisk the buttermilk or whole milk, vanilla, and eggs into the small bowl until combined. Add this wet mixture over the dry mixture and whisk it well.
4. Then, drizzle in melted butter. Add banana and stir until combined.
5. Let coat the waffle maker with non-stick spray.
6. Place batter into the preheated waffle iron and cook until crispy and golden brown for four minutes. Keep warm waffles in the oven.
7. Top with butter and pure maple syrup.

Nutrition: Calories; 407kcal, carbohydrates; 60g, protein; 10g, fat; 13g

77. Hash brown potatoes

Preparation time: 10 minutes | **Cooking time:** 25 minutes | **Serving:** 4

Ingredients:

- Russet or all-purpose potatoes – 1 ½ pounds, peeled
- Scallion greens – two tbsp, chopped
- Kosher salt and ground black pepper – to taste
- Unsalted butter – three tbsp, melted
- Vegetable oil – three tbsp

Directions:
1. Firstly, grate the potatoes with a box grater and then add to the bowl of cold water. Stir until the water looks cloudy.
2. Then, drain into the colander and pressing out as much as possible.
3. Place onto the clean-lined towel.
4. Transfer the potatoes into the mixing bowl. Then, add scallions and toss to combine. Sprinkle with pepper and salt.
5. Add half of the oil and butter into the skillet and heat it.
6. When heated, add potato mixture and toss to coat in the oil.
7. Cook over medium flame for ten to fifteen minutes until golden brown.

8. Flip over potatoes with a sturdy spatula. Add additional butter and oil when the pan looks dry. Do not worry if the potatoes break up and cook over medium flame until browned for ten minutes.
9. Serve and enjoy!

Nutrition: Calories; 304kcal, carbohydrates; 30g, protein; 3g, fat; 18g

78. Savory Breakfast Bowl

Preparation time: 20 minutes | **Cooking time:** 20 minutes | **Servings:** 1

Ingredients
- ½ C. oats, rolled
- ½ C. almond milk, unsweetened
- ½ C. water
- ¼ tsp. Himalayan salt
- ¼ tsp. black pepper, crushed
- 1 C. spinach
- 1 tbsp. nutritional yeast
- 1 tsp. lemon zest
- ½ tsp. turmeric
- ¼ tsp. red chili flakes
- ⅓ C. lentils, cooked

Directions
1. In a medium saucepan over medium heat, add oats, almond milk, water, salt, and pepper. Bring to a boil and then reduce heat to low and simmer 5–10 minutes or until liquid is absorbed.
2. Stir in spinach, nutritional yeast, lemon zest, turmeric, chili flakes, and lentils.
3. Remove from heat and serve.

Nutrition: Calories: 700, Carbs 22g, Protein 25g, Fat 50g.

79. Fruit and Millet Breakfast

Preparation time: 30 minutes | **Cooking time:** 15 minutes | **Servings:** 2

Ingredients
- ½ C. millet
- 1 C. water
- 2 tbsp. raisins
- 1 tbsp. currants

- ⅛ tsp. cinnamon
- ⅛ tsp. vanilla extract
- 1 C. coconut milk, unsweetened and divided
- 1 tsp. maple syrup
- ½ C. raspberries
- ½ C. blueberries
- 1 tsp. hemp hearts
- 1 tsp. chia seeds
- 1 tsp. mint, chopped

Directions
1. Place millet and water in a medium saucepan over medium heat. Bring to a boil, and then add the raisins, currants, cinnamon, and vanilla. Cover with a lid, reduce heat to low, and let cook for another 10 minutes until liquid is absorbed.
2. Turn heat off and let sit for 10 minutes
3. Add coconut milk, maple syrup, raspberries, blueberries, hemp hearts, and chia seeds. Turn heat to low and let cook for 2 minutes.
4. Transfer to bowls and garnish with mint.

Nutrition: Calories: 129, Carbs 57g, Protein 49g, Fat 36g.

80. Breakfast Squash Bread

Preparation time: 40 minutes | **Cooking time:** 20–30 minutes | **Servings:** 2

Ingredients
- 1 C. almond meal
- 1 tbsp. flax meal
- ⅓ C. arrowroot flour
- ½ tbsp. chia seeds
- ½ tsp. baking soda
- 1 tbsp. oregano, dried
- ½ tsp. Himalayan salt
- 1 egg
- ½ zucchini, finely grated
- ½ yellow squash, finely grated

- 2 tbsp. coconut milk
- 2 tbsp. coconut oil
- ½ tsp. apple cider vinegar

Directions
1. Preheat oven to 350°F/180°C. Line a mini loaf tin with parchment paper.
2. In a medium-sized bowl, combine the almond meal, flax meal, arrowroot, chia seeds, baking soda, oregano, and salt.
3. Beat the egg in a large bowl and add the zucchini, squash, coconut milk, coconut oil, and vinegar. Pour the dry ingredients into the large bowl with the wet ingredients and stir until well combined.
4. Pour mixture into the prepared mini loaf pan and bake in the oven for 20–30 minutes or until lightly golden brown and cooked in the center.

Nutrition: Calories: 216, Carbs 12g, Protein 15g, Fat 17g, Sodium 151 mg

81. Chia Breakfast Pudding With Cantaloupe

Preparation time: 5 minutes | **Cooking time:** 0 minutes | **Servings:** 4
Ingredients
- 2 C. low-fat rice milk
- ¼ C. maple syrup
- ½ tsp. vanilla extract
- ½ C. chia seeds
- 1 C. cantaloupe, chopped

Directions
1. In a bowl, whisk together the milk, maple syrup, and vanilla.
2. Stir in the chia seeds. Cover and refrigerate overnight (or for at least 4 hours).
3. Serve the cantaloupe spooned over the pudding.

Nutrition: Calories: 206, Protein 7g, Fat 7g, Carbs 34g.

82. Apple Parfait

Preparation time: 10 minutes | **Cooking time:** 0 minutes | **Servings:** 2
Ingredients
- 2 oz. cashews, soaked
- 2 oz. low-fat coconut milk
- ¼ tsp. vanilla extract
- 2 apples, chopped
- 1 tbsp. hemp seeds

Directions
1. Place the cashews, coconut milk, vanilla extract, and hemp seeds into the blender.
2. Blend the mixture until smooth and homogenous.
3. After this, place a small amount of the smooth mixture in the glass.
4. Then make a layer of the chopped apples.
5. Repeat the layers until you have put in all the ingredients.
6. Serve it!

Nutrition: Calories: 367, Fat 22g, Carbs 42g, Protein 6.8g

83. Mexican Breakfast Toast

Preparation time: 5 minutes | **Cooking time:** 20 minutes | **Servings:** 2
Ingredients
- 2 slices sprouted bread, toasted
- 2 tbsp. hummus
- ½ C. spinach, chopped
- Chives
- ½ C. sprouts
- 1 avocado, thinly sliced
- ¼ tsp. Himalayan salt
- Spicy Yogurt
- 3 tbsp. yogurt, unsweetened
- ½ lime, juiced
- 1 tsp. cumin
- 1 tsp. cayenne

Directions
1. In a small bowl, prepare the Spicy Yogurt by combining all the Spicy Yogurt ingredients and whisking well to combine.
2. Place toast slices on plates and spread a tbsp. of hummus on each. Place spinach

on each slice, and then Spicy Yogurt, chives, sprouts, and avocado. Sprinkle each with salt and serve.

Nutrition: Calories: 438, Carbs 15g, Protein 23g, Fat 36g, Saturated Fat 12g, Sodium 1457mg, Fiber 3g

84. Morning Sweet Bread

Preparation time: 30 minutes | **Cooking time:** 30 minutes | **Servings:** 2

Ingredients

- 1 tbsp. flaxseed, ground
- 3 tbsp. water
- 1 ½ C. almond meal
- 2 tbsp. coconut flour
- 1 tsp. Himalayan salt
- 2 tsp. cinnamon
- 1 tsp. vanilla extract
- 1 tsp. corn syrup
- 1 tbsp. olive oil
- 2 tbsp. raisins
- 1 tbsp. cashew butter, melted
- 1 pear, cored and sliced

Directions

1. Preheat oven to 350°F/180°C and line bottom of a small glass baking dish with parchment paper.
2. In a small bowl, mix together the flaxseeds and 3 tbsp. water from the flaxseeds gel. Set aside and let sit 10 minutes until it forms a gel.
3. In a large bowl, combine the almond meal, coconut flour, salt, cinnamon, vanilla, corn syrup, flaxseeds gel, olive oil, and raisins.
4. Place dough in the baking dish and press into an even layer. Bake in the oven for 15 minutes.
5. Remove and let cool. Top with cashew butter and pear slices before serving.

Nutrition: Calories: 509, Carbs 80g, Protein 33g, Fat 6g, Sodium 82mg, Fiber 4g.

85. Banana Breakfast Pudding

Preparation time: 5 minutes + 8 hours chill time | **Cooking time:** 0 minutes | **Servings:** 1

Ingredients

- 1 C. coconut milk
- 1 tbsp. maple syrup
- ½ tsp. vanilla extract
- ¼ tsp. cinnamon
- ¼ tsp. nutmeg
- ⅛ tsp. Himalayan salt
- 2 tbsp. chia seeds
- 1 banana, sliced
- 1 tbsp. walnuts, toasted and crushed
- 1 tbsp. cacao nibs

Directions

1. In a small bowl or jar with a cover, place coconut milk, maple syrup, vanilla, cinnamon, nutmeg, salt, and chia seeds.
2. Let sit in the fridge, covered, overnight.
3. In the morning, top with banana, walnuts, and cacao nibs before serving.

Nutrition: Calories 434, Carbs 27g, Protein 27g

86. Italian Breakfast Hash

Preparation time: 35 minutes | **Cooking time:** 30 minutes | **Servings:** 2

Ingredients

- 2 sweet potatoes, peeled and cubed into ½ inch pieces
- 2 tbsp. olive oil
- ½ red bell pepper, halved and sliced
- ½ green bell pepper, halved and sliced
- ½ tsp. Himalayan salt
- ½ tsp. black pepper, crushed
- ¼ tsp. paprika
- 4 fresh sage leaves, thinly sliced
- 1 tsp. oregano
- ¼ tsp. red chili flakes
- 1 C. tempeh, crumbled
- 1 tbsp. parsley, chopped

Directions

1. Place sweet potato cubes in a medium pot over medium-high heat. Bring to a boil and let cook for 5 minutes. Potatoes

should be tender, but not mushy. Drain and set aside.

2. Heat oil in a large skillet over medium-low heat. Add bell peppers, and sweet potatoes. Cook 10 minutes, stirring frequently.
3. Stir in the salt, pepper, paprika, sage, oregano, and chili flakes. Cook for 2 minutes, and then crumble in the tempeh. Cook another 2 minutes and then remove from heat.
4. Garnish with parsley before serving.

Nutrition: Calories: 43, Carbs 4g, Protein 1g, Fat 3g, Sodium 110mg.Fiber 1g, Sugar 1g.

87. Papaya Breakfast Boat

Preparation time: 5 minutes | **Cooking time:** 0 minutes | **Servings:** 2

Ingredients

- 1 papaya, cut lengthwise in half, and seeds removed
- 1 C. yogurt, unsweetened
- 1 lime, zested
- 3 tbsp. raw oats
- 1 tbsp. coconut, unsweetened, shredded
- ½ banana, sliced
- ¼ C. raspberries
- 1 tbsp. walnuts, chopped
- 1 tsp. chia seeds
- 1 tsp. maple syrup

Directions

1. Place papaya halves on plates and place yogurt on top of each.
2. Then top each half with lime zest, oats, coconut, banana, raspberries, walnuts, chia seeds.
3. Drizzle with maple syrup and serve.

Nutrition: Calories: 60, Carbs 5g, Protein 6g, Fat 3g, Sodium 90mg, Fiber 1g, sugar 1g.

88. Cherry Almond Bake

Preparation time: 50 minutes plus 30 minutes cooling | **Cooking time:** 45 minutes | **Servings:** 2

Ingredients

- 3 tbsp. almond milk, unsweetened
- ¼ C. dates, pitted
- ⅓ C. almond meal
- ¾ tsp. vanilla extract
- ¼ tsp. almond extract
- ⅛ tsp. Himalayan salt
- ¼ C. raw almonds, slivered and divided
- 1 ½ C. fresh cherries, pitted, divided
- 1 C. quinoa, cooked

Directions

1. Preheat oven to 350°F/180°C, and line a small baking dish with parchment paper.
2. Combine the almond milk, dates, almond meal, vanilla extract, almond extract, salt, half of the almonds, and half of the cherries in a food processor or blender.
3. Add mixture to a large bowl and stir in the quinoa. Pour into prepared baking dish and place remaining cherries and almonds on top.
4. Bake in the oven for 45 minutes or until lightly browned on top.
5. Remove from oven and let cool for 30 minutes before cutting into squares and serving.

Nutrition: Calories: 141, Protein 4g, Fat 12g, Saturated fat 1g, Sodium 170 mg.

89. Salmon and Cabbage Hash

Preparation time: 12 minutes | **Cooking time:** 15 minutes | **Servings:** 2

Ingredients:

- 1 tbsp. olive oil
- 1 C. green cabbage, thinly shredded
- 1 C. sweet potato, shredded
- 4 oz. salmon, smoked, flaked into bite-size pieces
- ¼ tsp. black pepper, ground
- 1 tbsp. fresh dill, chopped

Directions:

LOW FODMAP COOKBOOK - SUZANNE SCARRETT

1. In a medium-sized skillet over medium heat, add olive oil, cabbage, sweet potato. Sauté for 8 minutes until cabbage is soft, and sweet potato is tender.
2. Add smoked salmon, pepper, and dill. Cook 2 minutes.
3. Remove from heat and serve.

Nutrition: Calories: 15, Carbs 3g, Protein 1g, Fat 1g, Saturated Fat 1g, Sodium 1164 mg.

90. Summer Medley Parfait

Preparation time: 10 minutes | **Cooking time:** 0 minutes | **Servings:** 2
Ingredients:
- ⅓ C. raw cashews
- ½ tbsp. corn syrup
- ½ tsp. vanilla extract
- ¼ tsp. almond extract
- 1 tsp. lemon juice
- ⅛ tsp. Himalayan salt
- 1 ½ C. strawberries, hulled, chopped, and divided
- ½ tbsp. fresh mint, thinly sliced
- 1 tsp. lemon zest
- ⅓ C. almonds, slivered and toasted

Directions:
1. In a food processor, combine the drained cashews, corn syrup, vanilla extract, almond extract, lemon juice, and salt. Add half of the strawberries and pulse until everything is combined thoroughly.
2. Pour cashew mixture into serving bowls or glasses and top with remaining strawberries, mint, lemon zest, and almonds.
3. Serve immediately.

Nutrition: Calories: 11, Carbs 2g, Protein 1g, Fat 1g.

Lunch

91. Antipasto on a Stick

Preparation Time: 5 minutes | **Cooking Time:** 0 minutes | **Servings:** 1
Ingredients:

- 1 small jar pepperoncini
- 1 small jar pitted Kalamata olives
- Fresh mozzarella balls, small, 2 for each skewer
- Thinly sliced ham or Canadian bacon
- Basil leaves or spinach leaves
- Grape tomatoes
- Skewers about 6 inches long

Directions:

1. Cut the pepperoncini in half so that it will fit evenly on the skewer.
2. Fold the ham into quarters to fit on the skewer.
3. Layer the ingredients on the skewer, placing 2 mozzarella balls, 2 slices of ham, 1 whole pepperoncino, and 2 grape tomatoes on each skewer. Add olives between the Ingredients as you desire.
4. Nutrition Information is based on 5 olives per skewer.
5. Serve on a platter with spinach leaves scattered around for a beautiful presentation.

Nutrition: Calories: 263, Fat: 17g, Carbs: 8g, Protein: 22 g

92. Crab and Miso Soup

Preparation Time: 10 minutes | **Cooking Time:** 20-25 minutes | **Servings:** 4
Ingredients:

- 2 x 250g pots Instant Brown
- Medium Grain Rice in 90 seconds
- 2 bunches broccoli, stems sliced
- 2 corn cobs

- 1/3 cup white miso paste
- 1/4 cup tahini
- 200g fresh crab meat, cooked
- 1/3 cup chopped chives
- 2 teaspoons black sesame seeds, toasted

Directions:

1. Cook rice following the package directions.
2. Add 6 cups of water in a large saucepan.
3. Bring the water to boil over high heat.
4. Add the broccoli and cook for 1 min.
5. Meanwhile, cut corn kernels from the fresh cobs.
6. Add to the pan with rice and cook for 1 minute.
7. Remove from heat.
8. Add miso paste and tahini and stir until well combined—divide between 4 serving bowls.
9. Add the crab and sprinkle with chives and sesame seeds.

Nutrition: Calories: 514, Fat: 15g, Carbs 82.60g, Protein: 22.5

93. Mexican Lime Chicken

Preparation Time: 5 Minutes | **Cooking Time:** 30 minutes | **Servings:** 4
Ingredients:

- 1 Lb. boneless, and skinless chicken breasts, pounded to an even thickness
- 1/4 cup fresh lime juice
- 2 tablespoons olive oil
- 1/2 teaspoon ancho chili powder
- 1/2 teaspoon salt
- 1/4 teaspoon fresh ground black pepper

Directions:

1. Make a marinade of lime juice, ancho chili powder, salt, and pepper.

2. Pour this into a sealable plastic bag or bowl and place the chicken breasts inside, poking them first with a fork so they will absorb more marinade.

3. Refrigerate for two hours, turning the chicken over every 30 minutes to ensure it is coated evenly.

4. Drain the chicken and grill over medium until the chicken is done.

Nutrition: Calories: 204, Fat: 10g, Carbs: 1g, Protein: 26g

94. Pad Thai Noodles

Preparation Time: 20 Minutes | **Cooking Time:** 15 Minutes | **Servings:** 4

Ingredients:
- 250g rice stick noodles
- 2 tablespoons Rice Oil
- 2 eggs, scrambled a bit • 1/3 cup pad Thai paste
- 250g firm tofu, chopped into fine pieces
- 100g beansprouts end trimmed
- 2 tablespoons peanuts, chopped coarsely
- Lime wedges, for garnish

Directions:
1. Add the rice noodles in a heatproof bowl.
2. Cover w/ boiling hot water.
3. Stand for 10 minutes until softened.
4. Drain the noodles in a colander. Set the noodles aside.
5. Heat 1 Tsp. Of oil in a large frying pan.
6. Add egg and fry softly enough that the white is set. Cook for 2 minutes and remove to a plate.
7. Roughly chop the egg.
8. Heat the remaining oil in the pan.
9. Add the Thai paste and tofu. Stir together in the oil for 1 minute or until fragrant. Add the rice noodles. Cook, stirring, for 1 minute or until the noodles are warmed.
10. Remove from heat.
11. Divide the noodle mixture between the serving bowls. Place the beansprouts on top, then the pieces of egg, then the

peanuts. Squirt a spritz of lime juice into the noodles and serve with decorative lime pieces.

Nutrition: Calories: 380, Fat: 21g, Carbs: 28g, Protein: 16g

95. Parmesan Coated Wings

Preparation Time: 10 Minutes | **Cooking Time:** 60 Minutes | **Servings:** 2

Ingredients:
- 24 chicken wings
- Olive oil cooking spray
- 3 tablespoons butter
- 1/4 teaspoon salt
- 1/4 teaspoon ground black pepper
- 1/2 cup finely shredded
- Parmesan cheese
- Chopped fresh parsley

Directions:
1. Preheat oven to 370° F.
2. Line a large baking sheet with aluminum foil, shiny side up, and spritz with olive oil cooking spray.
3. Place the wings on the prepared sheet and season with salt and pepper.
4. Bake for 1 hour, or until golden brown.
5. In a small saucepan, heat olive oil.
6. Add butter and melt to combine with the oil.
7. Stir in salt and pepper.
8. Arrange wings on a serving plate and drizzle with the butter and oil mixture.
9. Sprinkle with Parmesan cheese and chopped parsley and serve.

Nutrition: Calories: 142, Fat: 11g, Carbs: 0g, Protein: 11g

96. Pina Colada Bites

Preparation Time: 15 Minutes | **Cooking Time:** 75 Minutes | **Servings:** 4

Ingredients:
- 1.3kg pineapple
- 1 1/2 cups agave syrup
- 1 cup of water

- 1 tablespoon of liquid glucose
- 2 teaspoons Coconut extract

Directions:
1. Cut the pineapple slices into smaller bits.
2. Combine the agave syrup and water into a saucepan, stirring until all the agave syrup are melted.
3. Bring the liquid to a simmer.
4. Add the pineapple and 2 teaspoons coconut extract.
5. Slowly continue to simmer for 40 minutes or until the pineapple is opaque.
6. Use a slotted spoon to transfer to a rack placed over a baking tray lined with baking paper.
7. Preheat oven to 225F. Bake for 1 1/4 hours, to dry the pineapple. Allow the pineapple to cool. Store in an airtight container at room temperature or refrigerate if the atmosphere is humid.

Nutrition: Calories: 460, Fat: 4g, Carbs: 107g, Protein: 1.8 g

97. Savory Chicken and Rice Muffins

Preparation Time: 10 Minutes | **Cooking Time:** 20 Minutes | **Servings:** 8
Ingredients:
- 2/3 cup Basmati Rice
- 250g skinless smoked chicken breast, chopped finely
- 2/3 cup dried tomatoes, coarsely chopped
- 1 1/3 cups grated fresh mozzarella cheese
- 1/4 cup basil leaves, chopped finely
- 3 eggs, lightly beaten

Directions:
1. Preheat oven to 400F.
2. Grease Texas-sized muffin tin.
3. Line the muffin tin with liners.
4. Cook the basmati rice as the package suggests.
5. Rinse the rice and let cool.
6. Place all ingredients into a bowl, with the exception of 1/3 cups of the mozzarella cheese.

7. Spoon the mixture of chicken and rice into the prepared muffin pan.
8. Sprinkle with remaining cheese.
9. Bake for 15 to 20 mins. or until the muffins are firm & light golden in color.
10. Stand in pan for 5 minutes. Dump the muffins onto a plate and allow it to cool. Store in an airtight container.
11. Refrigerate until ready to serve. Enjoy for breakfast or as a light tea snack.

Nutrition: Calories: 229, Fat: 8g, Carbs: 18g, Protein: 20g

98. Tuesday Tacos

Preparation Time: 5 Minutes | **Cooking Time:** 20 Minutes | **Servings:** 4
Ingredients:
- 1 jalapeno chilies (diced) optional
- 1 handful chives (diced)
- 2 red pepper (green and, diced)
- 2 Lbs. ground chicken (or turkey)
- 1 can diced tomatoes (with or without chilies)
- 2 tbsps. Cumin
- 2 tbsps. Paprika
- 1 tbsp. cayenne pepper
- 1 tbsp. oregano

Directions:
1. Start with placing the chives, bell pepper pieces, and the ground chicken, with a tablespoon of olive into a skillet and beginning to fry.
2. Fry the meat and the peppers until the meat is no longer pink, the meat is crumbled, and the peppers are soft.
3. Sprinkle spices into your meat and mix, occasionally tasting for flavor.
4. When the meat has the desired flavor, add the can of diced tomatoes and serve.

Nutrition: Calories: 390, Fat: 20g, Carbs: 11g, Protein: 41g

99. Turkey Burgers with Spinach and Feta

Preparation Time: 5 Minutes | **Cooking Time:** 14 Minutes | **Servings:** 4

Ingredients:

- 1 Lb. ground turkey
- 1 egg beaten
- 1 cup crumbled feta cheese
- 3 cups frozen spinach, defrosted
- Spices of your choice: paprika, oregano, cayenne pepper, salt, pepper
- Olive oil

Directions:

1. Place your ingredients into a bowl and mix together.
2. Scoop one Pattie together and press until firm.
3. Place gently into the cooking oil in a skillet on medium.
4. Place each Pattie into the pan in this manner. Let the patties cook for 7 minutes on one side, then gently turn so the patties will stay firm and shaped.
5. Flip the patties & cook for another 6 or 7 minutes.
6. Serve

Nutrition: Calories: 360, Fat: 24g, Carbs: 9g, Protein: 28g

100. Minestrone

Preparation Time: 10 minutes | **Cooking Time:** 40 minutes | **Servings:** 4

Ingredients:

- 65 grams middle bacon
- 80 grams leek
- 75 grams shell pasta, gluten-free
- 240 grams carrots, diced
- 12 grams fresh basil, chopped
- 160 grams potato, diced
- 310 milliliters boiling water
- 50 grams celery, sliced
- 160 grams zucchini, diced
- 400 grams canned plain tomatoes, chopped
- 60 grams spinach, sliced
- 3 tablespoons parmesan cheese
- Olive oil
- Salt and pepper
- 500 milliliters low FODMAP vegetable stock
- 168 grams canned chickpeas, rinsed and drained

Directions:

1. Remove the white stem of the leeks.
2. Chop the green tips finely and set aside.
3. Slice the bacon into small pieces after removing the rind.
4. Over medium heat, saute carrots, potato, leeks, bacon and celery in a large saucepan for about 20 minutes.
5. Add tomatoes, boiling water, chickpeas, vegetable stock, spinach and zucchini into the pan.
6. Turn down the heat to medium-low and let it simmer.
7. After 10 minutes, put the pasta and basil in the pan.
8. Allow the pasta to cook in the soup. Sprinkle salt and pepper to taste.
9. Adjust the soup's consistency by adding water, if desired.
10. Serve with parmesan cheese, baby basil leaves

Nutrition: Calories: 386, Total Fat: 17g, Saturated Fat: 0g, Cholesterol: 0 mg, Sodium: 0mg, Total Carbs: 50.4g, Fiber: 10.6g, Sugar: 11.8g, Protein: 11.9g

101. Cheesy Chicken Fritters

Preparation Time: 10 minutes | **Cooking Time:** 20 minutes | **Servings:** 4

Ingredients:

- 500 grams chicken, ground
- 84 grams mozzarella cheese, grated
- ¼ teaspoon salt
- 2 large eggs
- 2 teaspoons chives, dried
- 60 milliliters mayonnaise
- 2 tablespoons fresh basil, chopped
- 35 grams plain flour, gluten-free
- Olive oil
- Black pepper

Directions:

1. Mix all of the ingredients thoroughly in a large bowl.
2. Season with salt and pepper.
3. Place a large frying pan with olive oil over medium heat.
4. Scoop about ¼ cup of the chicken mixture and place it in the pan.
5. Flatten the mixture slightly using a spatula and let it cook for about 4 minutes on each side.
6. Line a plate with paper towel.
7. Once cooked thoroughly, transfer the fritters into the plate to remove excess oil.
8. Repeat the process for the remaining chicken mixture.

Nutrition: Calories: 415, Total Fat: 26.8g, Saturated Fat: 0g, Cholesterol: 0 mg, Sodium: 0 mg, Total Carbs: 11.4 g, Fiber: 0.4g, Sugar: 1.7g, Protein: 31.3 g

102.   Crispy Falafel

Preparation Time: 10 minutes | **Cooking Time:** 25 minutes | **Servings:** 5
Ingredients:

- 120 grams carrots, grated and peeled
- 2 tablespoons olive oil
- 5 tablespoons plain flour, gluten-free
- ¾ teaspoon cumin, ground
- 25 grams fresh parsley, chopped
- 2 teaspoons paprika
- 80 grams leek
- Zest and juice of 1 large lime
- Salt and pepper
- 182 grams microwavable brown rice, pre-cooked
- 168 grams canned chickpeas, rinsed and drained

Directions:

1. Set the oven to 380°F.
2. Prepare a roasting tray lined with baking paper.
3. Remove the white stems of the leek and chop the green tips roughly.
4. Except for the plain flour, blend all of the ingredients using a food processor.
5. Once the mixture becomes a smooth paste, add the plain flour and mix well.
6. Use 1 tablespoon of olive oil to grease the baking paper.
7. Form small falafel patties using a tablespoon and place them on the roasting tray.
8. Make sure to allocate enough space between each patty.
9. Coat the top of the patties with olive oil.
10. Place the tray in the oven and cook for about 12 minutes on each side.
☐

Nutrition: Calories: 187, Total Fat: 7.1g, Saturated Fat: 0g, Cholesterol: 0 mg, Sodium: 0 mg, Total Carbs: 27.7g, Fiber: 4.5g, Sugar: 3.6 g, Protein: 4.4 g

103.   Chicken Alfredo Pasta Bake

Preparation Time: 10 minutes | **Cooking Time:** 50 minutes | **Servings:** 4
Ingredients:

- 450 grams chicken breast
- 3 tablespoons fresh sage, chopped
- 5 tablespoons butter
- 114 grams cheddar cheese, grated
- ¼ cup plain flour, gluten-free
- 750 milliliters rice milk
- 180 grams broccoli florets
- 3 tablespoons parmesan cheese, grated
- 120 grams baby spinach, chopped
- ½ teaspoon basil, dried
- 240 grams pasta, gluten-free
- Salt and pepper
- Olive oil

Directions:

1. Heat the oven to 360°F.
2. Apply olive oil on a large oven dish to grease it. Slice the chicken breast fillet into small pieces.
3. Sear the chicken using olive oil in a large frying pan over medium-high heat.

4. Once the meat is golden brown, remove it from the flame and set aside for later.
5. .
6. Place the spinach leaves in a hot pan until slightly wilted.
7. Remove from heat and place it on one side for later use.
8. Over medium heat, melt the butter in a medium-sized saucepan.
9. Add plain flour into the saucepan and stir continuously for a minute while cooking.
10. Once slightly frothy, add ½ cup of milk into the saucepan and stir until smooth.
11. Pour 1 cup of milk at a time into the mixture while stirring continuously.
12. Season to taste.
13. Add parmesan cheese, basil and 57 grams of cheddar cheese into the sauce.
14. Give the mixture an occasional stir until it gained a thick consistency.
15. Prepare a large saucepan of boiling water and cook the pasta.
16. After 5 minutes, drain the pasta and drizzle with olive oil.
17. Add Alfredo sauce, broccoli, chicken and spinach into the pasta and mix well.
18. Transfer everything to the greased oven dish and sprinkle the remaining cheese on top.
19. Let it cook in the oven for 10 minutes without cover.
20. Place the pasta bake in an oven grill and cook for another 3 minutes. Garnish with sage.

Nutrition: Calories: 743, Total Fat: 29.9g, Saturated Fat: 0g, Cholesterol: 0 mg, Sodium: 0 mg, Total Carbs: 78.8g, Fiber: 10g, Sugar: 11.4g, Protein: 41g

104.   Rosemary Beef Stew

Preparation Time: 10 minutes | **Cooking Time:** 20 minutes | **Servings:** 4
Ingredients:
- 2 sprigs rosemary
- 1 tablespoon olive oil
- 1 tablespoon almond butter
- 8 ounces shallots
- 2 carrots, chopped
- 2 tablespoons almond flour
- 1 1/8 kilograms beef
- Water as needed
- 2 teaspoons salt

Directions:
1. While many people don't really like the flavor of the Rosemary, the balance here is just too perfect to ignore! It's awesome in all the right places.
2. Set the pot to Sauté mode and add olive oil, allow the oil to heat up.
3. Add butter and chopped rosemary and stir.
4. Add shallots, carrots and sauté for a while.
5. Shove the veggies on the side and add the meat cubes, brown them slightly and pour just enough stock to cover them, season with salt gently.
6. Lock up the lid and cook on 20 minutes on HIGH pressure.
7. Release the pressure naturally over 10 minutes.
8. Open and set the pot to Sauté mode, allow it to simmer.
9. Enjoy!

Nutrition: Calories: 330, Total Fat: 10, Saturated Fat: 1g, Cholesterol: 0 mg, Sodium: 0 mg, Total Carbs: 3g, Fiber: 1g, Sugar: 1g, Protein: 10g

105.   Shrimp with Beans

Preparation time: 10 minutes | **Cooking time:** 10 minutes | **Servings:** 4
Ingredients:
- 1 lb. Shrimp, peeled and deveined
- 2 tbsp. Soy sauce
- 2 tbsp. Olive oil
- Salt
- ½ lb. Green beans, washed and trimmed

Directions:
1. Heat oil in a pan over medium-high heat.

2. Add beans to the pan and sauté for 5-6 minutes or until tender.
3. Remove pan from heat and set aside.
4. Add shrimp in the same pan and cook for 2-3 minutes each side.
5. Return beans to the pan along with soy sauce.
6. Stir well and cook until shrimp is done.
7. Season with salt and serve.

Nutrition: Calories: 217, Total Fat: 9g, Saturated Fat: 1.6g, Cholesterol: 0 mg, Sodium: 0 mg, Total Carbs: 6.4g, Fiber: 2g, Sugar: 0.9g, Protein: 27.4 g

106. Broccoli Fritters

Preparation time: 10 minutes | **Cooking time:** 15 minutes | **Servings:** 4
Ingredients:
- 3 cups broccoli florets
- 1/3 cup parmesan cheese, grated
- ½ cup flour, gluten-free
- 1 large egg, lightly beaten
- 2 tbsp. Olive oil
- Pepper
- Salt

Directions:
1. Steam broccoli florets until tender.
2. Let it cool completely and chop. In a bowl, add egg, cheese, flour, pepper, and salt. Mix well.
3. Add chopped broccoli into the egg mixture and mix well. If the mixture is too dry, then add a tablespoon of water.
4. Heat the olive oil in a pan over medium heat.
5. Make patties from the mixture and cook on the hot pan for 3 minutes each side. Serve and enjoy.

Nutrition: Calories: 208, Total Fat: 11.6g, Saturated Fat: 3.4g, Cholesterol: 0 mg, Sodium: 0 mg, Total Carbs: 16.6g, Fiber: 2.2g, Sugar: 1.3g, Protein: 9.1g

107. Roasted Broccoli

Preparation time: 10 minutes | **Cooking time:** 15 minutes | **Servings:** 8
Ingredients:
- 8 cups broccoli florets
- ½ tsp red chili flakes
- 2 tbsp. Soy sauce
- ¼ cup olive oil

Directions:
1. Preheat the oven to 425°F.
2. Spray a baking tray with cooking spray and set aside.
3. Add all ingredients to the large mixing bowl and toss well.
4. Transfer broccoli mixture on a prepared baking tray.
5. Roast in preheated oven for 15 minutes.
6. Serve and enjoy.

Nutrition: Calories: 87, Total Fat: 6.6g, Saturated Fat: 0.9g, Cholesterol: 0 mg, Sodium: 0 mg, Total Carbs: 6.3g, Fiber: 2.4g, Sugar: 1.6g, Protein: 2.8g

108. Roasted Maple Carrots

Preparation time: 10 minutes | **Cooking time:** 25 minutes | **Servings:** 3
Ingredients:
- 1 lb. Baby carrots
- 2 tsp fresh parsley, chopped
- 1 tbsp. Dijon mustard
- 2 tbsp. Butter, melted
- 3 tbsp. Maple syrup
- Pepper
- Salt

Directions:
1. Preheat the oven to 400 °F.
2. In a large bowl, toss carrots with dijon mustard, maple syrup, butter, pepper, and salt.
3. Transfer carrots to baking tray and spread evenly.
4. Roast carrots in preheated oven for 25-30 minutes.
5. Serve and enjoy.

Nutrition: Calories: 177, Total Fat: 8.1g, Saturated Fat: 4.9g, Cholesterol: 0 mg, Sodium: 0 mg, Total Carbs: 26.2 g, Fiber: 4.6g, Sugar: 19.2g, Protein: 1.3g

109. Sweet & Tangy Green Beans

Preparation time: 10 minutes | **Cooking time:** 15 minutes | **Servings:** 6
Ingredients:

- 680 grams Green beans, trimmed
- 1 tbsp. Maple syrup
- 2 tbsp. Dijon mustard
- 2 tbsp. Rice wine vinegar
- ¼ cup olive oil
- ½ cup pecans, chopped
- Pepper
- Salt

Directions:
1. Preheat the oven to 400°F.
2. Place pecans on baking tray and toast in preheated oven for 5-8 minutes.
3. Remove from oven and let it cool. Boil water in a large pot over high heat.
4. Add green beans in boiling water and cook for 4-5 minutes or until tender.
5. Drain beans well and place in a large bowl. In a small bowl, whisk together oil, maple syrup, mustard, and vinegar.
6. Season beans with pepper and salt. Pour oil mixture over green beans.
7. Add pecans and toss well.
8. Serve and enjoy.

Nutrition: Calories: 139, Total Fat: 10.4g, Saturated Fat: 1.4g, Cholesterol: 0 mg, Sodium: 0 mg, Total Carbs: 10.9g, Fiber: 4.3g, Sugar: 3.7g, Protein: 2.5g

110. Easy Lemon Chicken

Preparation Time: 5 Minutes | **Cooking Time:** 15 Minutes | **Servings:** 1
Ingredients:

- 1 chicken breast, boneless and skinless
- 1 fresh lemon, sliced
- 1/2 tbsp Italian seasoning
- 1 fresh lemon juice
- Pepper
- Salt

Directions:
1. Preheat the oven to 350°F.
2. Season chicken with Italian season, pepper and salt.
3. Place chicken breast onto the foil piece.
4. Pour lemon juice over chicken and arrange lemon slices on top of chicken.
5. Tightly fold foil around the chicken breast and place in air fryer basket and cook for 15 minutes.
6. Serve and enjoy.

Nutrition: Calories: 179, Total Fat: 5.5g, Saturated Fat: 0.7g, Protein: 25.1g, Carbs: 7.2g, Fiber: 1.8g, Sugar: 3.1g

111. Flavorful Greek Chicken

Preparation Time: 10 Minutes | **Cooking Time:** 10 Minutes | **Servings:** 6
Ingredients

- 900 grams chicken thighs, skinless
- 1/2 cup olives
- 1/2 tsp ground coriander
- 3/4 tsp chili pepper
- 1/2 tsp paprika
- 2 tbsp olive oil
- 28 oz can tomato, diced
- 2 tsp dried oregano
- 2 tsp dried parsley
- Pepper
- Salt

Directions:
1. Add oil in the instant pot and set the pot on sauté mode.
2. Add chicken to the pot and sauté until brown. Transfer chicken on a plate.
3. Add tomatoes, spices, pepper, and salt and cook for 2-3 minutes.
4. Return chicken to the pot and stir well to combine.
5. Seal pot with lid and cook on manual mode for 8 minutes.

6. Once done then release pressure using quick-release method than open the lid.
7. Add olives and stir well.
8. Serve and enjoy.

Nutrition: Calories: 275, Total Fat: 12.9g, Saturated Fat: 2.9g, Protein: 33.7g, Carbs: 4.5g, Fiber: 1.2g

112.   Herb-Stuffed Pork Loin Roast

Preparation Time: 20 minutes | **Cooking Time:** 2 hours | **Servings:** 10

Ingredients:

- 2.5 kilograms pork loin roast
- 3 tablespoons pumpkin seeds
- 200 grams risotto rice
- ½ teaspoon thyme, dried
- 500 milliliters chicken stock
- 1 teaspoon oregano, dried
- 120 grams leek
- 1 tablespoon olive oil
- 1 cup fresh parsley, chopped
- Rock salt

Directions:

1. Remove the white stems of the leeks and chop the green tips.
2. Cook in olive oil over medium heat for about 2 minutes.
3. Add rice into the saucepan and stir for a minute.
4. Pour 125 milliliters of the chicken stock into the rice and leek mixture.
5. Stir occasionally.
6. Reduce heat to medium low. Continue adding chicken stock in batches while stirring until the rice is cooked. Remove from heat once done.
7. Add parsley, pumpkin seeds, thyme and oregano to the rice. Put the risotto in a bowl and set aside to cool.
8. Use a sharp knife to make ½ inch deep slices on the pork skin that are 1/2 inch apart.
9. Stuff the pork loin with the rice mixture and tie it properly.

10. Coat with olive oil and season with salt. Roast pork in a preheated oven at 430°F for 30 minutes.
11. Sprinkle the pork juices over the roast a few times during the cook.
12. Reduce the heat to 400 °F and return the pork roast to the oven and cook for another 1 ½ hour.
13. Drizzle the meat juices over the roast every 30 minutes. Allow to rest for 10 minutes before serving.

Nutrition: Calories: 434 kcal, Total Fat: 14.2g, Saturated Fat: 0g, Cholesterol: 0 mg, Sodium: 0 mg, Total Carbs: 20.5g, Fiber: 0.6 g, Sugar: 0.7g, Protein: 56.1g
□

113.   Low Fodmap Stuffing

Preparation Time: 10 minutes | **Cooking Time:** 30 minutes | **Servings:** 12

Ingredients:

- 10 slices bread, shredded
- 125 milliliters chicken stock
- 4 tablespoons butter, melted
- ¼ teaspoon black pepper
- ¼ teaspoon sea salt
- 120 grams green leek leaves, chopped
- ½ teaspoon thyme, dried
- 13 grams fresh parsley, chopped
- 1 teaspoon oregano, dried
- 1 teaspoon sage, dried

Directions:

1. Set the oven to 360°F.
2. Coat bread pieces with oil mixture.
3. Arrange the bread in a baking tray. Cook in the oven for 5 minutes.
4. Turn the bread and bake for another 5 minutes.
5. Remove from oven. Place bread in a bowl with the remaining ingredients.
6. Mix well.

Nutrition: Calories: 120, Total Fat: 5.6g, Saturated Fat: 0g, Cholesterol: 0 mg, Sodium:

0 mg, Total Carbs: 14.8g, Fiber: 0.9g, Sugar: 1.6g, Protein: 3 g

☐

114. Chili Coconut Crusted Fish

Preparation Time: 15 minutes | **Cooking Time:** 45 minutes | **Servings:** 4

Ingredients:

- 20 grams dried coconut, shredded
- 57 grams cheddar cheese, grated
- 1 tablespoon sesame oil
- 460 grams cod
- 4 kaffir lime leaf, sliced
- 1 mild green chili, deseeded and sliced

Directions:

1. Soak coconut in water for 10 minutes.
2. Remove excess water.
3. Fry chili, and lime leaves in 1 tablespoon sesame oil over medium-high heat.
4. Once fragrant, add coconut and cook for another minute.
5. Remove from heat and set aside for later.
6. Fry the fish for 2 minutes on each side. Transfer fish to a baking tray.
7. Sprinkle cheese on top and coat with coconut mixture.
8. Grill on high in the oven for 2 minutes.

Nutrition: Calories: 227, Total Fat: 10.8g, Saturated Fat: 0g, Cholesterol: 0 mg, Sodium: 0 mg, Total Carbs: 1.4g, Fiber: 0.7g, Sugar: 0.5g, Protein: 30 g

115. Spicy Chicken Drumsticks

Preparation Time: 10 minutes | **Cooking Time:** 45 minutes | **Servings:** 4

Ingredients:

- 8 pieces chicken drumsticks
- ½ teaspoon black pepper, ground
- 1 ½ tablespoon pure maple syrup
- 1 teaspoon coriander
- ¼ teaspoon cloves, ground
- ¼ teaspoon cumin, ground
- ½ teaspoon turmeric, ground
- ¼ teaspoon paprika
- ½ teaspoon yellow mustard powder

Directions:

1. Combine oil and maple syrup together in a bowl. Mix the dried spices in a separate bowl.
2. Rub each chicken with the oil mixture then completely coat with the spice rub.
3. Bake chicken in a preheated oven at 360°F for 45 minutes.

Nutrition: Calories: 492, Total Fat: 31.1g, Saturated Fat: 0g, Cholesterol: 0 mg, Sodium: 0 mg, Total Carbs: 2.4g, Fiber: 0.2g, Sugar: 1.5g, Protein: 46.1g

☐

116. Paprika Calamari With Garden Salad

Preparation Time: 5 minutes | **Cooking Time:** 10 minutes | **Servings:** 5

Ingredients:

- ½ teaspoon finely ground black pepper
- 1 teaspoon paprika
- ⅓ cup cornstarch
- 4 large or 8 regular squid bodies, cleaned
- ½ teaspoon salt
- Olive oil
- Garden Salad
- ½ green bell pepper, seeded and sliced
- 1 cup snow pea shoots
- 2 stalks celery, thinly sliced
- Dressing
- 1½ tablespoons lemon juice
- ½ teaspoon Stevia extracts
- Salt
- 1 small head romaine lettuce, roughly chopped
- ½ large cucumber halved lengthwise and sliced

Directions:

1. Slice the squid bodies down to two large pieces (slice them into quarters if you use big squid).

2. Cut the squid bits in a 1⁄2-inch (1 cm) cross pattern with a sharp knife, making sure it is not cut through all the time. Pat dry on towels of paper.
3. Combine the pepper, paprika, salt, and corn starch in a fairly large bowl and mix thoroughly.
4. Cover for 3 to 4 hours and cool.
5. To cook the salad, combine in a large salad bowl the shoots of latch, cucumber, celery, snow pepper, and snow pea.
6. In order to dress in the size of the dressing, add prune puree, lemon juice, and Stevia extracts.
7. Taste salt for season. Preheat the grill to warm or heat a saucepan or grill over high temperatures.
8. Brush with oil the grill or bowl.
9. Add the calamari, rate, and cook for 2 to 3 minutes.
10. Turn and cook for another 1-2 minutes until the squid is opaque in white.
11. Wash the dressing and spread the salad into four bowls or plates.
12. Arrange and serve the calamari warm on top.

Nutrition: Calories: 229.2, Total Fat: 15.1, Saturated Fat: 2.2, Cholesterol: 264.1 mg, Sodium: 50.9 mg, Total Carbs: 5.1g, Fiber: 0.1g, Sugar: 0.3g, Protein: 17.8g

117. Chili Salmon With Cilantro Salad

Preparation Time: 5 minutes | **Cooking Time:** 10 minutes | **Servings:** 5
Ingredients:
- 1 tablespoon garlic-free sweet chili sauce
- Four 5½-ounce salmon fillets
- Salt and freshly ground black pepper
- Cilantro Salad
- 1 tablespoon rice vinegar
- 2 tablespoons fish sauce
- ½ green bell pepper, thinly sliced
- ½ cup firmly packed chopped cilantro
- ½ small red chile, finely chopped
- 5 cups roughly chopped lettuce leaves
- 2 tablespoons lime juice
- 2 tablespoons Stevia extracts
- 2 stalks celery, thinly sliced on the diagonal
- ½ large cucumber halved lengthwise and sliced

Directions:
1. Line the broiler with the sheet of foil and put the oven in the grill 5 inches away.
2. Place the fillets of salmon in the crust, skin-side up, and coat until crispy for 1 to 2 minutes.
3. Try turning on the fillets and brush the sweet chili sauce with 3⁄4 teaspoon.
4. Salt and pepper season. Season.
5. Alternatively, fry for 3 to 4 minutes or until properly cooked.
6. Mix the celery, bell pepper, lettuce, cucumber, and cilantro together in a big bowl to make the salad.
7. In a small bowl, add the chili, the lime juice, rice vinegar, the fish sauce, and the Stevia extracts.
8. Serve with fish.

Nutrition: Calories: 293.7, Total Fat: 14.2g, Saturated Fat: 2.8g, Cholesterol: 80.8 mg, Sodium: 366.2 mg, Total Carbs: 1g, Fiber: 0g, Sugar: 0.2g, Protein: 38.9g,

118. Dukkah-Crusted Snapper

Preparation Time: 5 minutes | **Cooking Time:** 10 minutes | **Servings:** 4
Ingredients:
- Dukkah
- Cooked basmati rice
- Lemon wedges
- ½ cup blanched almonds
- ¼ cup pine nuts
- 2 tablespoons canola oil
- Cilantro leaves
- 1 teaspoon cumin seeds
- 1 teaspoon sesame seeds
- ½ teaspoon chili powder
- 1 teaspoon ground coriander

- Four 7-ounce snapper fillets or other lean fish

Directions:

1. Preheat oven to 330°F when preparing the dukkah and line the parchment paper on a baking sheet.
2. Place almonds and pine nuts on the baker and bake 5 minutes or until golden.
3. Bake for 5 minutes.
4. Refrigerate to room temperature.
5. In a food processor, put all nuts and spices and pulse until the crumbs have been thin.
6. Retention of four tablespoons and pass the remainder to a pot.
7. Brush the fillets with gasoline, drive them all over to cover the dukkah.
8. Thermally heat a grilled grill or cast iron saucepan. Add the fish and cook on each side for 3 to 4 minutes before frying.
9. Sprinkle the coriander and the dukkah reserved.
10. Serve with rice basmati and wedges of lemon.

<u>Nutrition:</u> Calories: 580, Total Fat: 23g, Saturated Fat: 9g, Cholesterol: 110 mg, Sodium: 410 mg, Total Carbs: 60g, Fiber: 10g, Sugar: 16g, Protein: 38g

119. Balsamic Sesame Swordfish

Preparation Time: 5 minutes | **Cooking Time:** 15 minutes | **Servings:** 4

Ingredients:

- 3 tablespoons balsamic vinegar
- 1½ tablespoons sesame seeds
- Steamed Asian greens
- 2 tablespoons soy sauce
- 2 tablespoons Stevia extracts
- 4 large swordfish steaks

Directions:

1. In a non-metallic dish, mix balsamic, soy, and Stevia extracts.
2. Attach the steaks of swordfish and transform the marinade into coat.

3. Cover and cool, turn periodically for 3-4 hours. To 450 ° F, preheat the oven—line a large parchment paper baking sheet.
4. Place the steaks of swordfish on a bakery book and book the marinade for 10 minutes.
5. Turn over the steaks and add the marinade. Sprinkle with sesame seeds and cook until cooked for another 5 to 10 minutes.
6. Serve with the Asian greens steamed.

<u>Nutrition:</u> Calories: 95, Total Fat: 11g, Saturated Fat: 1g, Cholesterol: 0 mg, Sodium: 122 mg, Total Carbs: 0g, Fiber: 0g, Sugar: 0g, Protein: 0g

120. Lemon-Oregano Chicken Drumsticks

Preparation Time: 10 minutes | **Cooking Time:** 15 minutes | **Servings:** 4

Ingredients:

- 18 skinless chicken drumsticks
- Salt and freshly ground black pepper
- ¼ cup finely chopped oregano
- 1 tablespoon finely grated lemon zest
- 2 tablespoons extra virgin olive oil
- Greek Salad
- 2 cups shredded iceberg lettuce
- 12 cherry tomatoes, cut in half
- ½ cup pitted kalamata olives
- 4 ounces feta
- 2 tablespoons olive oil
- 2 teaspoons balsamic vinegar

Directions:

1. Use a little knife to pierce the chicken evenly. In a large bowl, add the oregano, citrus fruit, and oil.
2. Add the chicken, salt, and pepper season and cover with the meat. Cover, cool, turn periodically for 3 to 4 hours. To 450 ° F, preheat the oven—cover two parchment paper bakery boards.
3. Place the drumsticks on the slabs and

cook until golden brown and cooked for 10 to 15 minutes.

4. n the meantime, put the salad in a large bowl and gently toss the lettuce, tomatoes, olives, and feta.

5. Place the olive oil and vinegar in a tiny glass and blend well.

6. Place the salad over and throw it quickly. Eat with chicken, with the extra oregano.

7. Serve.

Nutrition: Calories: 35, Total Fat: 35g, Saturated Fat: 0g, Cholesterol: 0 mg, Sodium: 470 mg, Total Carbs: 2g, Fiber: 0g, Sugar: 0g, Protein: 0g☐

121. LowFodmap Carrot & Corn Fritters

Preparation time: 10 minutes | Cooking time: 20 minutes | Servings: 4

Ingredients:

- Carrot & corn fritters
- 2-large egg
- 63ml-(1/4 cup) low fodmap milk
- ½-tsp ground cumin
- 1 ½-tsp paprika
- 240g-(2 large) carrot
- 1-red bell peppers (large)
- 12g-(1/4 cup) fresh chives
- 2-tbsp fresh parsley
- 128g-(3/4 cup) sweet corn
- 70g-(1/2 cup) gluten free all-purpose flour

Directions:

1. Mesh the carrots, deseed and dice the crimson ringer peppers, and degree out the corn quantities.

2. Nicely cleave the chives and parsley.

3. In a big bowl mix the eggs and espresso milk (fodmap) together.

4. Whilst you are carried out with that mixture inside the flour, paprika, and cumin.

5. Mix the corn, carrot, pink ringer peppers, chives, and parsley until they form.

6. Season with salt and pepper. Spot a massive non-stick fry container over

medium warm temperature and shower with oil.

7. Spoon 1/four cup combo for each waste into the container.

8. Cook 4 to six wastes one after some other-leveling them marginally so they are not very thick.

9. Permit to cook dinner for 3 to 4mins for every aspect, till extremely good dark-colored and cooked through.

10. Ensure you blend the blend before cooking each bunch.

11. Serve 3 wastes for everybody.

Nutrition: Calories: 187, Total Fat: 4g, Saturated Fat: 0g, Cholesterol: 0 mg, Sodium: 0 mg, Total Carbs: 30.g, Fiber: 0g, Sugar: 8.2g, Protein: 7.4g☐

122. Low Fodmap Hawaiian Toasties

Preparation time: 4 minutes | Cooking time: 6 minutes | Servings: 1

Ingredients:

- 2-slices low fodmap bread
- 1-tbsp dairy free spread
- 35g-cheddar cheese
- 30g-shaved ham
- 1 tbsp scallions
- Season with black pepper
- 40g-canned pineapple chunks in syrup

Directions:

1. Preheat medium frypan over medium warmth. Spread the outside of the low fodmap bread.

2. Mesh the cheddar and cut the ham.

3. Channel, wash and finely hack the tinned pineapple.

4. Finely slash the scallions.

5. Collect your cheddar toasties.

6. Make certain to put buttered sides outwardly, at that point include the cheddar, ham, pineapple, scallions and a sprinkle of dark pepper.

7. Cook each side for around 3 minutes until brilliant darker.

8. Serve hot, unwind, and appreciate!

Nutrition: Calories: 454, Total Fat: 26.5g, Saturated Fat: 0g, Cholesterol: 0 mg, Sodium: 0 mg, Total Carbs: 33.7g, Fiber: 0g, Sugar: 3g, Protein: 19.9 g

123. Roasted Pepper Pasta

Preparation Time: 10 minutes | **Cooking Time:** 10 minutes | **Servings:** 4

Ingredients:
- 4 cups gluten-free pasta, cooked
- 3 Tbsp. parmesan cheese, grated
- 3 Tbsp. fresh basil leaves, chopped
- 1 Tbsp. tapioca starch
- 1 cup unsweetened almond milk
- 2 Tbsp. olive oil
- ¼ cup pumpkin puree
- 2 cups red bell peppers, roasted
- Salt

Directions:
1. Add roasted bell peppers, parmesan cheese, basil leaves, tapioca starch, almond milk, olive oil, and pumpkin puree into a blender and blend until smooth.
2. Pour blended sauce into a large pan and heat over medium-high heat.
3. Stir well and cook the sauce until slightly thickens.
4. Add cooked pasta to the sauce and toss well. Season with salt and serve.

Nutrition: Calories: 308, Total Fat: 10g, Saturated Fat: 2g, Cholesterol: 0 mg, Sodium: 0 mg, Total Carbs: 47.5g, Fiber: 8.3g, Sugar: 3.6g, Protein: 7g

124. Lemon Butter Shrimp Over Vegetable Noodles

Preparation Time: 8 minutes | **Cooking Time:** 12 minutes | **Servings:** 4

Ingredients:
- 1 lb. shrimp, cleaned and deveined
- ¼ cup butter
- 1 tablespoon lemon juice
- 1 tablespoon capers
- ½ teaspoon salt
- ½ teaspoon black pepper
- 4 cups zucchini, spiral sliced into noodles

Directions:
1. Bring a lightly salted pot of water to a boil. Add the zucchini spirals to the water and cook for 2-3 minutes.
2. Carefully remove the zucchini from the cooking water and transfer it to a bowl of ice water to stop the cooking.
3. Let sit for 1-2 minutes before draining.
4. Heat the butter in a skillet over medium heat. Sprinkle the shrimp with lemon juice and season it with the salt and black pepper.
5. Place the shrimp in the skillet with the butter, along with the capers.
6. Cook for 2-3 minutes per side, or until cooked thoroughly.
7. Add the zucchini noodles to the skillet and toss to coat in the warm butter.
8. Transfer to serving plates and enjoy.

Nutrition: Calories: 431, Total Fat: 20.4g, Saturated Fat: 4.9g, Cholesterol: 0 mg, Sodium: 0 mg, Total Carbs: 7.1g, Fiber: 1.3g, Sugar: 3.5g, Protein: 53.4g

125. Pasta With Salmon And Dill

Preparation Time: 10 minutes | **Cooking Time:** 15 minutes | **Servings:** 3

Ingredients:
- 1 packet gluten-free pasta
- 1 tablespoon olive oil
- 1/3 mushrooms
- zest of 1 lime
- ½ smoked salmon
- 3 cups baby spinach
- 250 ml low fodmap chicken stock
- 1 tablespoon cornflour
- 1 cup fat milk
- 1 bunch of dill

Directions:

1. In a pan heat oil over medium heat, add mushrooms and sauté for 2-3 minutes.
2. Add lime juice, lime zest, salmon, chicken stock and baby spinach leaves.
3. In a bowl add milk, cornflour and whisk until dissolved.
4. Pour mix into the pan, add cooked pasta and dill.
5. Toss until pasta is coated.
6. When ready serve with grated cheese

Nutrition: Calories: 162, Total Fat: 3.1g, Saturated Fat: 0g, Cholesterol: 23 mg, Sodium: 43 mg, Total Carbs: 18 g, Fiber: 0g, Sugar: 0, Protein: 9.3 g

126.   Greek Pasta Salad

Preparation Time: 5 minutes | **Cooking Time:** 5 minutes | **Servings:** 4

Ingredients:

- 4 oz. gluten-free pasta
- 1 cup canned chickpeas
- ¼ cup feta cheese
- ¼ cup Kalamata olives
- 2 cups tomatoes
- 2 tablespoons oregano
- 1 tablespoon lemon juice
- ½ cup low fodmap dressing

Directions:

1. In a bowl add all Ingredients and mix well.
2. Serve with dressing

Nutrition: Calories: 132, Total Fat: 6.2g, Saturated Fat: 2.3g, Cholesterol: 0 mg, Sodium: 0 mg, Total Carbs: 15.7g, Fiber: 5.4g, Sugar: 1.1g, Protein: 3.2g

127.   Salmon And Spinach

Preparation Time: 10 minutes | **Cooking Time:** 20 minutes | **Servings:** 4

Ingredients:

- 1 package gluten-free spaghetti noodles
- 1 tablespoon olive oil
- 1 ½ cup fresh spinach
- 1 can canned sliced mushrooms
- 2 cups lactose-free cream cheese
- 1 cup smoked salmon flakes
- Juice from 1 lemon
- Water
- Salt and pepper to taste

Directions:

1. Place water in a deep pot and bring to a boil.
2. Cook spaghetti noodles according to package instructions.
3. Drain the noodles and set aside once cooked. Heat olive oil in a pan over medium heat and wilt the spinach and set aside.
4. Using the same pan, stir in the mushrooms.
5. Add in the cream cheese and pour water. Season with salt and pepper to taste.
6. Bring to a boil and add in the salmon flakes. Stir in the spaghetti noodles.
7. Add the wilted spinach.
8. Drizzle with lemon juice before serving.

Nutrition: Calories: 406, Total Fat: 5.9g, Saturated Fat: 1.5g, Cholesterol: 0 mg, Sodium: 125 mg, Total Carbs: 59.3g, Fiber: 8.3g, Sugar: 9.7g, Protein: 32.5g

128.   Spaghetti Bolognese

Preparation Time: 10 minutes | **Cooking Time:** 20 minutes | **Servings:** 5

Ingredients:

- 1 package gluten-free spaghetti noodles
- 1 tablespoon olive oil
- ½ lb. minced beef
- 1 cup green leeks, chopped
- 1 can crushed tomatoes
- 2 teaspoons Italian herbs
- 2 large carrots, grated
- 1 ½ cups chopped green beans
- 4 cups baby spinach, chopped
- 1 cup parmesan cheese
- A handful of basil, torn
- Salt and pepper to taste

Directions:

1. Cook the spaghetti noodles according to package instructions.
2. Once cooked, drain the noodles and set aside.
3. Heat the olive oil over medium heat. Stir in the beef and leeks and cook for 3 minutes while stirring constantly.
4. Add in the tomatoes, herbs, carrots, and green beans.
5. Season with salt and pepper to taste and adjust the moisture by adding more water if needed.
6. Allow to simmer for 10 minutes until the vegetables are soft.
7. Stir in the spinach and cooked noodles last.
8. Garnish with parmesan and basil leaves.

Nutrition: Calories: 388, Total Fat: 12.2g, Saturated Fat: 4.4g, Cholesterol: 0 mg, Sodium: 491 mg, Total Carbs: 49.9g, Fiber: 9.7g, Sugar: 4.6g, Protein: 24.9g

129. Pad Thai With Shrimps

Preparation Time: 10 minutes | Cooking Time: 6 minutes | Servings: 4

Ingredients:

- 1 package rice noodle
- 2 tablespoons olive oil
- 1 lb. large shrimps, peeled and deveined
- 1 red bell pepper, thinly sliced
- ¼ cup fish sauce
- ¼ cup glucose syrup
- 2 tablespoons rice vinegar
- 1 tablespoons ground paprika
- 2 teaspoons low sodium tamari
- 1 large egg, fried and cut into strips
- 1 cup fresh bean sprouts
- 1 teaspoon sesame seeds
- Freshly chopped cilantro leaves
- Salt to taste

Directions:

1. Cook the rice noodles according to package instructions.
2. Drain and set aside.

3. Heat the olive oil in pan over medium heat and stir in the shrimps and bell pepper.
4. Season with salt to taste and cook for 4 minutes until the shrimps turn red.
5. Set aside. In a mixing bowl, combine the fish sauce, glucose syrup, rice vinegar, and paprika.
6. Add in the tamari.
7. Assemble the Pad Thai.
8. Place the noodles at the bottom of the bowl and place the shrimps and bell pepper on top.
9. Add egg strips, and bean sprouts.
10. Drizzle with the sauce.
11. Garnish with sesame seeds and cilantro seeds.

Nutrition: Calories: 429, Total Fat: 13.5g, Saturated Fat: 2g, Cholesterol: 0 mg, Sodium: 215 mg, Total Carbs: 52.7g, Fiber: 4.2g, Sugar: 4.7g, Protein: 24.4g

130. Coconut Chicken Rice Noodle

Preparation Time: 5 minutes | Cooking Time: 10 minutes | Servings: 4

Ingredients:

- 1 package rice noodle
- 2 tablespoons coconut oil
- 1 lb. chicken breasts
- 1 zucchini, sliced
- 1 bell pepper, seeded and sliced
- 2 carrots, peeled and sliced
- 1 can coconut milk
- Salt and pepper to taste

Directions:

1. Cook the rice noodles according to package instructions.
2. Drain and set aside.
3. Heat coconut oil in a deep pan over medium heat and fry the chicken breasts for 3 minutes on each side or until they turn golden brown.
4. Stir in the zucchini, bell pepper, and

carrots. Season with salt and pepper to taste.

5. Stir for 1 minute.
6. Add in the coconut milk.
7. Cover the pan with lid and simmer for 6 minutes.
8. Add cooked noodles last.

Nutrition: Calories: 514, Total Fat: 13.9, Saturated Fat: 7.1g, Cholesterol: 0 mg, Sodium: 102 mg, Total Carbs: 22.5g, Fiber: 3.4g, Sugar: 1.2g, Protein: 19.6g

131. Tuna Noodle Casserole

Preparation Time: 10 minutes | **Cooking Time:** 20 minutes | **Servings:** 4
Ingredients:
- 1 package 7 ounces gluten-free pasta
- ¼ cup unsalted butter
- ½ cup green part of the leek, chopped
- ½ cup green scallions, green part chopped
- 3 ½ ounces oyster mushrooms
- ¼ cup peas
- ¼ cup tapioca starch
- ¾ cup coconut milk
- 2 teaspoons soy sauce
- 2 ounces mozzarella cheese
- Salt and pepper to taste

Directions:
1. Preheat the oven to 350°F.
2. Grease the casserole dish with non-stick spray.
3. Cook the pasta in a large pot with boiling water and cook according to package instructions.
4. Drain and set aside. Melt the butter over medium heat in a skillet and sauté the leeks and scallion for 30 seconds.
5. Stir in the oyster mushrooms and peas and cook for 2 minutes. Stir in the tapioca starch and coconut milk.
6. Allow to simmer and season with soy sauce, salt and pepper to taste.
7. Place the cooked pasta in the casserole dish and pour in the sauce.

8. Top with cheese. Bake in the oven for 15 minutes.

Nutrition: Calories: 262, Total Fat: 19. Saturated Fat: 14.4g, Cholesterol: 0 mg, Sodium: 205 mg, Total Carbs: 17.7g, Fiber: 2.7g, Sugar: 3.3g, Protein: 7.5g

132. Baked Shrimp Mix

Preparation time: 10 minutes | **Cooking time:** 32 minutes | **Servings:** 4
Ingredients
- 4 gold potatoes, peeled and sliced
- 2 fennel bulbs, trimmed and cut into wedges
- 2 shallots, chopped
- 3 tbsp. olive oil
- ½ C. Kalamata olives, pitted and halved
- 2 lb. shrimp, peeled and deveined
- 1 tsp. lemon zest, grated
- 2 tsp. oregano, dried
- 4 oz. feta cheese, crumbled
- 2 tbsp. parsley, chopped

Directions
1. In a roasting pan, combine the potatoes with 2 tbsp. oil, and the rest of the ingredients except the shrimp, toss, introduce in the oven and bake at 450°F for 25 minutes.
2. Add the shrimp, toss, bake for 7 minutes more, divide between plates and serve.

Nutrition: Calories: 341, Fat: 19g, Fiber: 9g, Carbs: 34, Protein: 10g

133. Shrimp and Lemon Sauce

Preparation time: 10 minutes | **Cooking time:** 15 minutes | **Servings:** 4
Ingredients
- 1-lb. shrimp, peeled and deveined
- ⅓ C. lemon juice
- 4 egg yolks
- 2 tbsp. olive oil
- 1 C. chicken stock
- Salt and black pepper to the taste

- 1 C. black olives, pitted and halved
- 1 tbsp. thyme, chopped

Directions
1. In a bowl, mix the lemon juice with the egg yolks and whisk well.
2. Heat up a pan with the oil over medium heat, add the shrimp and cook for 2 minutes on each side and transfer to a plate.
3. Heat up a pan with the stock over medium heat, add some of this over the egg yolks and lemon juice mix and whisk well.
4. Add this over the rest of the stock, also add salt and pepper, whisk well and simmer for 2 minutes.
5. Add the shrimp and the rest of the ingredients, toss and serve right away.

Nutrition: Calories: 237, Fat: 15.3g, Fiber: 4.6g, Carbs: 15.4g, Protein: 7.6g,

134. Shrimp and Beans Salad

Preparation time: 10 minutes | **Cooking time:** 4 minutes | **Servings:** 4
Ingredients
- 1-lb. shrimp, peeled and deveined
- 30 oz. cannellini beans, canned, drained and rinsed
- 2 tbsp. olive oil
- 1 C. cherry tomatoes, halved
- 1 tsp. lemon zest, grated
- A pinch salt and black pepper

For the dressing:
- 3 tbsp. red wine vinegar
- ½ C. olive oil

Directions:
1. Heat up a pan with 2 tbsp. oil over medium-high heat, add the shrimp and cook for 2 minutes on each side.
2. In a salad bowl, combine the shrimp with the beans and the rest of the ingredients except the ones for the dressing and toss.
3. In a separate bowl, combine the vinegar with ½ C. oil. Whisk well.
4. Pour over the salad, toss and serve right away.

Nutrition: Calories: 207, Fat: 12.3g, Fiber: 6.6g, Carbs: 15.4g, Protein: 8.7g

135. Pecan Salmon Fillets

Preparation time: 10 minutes | **Cooking time:** 15 minutes | **Servings:** 6
Ingredients
- 3 tbsp. olive oil
- 3 tbsp. mustard
- 5 tsp. maple syrup
- 1 C. pecans, chopped
- 6 salmon fillets, boneless
- 1 tbsp. lemon juice
- 3 tsp. parsley, chopped
- Salt and pepper, to the taste

Directions
1. In a bowl, mix the oil with the mustard and maple syrup and whisk well.
2. Put the pecans and the parsley in another bowl.
3. Season the salmon fillets with salt and pepper, arrange them on a baking sheet lined with parchment paper, brush with the maple syrup and mustard mix, and top with the pecans mix.
4. Introduce in the oven at 400°F, bake for 15 minutes, divide between plates, drizzle the lemon juice on top and serve.

Nutrition: Calories: 282, Fat: 15.5g, Fiber: 8.5g, Carbs: 20.9g, Protein: 16.8g,

136. Salmon and Broccoli

Preparation time: 10 minutes | **Cooking time:** 20 minutes | **Servings:** 4
Ingredients
- 2 tbsp. balsamic vinegar
- 1 broccoli head, florets separated
- 4 pieces salmon fillets, skinless
- ¼ C of chives
- 1 tbsp. olive oil
- Sea salt and black pepper, to the taste

Directions:

1. In a baking dish, combine the salmon with the broccoli and the rest of the ingredients, introduce in the oven and bake at 390°F for 20 minutes.
2. Divide the mix between plates and serve.

Nutrition: Calories: 302, Fat: 15.5g, Fiber: 8.5g, Carbs: 18.9g, Protein: 19.8g,

137. Dijon Fish Fillets

Preparation time: 15 minutes | **Cooking time:** 3 minutes | **Servings:** 2

Ingredients

- 2 white fish fillets
- 1 tbsp. Dijon mustard
- 1 C. water
- Pepper
- Salt

Directions

1. Pour water into the instant pot and place the trivet in the pot.
2. Brush fish fillets with mustard and season with pepper and salt and place on top of the trivet.
3. Seal pot with lid and cook on high for 3 minutes.
4. Once done, release pressure using quick release. Remove lid.
5. Serve and enjoy.

Nutrition: Calories: 270, Fat: 11.9g, Carbohydrates: 0.5g, Sugar: 0.1g, Protein: 38g, Cholesterol: 119 mg

138. Marinated Tuna Steak

Preparation time: 6 minutes | **Cooking time:** 18 minutes | **Servings:** 4

Ingredients

- 2 tbsp. olive oil
- ¼ C. orange juice
- ¼ C. soy sauce
- 1 tbsp. lemon juice
- 2 tbsp. fresh parsley
- ½ tsp. black pepper, ground
- ½ tsp. fresh oregano
- 4 (4 oz.) tuna steaks

Directions

1. Chop the oregano and parsley.
2. In a glass container, mix the pepper, oregano, parsley, lemon juice, soy sauce, olive oil, and orange juice.
3. Warm the grill using the high heat setting. Grease the grate with oil.
4. Add to tuna steaks and cook for 5–6 minutes. Turn and baste with the marinated sauce.
5. Cook another 5 minutes or until it's the way you like it. Discard the remaining marinade.

Nutrition: Calories 200, Protein 27.4g, Fat 7.9g

139. Shrimp Pasta

Preparation time: 4 minutes | **Cooking time:** 16 minutes | **Servings:** 4

Ingredients

- 6 oz. spaghetti high protein
- 12 oz. raw shrimp, peeled and deveined, cut into 1-inch pieces
- 1 bunch asparagus, trimmed
- 1 large bell pepper, thinly sliced
- 1 C. fresh peas
- 1 and ¼ tsp. kosher salt
- ½ and ½ C. non-fat plain yogurt
- 3 tbsp. lemon juice
- 1 tbsp. extra-virgin olive oil
- ½ tsp. fresh ground black pepper
- ¼ C. pine nuts, toasted

Directions

1. Take a large-sized pot and bring water to a boil.
2. Add your spaghetti and cook them for about minutes less than the directed package instruction.
3. Add shrimp, bell pepper, asparagus and cook for about 2–4 minutes until the shrimp are tender.
4. Drain the pasta and the contents well.
5. Whisk in yogurt, parsley, oil, pepper, and lemon juice.
6. Add pasta, mix and toss well.
7. Serve by sprinkling some pine nuts!

Nutrition: Calories: 406, Fat: 22g, Protein: 26g

140. Tuna With Vegetable Mix

Preparation time: 8 minutes | **Cooking time:** 16 minutes | **Servings:** 4

Ingredients

- ¼ C. extra-virgin olive oil, divided
- 1 tbsp. rice vinegar
- 1 tsp. kosher salt, divided
- ¾ tsp. Dijon mustard
- ¾ tsp. maple syrup
- 4 oz. baby gold beets, thinly sliced
- 4 oz. fennel bulb, trimmed and thinly sliced
- 4 oz. baby turnips, thinly sliced
- 6 oz. Granny Smith apple, very thinly sliced
- 2 tsp. sesame seeds, toasted
- 6 oz. tuna steaks
- ½ tsp. black pepper
- 1 tbsp. fennel fronds, torn

Directions:

1. Scourge 2 tbsp. of oil, ½ a tsp. of salt, maple syrup, vinegar, and mustard.
2. Give the mixture a nice mix.
3. Add fennel, beets, apple, and turnips; mix and toss until everything is evenly coated.
4. Sprinkle with sesame seeds and toss well.
5. Using a cast-iron skillet, heat 2 tbsp. of oil over high heat.
6. Carefully season the tuna with ½ a tsp. of salt and pepper
7. Situate the tuna in the skillet and cook for 4 minutes, giving 1½ minutes per side.
8. Remove the tuna and slice it up.
9. Place in containers with the vegetable mix.
10. Serve with the fennel mix and enjoy!

Nutrition: Calories 443, Fat 17g, Protein16.5g

141. Tuna Bowl With Kale

Preparation time: 4 minutes | **Cooking time:** 18 minutes | **Servings:** 6

Ingredients

- 3 tbsp. extra virgin olive oil
- ¼ C. capers
- 2 tsp. agave syrup
- 15 oz. can great northern beans, drained and rinsed
- 1-lb. kale, chopped with the center ribs removed
- ½ tsp. black pepper, ground
- ½ C. of chives
- 2 ½ oz. olives, drained and sliced
- ¼ tsp. sea salt
- ¼ tsp. red pepper, crushed
- 6 oz. tuna in olive oil, do not drain

Directions

1. Place a large pot, like a stockpot, on your stove and turn the burner to high heat.
2. Fill the pot about ¾ of the way full of water and let it come to a boil.
3. Cook the kale for 2 minutes.
4. Drain the kale and set it aside.
5. Set the heat to medium and place the empty pot back on the burner.
6. Add the oil and chives. Sauté for 3–4 minutes.
7. Add the capers, olives, and red pepper.
8. Cook the ingredients for another minute while stirring.
9. Pour in the agave syrup and stir while you toss in the kale. Mix all the ingredients thoroughly and ensure the kale is thoroughly coated.
10. Cover the pot and set the timer for 8 minutes.
11. Put off the heat and stir in the tuna, pepper, beans, salt, and any other herbs that will make this one of the best Mediterranean dishes you've ever made.

Nutrition: Calories: 265, Fat: 12g, Protein: 16g

142. Chicken and Olives Salsa

Preparation time: 10 minutes | **Cooking time:** 25 minutes | **Servings:** 4

Ingredients

- 2 tbsp. avocado oil
- 4 chicken breast halves, skinless and boneless
- Salt and black pepper, to the taste
- 1 tbsp. sweet paprika
- 1 tbsp. balsamic vinegar
- 2 tbsp. parsley, chopped
- 1 avocado, peeled, pitted, and cubed
- 2 tbsp. black olives, pitted and chopped

Directions:

1. Heat and set your grill over medium-high heat, add the chicken brushed with half of the oil and seasoned with salt, and pepper, cook for 7 minutes on each side, and divide between plates.
2. Meanwhile, in a bowl, mix the ingredients and the remaining oil, toss, add on top of the chicken and serve.

Nutrition: Calories: 289, Fat: 12.4g, Fiber: 9.1g, Carbs: 23.8g, Protein: 14.3g

143. Chili Chicken Mix

Preparation time: 10 minutes | **Cooking time:** 18 minutes | **Servings:** 4

Ingredients

- 2 lb. chicken thighs, skinless and boneless
- 2 tbsp. olive oil
- ½ C. of chives
- 1 tsp. smoked paprika
- 1 tsp. chili pepper
- ½ tsp. coriander seeds, ground
- 2 tsp. oregano, dried
- 2 tsp. parsley flakes
- 30 oz. tomatoes, canned and chopped
- ½ C. black olives, pitted and halved

Directions:

1. Set the instant pot on Sauté mode, then add the oil, heat it, add the chives, and the rest of the ingredients except the tomatoes, olives, and the chicken, stir, and sauté 10 minutes.

2. Add the chicken, tomatoes, and olives, put the lid on, and cook on High for 8 minutes.
3. Release the pressure naturally for 10 minutes, split the mix into bowls and serve.

Nutrition: Calories: 153, Fat: 8g, Fiber: 2g, Carbs: 9g, Protein: 12g

144. Duck and Orange Warm Salad

Preparation time: 10 minutes | **Cooking time:** 25 minutes | **Servings:** 4

Ingredients:
- 2 tbsp. balsamic vinegar
- 2 oranges, peeled and cut into segments
- 1 tsp. orange zest, grated
- 1 tbsp. orange juice
- 3 shallots, minced
- 2 tbsp. olive oil
- Salt and black pepper to the taste
- 2 duck breasts, boneless and skin scored
- 2 C. baby arugula
- 2 tbsp. chives, chopped

Directions:
1. Heat a pan with the oil over medium-high heat, add the duck breasts skin side down, and brown for 5 minutes.
2. Flip the duck, add the shallot and the other ingredients except for the arugula, orange, and chives, and cook for 15 minutes more.
3. Transfer the duck breasts to a cutting board, cool down, cut into strips, and put in a salad bowl.
4. Add the remaining ingredients, toss, and serve warm.

Nutrition: Calories: 304, Fat: 15.4g, Fiber: 12.6g, Carbs: 25.1g, Protein: 36.4g

145. Turmeric Baked Chicken Breast

Preparation time: 5 minutes | **Cooking time:** 40 minutes | **Servings:** 2

Ingredients

- 8 oz. chicken breast, skinless, boneless
- 2 tbsp. capers
- 1 tsp. olive oil
- ½ tsp. paprika
- ½ tsp. turmeric, ground
- ½ tsp. salt

Directions

1. Make the lengthwise cut in the chicken breast.
2. Rub the chicken with olive oil, paprika, capers, ground turmeric, salt.
3. Then fill the chicken cut with capers and secure it with toothpicks.
4. Bake the chicken breast for 40 minutes at 350°F.
5. Remove the toothpicks from the chicken breast and slice it.

Nutrition: Calories: 156, Fat: 5.4g, Fiber: 0.6g, Carbs: 1.3, Protein: 24.4g

146. Balsamic Chicken

Preparation time: 10 minutes | **Cooking time:** 30 minutes | **Servings:** 4

Ingredients

- 3 chicken breasts
- ¼ C. olive oil
- ¼ C. balsamic vinegar

Directions:

1. In a bowl, add all ingredients.
2. Add chicken and the marinade for 3–4 hours.
3. Grill and serve with vegetables.

Nutrition: Calories: 200, Fat: 8g, Fiber: 4g, Carbs: 8g, Protein: 3g

147. Lemon Chicken Mix

Preparation time: 10 minutes | **Cooking time:** 10 minutes | **Servings:** 2

Ingredients

- 8 oz. chicken breast, skinless, boneless

- 1 tsp. Cajun seasoning
- 1 tsp. balsamic vinegar
- 1 tsp. olive oil
- 1 tsp. lemon juice

Directions

1. Cut the chicken breast on the halves and sprinkle with Cajun seasoning.
2. Then sprinkle the poultry with olive oil and lemon juice.
3. Then sprinkle the chicken breast with balsamic vinegar.
4. Preheat the grill to 385°F.
5. Grill the chicken breast halves for 5 minutes from each side.
6. Slice Cajun chicken and place it on the serving plate.

Nutrition: Calories: 150, Fat: 5.2g, Fiber: 0g, Carbs: 0.1g, Protein: 24.1g

148. Chicken Shawarma

Preparation time: 15 minutes | **Cooking time:** 30 minutes | **Servings:** 8

Ingredients

- 2 lb. chicken breast, sliced into strips
- 1 tsp. paprika
- 1 tsp. cumin, ground
- ½ tsp. turmeric
- ¼ tsp. allspice, ground

Directions

1. Season the chicken with spices, and a little salt and pepper.
2. Pour 1 C. chicken broth into the pot.
3. Seal the pot.
4. Choose a poultry setting.
5. Cook for 15 minutes.
6. Release the pressure naturally.

Nutrition: Calories: 132, Total Fat: 3g, Saturated Fat: 0g, Cholesterol: 73 mg, Sodium: 58 mg, Total Carbohydrates: 0.5g, Dietary Fiber: 0.2g, Total Sugar: 0.1g, Protein: 24.2g, Potassium: 435 mg

149. Lemon Chicken

Preparation time: 10 minutes | **Cooking time:** 20 minutes | **Servings:** 4

Ingredients

- 1-lb. chicken breast, skinless, boneless
- 3 tbsp. lemon juice
- 1 tbsp. olive oil
- 1 tsp. black pepper, ground

Directions

1. Cut the chicken breast into 4 pieces.
2. Sprinkle every chicken piece with olive oil, lemon juice, and ground black pepper.
3. Then place them in the skillet.
4. Roast the chicken for 20 minutes over medium heat.
5. Flip the chicken pieces every 5 minutes.

Nutrition: Calories: 163, Fat: 6.5g, Fiber: 0.2g, Carbs: 0.6g, Protein: 24.2g

150.   Pork Rind Salmon Cakes

Preparation time: 10 minutes | **Cooking time:** 10 minutes | **Servings:** 2

Ingredients

- 6 oz. Alaska wild salmon, canned and drained
- 2 tbsp. pork rinds, crushed
- 1 egg, lightly beaten
- 1 tbsp. ghee
- ½ tbsp. Dijon mustard

Directions:

1. In a medium bowl, incorporate salmon, pork rinds, egg, and 1½ tbsp. of mayonnaise, and season with pink Himalayan salt and pepper.
2. With the salmon mixture, form patties the size of hockey pucks or smaller. Keep patting the patties until they keep together.
3. Position the medium skillet over medium-high heat, melt the ghee. When the ghee sizzles, place the salmon patties in the pan. Cook for 6 minutes on both sides. Transfer the patties to a paper towel-lined plate.
4. In a small bowl, mix together the remaining 1½ tbsp. of mayonnaise and the mustard.
5. Serve the salmon cakes with the mayo-mustard dipping sauce.

Nutrition: Calories: 362, Fat: 31g, Protein: 24g

151.   Rosemary Pork Chops

Preparation time: 30 minutes | **Cooking time:** 35 minutes | **Servings:** 4

Ingredients

- 4 pork loin chops, boneless
- Salt and black pepper, to taste
- 1 tbsp. rosemary, chopped
- 1 tbsp. olive oil

Directions:

1. In a roasting pan, combine the pork chops with the rest of the ingredients, toss, and bake at 425°F for 10 minutes.
2. Reduce the heat to 350°F and cook the chops for 25 minutes more.
3. Divide the chops between plates and serve with a side salad.

Nutrition: Calories: 161, Fat: 5g, Fiber: 1g, Carbs: 1g, Protein: 25g

152.   Tender Lamb

Preparation time: 2 hours | **Cooking time:** 2 Hours and 5 minutes | **Servings:** 6

Ingredients

- 3 lamb shanks
- Seasoning mixture (1 tbsp. oregano, ¼ tsp. cumin, ground, and 1 tbsp. paprika, smoked)
- 2 C. red wine
- 4 C. beef stock

Directions:

1. Coat the lamb shanks with the seasoning mixture.
2. Sprinkle with salt and pepper.
3. Marinate in half of the mixture for 30 minutes.
4. Set the Instant Pot to sauté.
5. Pour in 2 tbsp. of olive oil.
6. Brown the lamb on all sides. Remove and set aside.
7. Add the rest of the ingredients.
8. Put the lamb back to the pot.
9. Cover the pot and set it to manual.

10. Cook at high pressure for 30 minutes.
11. Release the pressure naturally.
12. Set the Instant Pot to sauté to simmer and thicken the sauce.

Nutrition: Calories: 566, Total Fat: 29.4g, Saturated Fat: 6.9g, Cholesterol: 147 mg, Sodium: 700 mg, Total Carbohydrates: 12g, Dietary Fiber: 2.2g, Total Sugar: 6g, Protein: 48.7g, Potassium: 890 mg

153. Worcestershire Pork Chops

Preparation time: 15 minutes | **Cooking time:** 15 minutes | **Servings:** 3

Ingredients
- 2 tbsp. Worcestershire sauce
- 8 oz. pork loin chops
- 1 tbsp. lemon juice
- 1 tsp. olive oil

Directions:
1. Mix up together Worcestershire sauce, lemon juice, and olive oil.
2. Brush the pork loin chops with the sauce mixture from each side.
3. Preheat the grill to 395°F.
4. Place the pork chops in the grill and cook them for 5 minutes.
5. Then flip the pork chops on another side and brush with the remaining sauce mixture.
6. Grill the meat for 7–8 minutes more.

Nutrition: Calories: 267, Fat: 20.4g, Fiber: 0g, Carbs: 2.1g, Protein: 17g

Snacks

154. Healthy coconut blueberry balls

Preparation time: 10 minutes | **Cooking time:** 10 minutes | **Servings:** 12

Ingredients:
- ¼ cup flaked coconut
- ¼ cup blueberries
- ½ teaspoon vanilla
- ¼ cup maple syrup
- ½ cup creamy almond butter
- ¼ teaspoon cinnamon
- 1 ½ tablespoon chia seeds
- ¼ cup flaxseed meal
- 1 cup rolled oats, gluten-free

Directions:
1. Add oats, cinnamon, chia seeds, and flaxseed meal in a large bowl and mix well.
2. Add almond butter to the microwave-safe bowl and microwave for 30 seconds. Stir until smooth.
3. Add vanilla and maple syrup in melted almond butter and stir well.
4. Pour almond butter mixture over oat mixture and stir to combine.
5. Add coconut and blueberries and stir well.
6. Make small balls from the oat mixture, place them onto the baking tray, and place them in the refrigerator for 1 hour.
7. Serve and enjoy.

Nutrition: Calories: 145, Carbs: 15.97g, Cholesterol: 0 mg, Fat: 8g, Fiber: 3.2g, Protein: 4g, Sugar: 7.4g

155. Crunchy roasted chickpeas

Preparation time: 10 minutes | **Cooking time:** 25 minutes | **Servings:** 4

Ingredients:
- 15 oz can chickpeas, drained, rinsed, and pat dry
- ¼ teaspoon paprika
- 1 tablespoon olive oil
- ¼ teaspoon pepper
- Pinch of salt

Directions:
1. Preheat the oven to 450 degrees.
2. Spray a baking tray with spray and set aside.
3. In a large bowl, toss chickpeas with olive oil and spread chickpeas onto the prepared baking tray.
4. Roast chickpeas in a preheated oven for 25 minutes. Shake after every 10 minutes.
5. Once chickpeas are done, then immediately toss with paprika, pepper, and salt.
6. Serve and enjoy.

Nutrition: Calories: 126, Carbohydrates: 15.33g, Cholesterol: 0mg, Fat: 5.45g, Fiber: 4.39g, Protein: 4.7g, Sugar: 2.7g

156. Tasty zucchini chips

Preparation time: 10 minutes | **Cooking time:** 15 minutes | **Servings:** 2

Ingredients:
2 medium zucchini, sliced 4mm thick
½ teaspoon paprika
¾ cup parmesan cheese, grated
4 tablespoon olive oil
¼ teaspoon pepper
Pinch of salt

Directions:
1. Preheat the oven to 375 degrees.
2. Spray a baking tray with cooking spray and set it aside.
3. In a bowl, combine the oil, paprika, pepper, and salt.
4. Add sliced zucchini and toss to coat.
5. Arrange zucchini slices onto the prepared baking tray and sprinkle grated cheese on top.

6. Bake in a preheated oven for 15 minutes or until lightly golden brown.
7. Serve and enjoy.

Nutrition: Calories: 405, Carbohydrates: 7.5g, Fat: 36.68g, Fiber: 2.17g, Protein: 13.14g, Sugar: 4.7g

157. Bagel, Salmon Cream Cheese

Preparation Time: 15 minutes | **Cooking Time:** 10 minutes | **Servings:** 2

Ingredients:

- 8 ounces (250 g) smoked salmon fillet, thinly sliced
- 1/2 cup (125 g) cream cheese
- 50 g of chives
- 4 bagels (about 80g each), split
- 2 tablespoons (7 g) fresh parsley, chopped
- Freshly ground black pepper, to taste

Directions:

1. Spread the cream cheese on each bottom's half of the bagel.
2. Top with salmon and chives, season with pepper, sprinkle with parsley and cover with bagel tops.
3. Serve and enjoy.

Nutrition: Calories: 911, Fat: 37g, Fiber: 7.6g, Carbohydrates: 86.7g, Protein: 54.7g, Sodium: 985mg

158. Greek Baklava

Preparation Time: 20 minutes | **Cooking Time:** 20 minutes | **Servings:** 12

Ingredients:

- 1 (16 oz.) package phyllo dough
- 1 lb. chopped nuts
- 1 cup butter
- 1 teaspoon ground cinnamon
- 1 cup water
- 1 cup corn syrup
- 1 teaspoon. vanilla extract
- 1/2 cup maple syrup

Directions:

1. Preheat the oven to 175°C or 350°Fahrenheit. Spread butter on the sides and bottom of a 9-in by the 13-in pan.
2. Chop the nuts, then mix with cinnamon; set it aside. Unfurl the phyllo dough, then halve the whole stack to fit the pan. Use a damp cloth to cover the phyllo to prevent drying as you proceed.
3. Put two phyllo sheets in the pan, then butter well.
4. Repeat to make eight layered phyllo sheets.
5. Scatter 2-3 tablespoons of nut mixture over the sheets, place two more phyllo sheets on top, butter, and then sprinkle with nuts. Layer as you go.
6. The final layer should be six to eight phyllo sheets deep.
7. Make square or diamond shapes with a sharp knife up to the bottom of the pan. You can slice into four long rows for diagonal shapes.
8. Bake until crisp and golden for 50 minutes.
9. Meanwhile, boil water and corn syrup until the syrup melts to make the sauce; mix in maple syrup and vanilla. Let it simmer for 20 minutes.
10. Take the baklava out of the oven, then drizzle with sauce right away; cool.
11. Serve the baklava in cupcake papers. You can also freeze them without cover. The baklava will turn soggy when wrapped.

Nutrition: Calories: 581, Carbohydrate: 56.26g, Cholesterol: 40mg, Fat: 37.44g, Fiber: 3.5g, Protein: 10.4g, Sodium: 288.95mg

159. Glazed Bananas in Phyllo Nut Cups

Preparation Time: 30 minutes | **Cooking Time:** 45 minutes | **Servings:** 6

Ingredients:

- 3/4 cup shelled pistachios
- 1/2 cup corn syrup
- 1 teaspoon. ground cinnamon
- 4 sheets phyllo dough (14 inches x 9 inches)

- 1/4 cup butter, melted

Sauce:

- 3/4 cup butter, cubed
- 3/4 cup corn syrup
- 3 medium firm bananas, sliced
- 1/4 teaspoon. ground cinnamon
- 3 to 4 cups vanilla ice cream

Directions:

1. Finely chop corn syrup and pistachios in a food processor; move to a bowl, then mix in cinnamon.
2. Slice each phyllo sheet into 6 four-inch squares, get rid of the trimmings. Pile the squares, then use plastic wrap to cover.
3. Slather melted butter on each square one at a time, then scatter a heaping tablespoonful of pistachio mixture.
4. Pile 3 squares, flip each at an angle to misalign the corners. Force each stack on the sides and bottom of an oiled eight-oz. Custard cup.
5. Bake for 15-20 minutes in a 350 degrees F oven until golden; cool for 5 minutes. Move to a wire rack to cool completely.
6. Melt and boil corn syrup and butter in a saucepan to make the sauce; lower heat.
7. Mix in cinnamon and bananas gently; heat completely.
8. Put ice cream in the phyllo cups until full, then put banana sauce on top. Serve right away.

Nutrition: Calories: 724.96, Carbohydrates: 81g, Cholesterol: 104mg, Fat: 43.65g, Fiber: 3.7g, Protein: 7 g, Sodium: 468 mg

160. Salmon Apple Salad Sandwich

Preparation Time: 15 minutes | **Cooking Time:** 10 minutes | **Servings:** 2

Ingredients:

4 ounces (125 g) canned pink salmon, drained and flaked
1 medium (180 g) red apple, cored and diced
1 celery stalk (about 60 g), chopped
1 shallot (about 40 g), finely chopped
1/3 cup (85 g) light mayonnaise

8 slices whole-grain bread (about 30 g each), toasted
8 (15 g) Romaine lettuce leaves
Salt and freshly ground black pepper

Directions:

1. Combine the salmon, apple, celery, shallot, and mayonnaise in a mixing bowl.
2. Season with salt and pepper.
3. Place 1 slice of bread on a plate, top with lettuce and salmon salad, and then cover with another slice of bread.
4. Repeat the procedure for the remaining ingredients.
5. Serve and enjoy.

Nutrition: Calories: 298, Carbs: 25.33g, Fat: 14.21g, Fiber: 6.54g, Protein: 16.59g, Sodium: 1100.94mg

161. Smoked Salmon & Cheese on Bread

Preparation Time: 15 minutes | **Cooking Time:** 10 minutes | **Servings:** 2

Ingredients:

- 8 ounces (250 g) smoked salmon, thinly sliced
- 1/3 cup (85 g) mayonnaise
- 2 tablespoons (30 ml) lemon juice
- 1 tablespoon (15 g) Dijon mustard
- 4 slices of cheddar cheese (about 2 oz. or 30 g each)
- 8 slices rye bread (about 2 oz. or 30 g each)
- 8 (15 g) Romaine lettuce leaves
- Salt and freshly ground black pepper

Directions:

1. Mix the mayonnaise, lemon juice and mustard in a small bowl. Flavor with salt and pepper and set aside.
2. Spread dressing on 4 bread slices. Top with lettuce, salmon, and cheese. Cover with remaining rye bread slices.
3. Serve and enjoy.

Nutrition: Calories: 620, Carbohydrates:

12.32g, Fat: 49g, Fiber: 2.41g, Protein: 32g, Sodium: 1732mg

162. Pan-Fried Trout

Preparation Time: 15 minutes | **Cooking Time:** 10 minutes | **Servings:** 2

Ingredients:
- 1 ¼ pounds trout fillets
- 1/3 cup white or yellow, cornmeal
- ¼ teaspoon anise seeds
- ¼ teaspoon black pepper
- ½ cup minced cilantro, or parsley
- Vegetable cooking spray
- Lemon wedges

Directions:
1. Coat fish with combined cornmeal, spices, and cilantro, pressing it gently into the fish. Spray a large skillet with cooking spray; heat over medium heat until hot.
2. Add fish and cook until fish is tender and flakes with a fork, about 5 minutes on each side. Serve with lemon wedges.

Nutrition: Calories: 502, Carbohydrate: 21.57g, Cholesterol: 193mg, Fat: 17.23g, Fiber: 3g, Protein: 65g

163. Greek Tuna Salad Bites

Preparation Time: 5 Minutes | **Cooking Time:** 10 Minutes | **Servings:** 2
Ingredients:
- Cucumbers (2 medium)
- White tuna (2 - 6 oz. cans.)
- Lemon juice (half of 1 lemon)
- Red bell pepper (0.5 cup)
- Black olives (0.25 cup)
- Olive oil (2 tablespoons.)
- Fresh parsley (2 tablespoons.)
- Dried oregano - salt & pepper (as desired)

Directions:
1. Drain and flake the tuna. Juice the lemon. Add olives, pepper, and parsley. Slice each of the cucumbers into thick rounds (skin off or on).

2. In a mixing container, combine the rest of the fixings.
3. Place a heaping spoonful of salad onto the rounds and enjoy it for your next party or just a snack.

Nutrition: Calories: 252, Carbs: 15g, Fats: 18.92g, Fiber: 2.5g, Protein: 8.75g

164. Stuffed Chicken Breasts

Preparation Time: 15 Minutes | **Cooking Time:** 15 Minutes | **Servings:** 2
Ingredients:
- ¼ cup Greek yogurt
- ¼ cup spinach, thawed & drained
- ½ cup artichoke hearts, thinly sliced
- ½ cup mozzarella cheese, shredded
- 1 ½ lb. chicken breasts
- 2 tablespoons. olive oil
- 4 ozs. cream cheese
- Sea salt & pepper, to taste

Directions:
1. Pound the chicken breasts to a thickness of about one inch. Using a sharp knife, slice a "pocket" into the side of each. That is where you will put the filling.
2. Sprinkle the breasts with salt and pepper and set aside.
3. Combine cream cheese, yogurt, mozzarella, spinach, artichoke, salt, and pepper in a medium bowl, and mix thoroughly. A hand mixer may be the easiest way to combine all the ingredients thoroughly.
4. Spoon the mixture into the pockets of each breast and set aside while you heat a large skillet over medium heat and warm the oil in it. If you have an extra filling, you can't fit into the breasts, set it aside until just before your chicken is done cooking.
5. Cook each breast for about eight minutes per side, then pull off the heat when it

reaches an internal temperature of about 165° Fahrenheit.

6. Before you pull the chicken out of the pan, heat the remaining filling to warm it through and rid it of any cross-contamination from the chicken. Once hot, top the chicken breasts with it.
7. Serve!

Nutrition: Calories: 885, Carbs: 10g, Fat: 64.48g, Fiber: 2.6g, Protein: 65.28g

165. Roasted green beans

Preparation time: 10 minutes | **Cooking time:** 15 minutes | **Servings:** 4
Ingredients:

- 1 lb green beans
- 4 tablespoon parmesan cheese
- 2 tablespoon olive oil
- Pinch of salt

Directions:

1. Preheat the oven to 400 degrees.
2. Add green beans to a large bowl.
3. Add remaining ingredients on top of green beans and toss to coat.
4. Spread green beans onto the baking tray and roast in a preheated oven for 15 minutes. Stir halfway through.
5. Serve and enjoy.

Nutrition: Calories: 118, Carbohydrates: 8.2g, Fat: 8.61g, Fiber: 3g, Protein: 3.8g, Sugar: 3.7g

166. Savory pistachio balls

Preparation time: 10 minutes | **Cooking time:** 5 minutes | **Servings:** 16
Ingredients:

- ½ cup pistachios, unsalted
- 1 cup dates, pitted
- ½ teaspoon ground fennel seeds
- ½ cup raisins
- Pinch of pepper

Directions:

1. Add all ingredients into the food processor and process until well combined.

2. Make small balls, place them onto the baking tray, and place them in the refrigerator for 1 hour.
3. Serve and enjoy.

Nutrition: Calories: 65, Carbs: 13.2g, Fat: 1.78g, Fiber: 1.32g, Protein: 1.3g, Sugar: 10g

167. Roasted almonds

Preparation time: 10 minutes | **Cooking time:** 20 minutes | **Servings:** 12
Ingredients:

- 2 ½ cups almonds
- ¼ teaspoon cayenne
- ¼ teaspoon ground coriander
- ¼ teaspoon cumin
- ¼ teaspoon chili powder
- 1 tablespoon fresh rosemary, chopped
- 1 tablespoon olive oil
- 2 ½ tablespoon maple syrup
- Pinch of salt

Directions:

1. Preheat the oven to 325 degrees.
2. Spray a baking tray with cooking spray and set it aside.
3. Whisk together oil, cayenne, coriander, cumin, chili powder, rosemary, maple syrup, and salt in a mixing bowl.
4. Add almond and stir to coat.
5. Spread almonds onto the prepared baking tray.
6. Roast almonds in a preheated oven for 20 minutes. Stir halfway through.
7. Serve and enjoy.

Nutrition: Calories: 224.6, Carbohydrates:10.42g, Fat: 18.7g, Fiber: 4.45g, Protein: 7.43g, Sugar: 4g

168. Banana strawberry popsicles

Preparation time: 5 minutes | **Cooking time:** 0 minutes | **Servings:** 2
Ingredients:

- ½ cup greek yogurt
- 1 banana, peeled and sliced
- 1 ¼ cup fresh strawberries
- ¼ cup of water

Directions:

1. Put all ingredients into the blender and blend until smooth.
2. Pour blended mixture into the popsicles molds and place in the refrigerator for 4 hours or until set.
3. Serve and enjoy.

Nutrition: Calories: 132, Carbs: 22.86g, Fat: 2.98g, Fiber: 3.46g, Protein: 5.79g, Sugar: 14g

169.   Chocolate matcha balls

Preparation time: 10 minutes | **Cooking time:** 5 minutes | **Servings:** 15

Ingredients:

- 2 tablespoon unsweetened cocoa powder
- 3 tablespoon oats, gluten-free
- ½ cup pine nuts
- ½ cup almonds
- 1 cup dates, pitted
- 2 tablespoon matcha powder

Directions:

1. Add oats, pine nuts, almonds, and dates into a food processor and process until well combined.
2. Place matcha powder in a small dish.
3. Make small balls from the mixture and coat with matcha powder.
4. Enjoy

Nutrition: Calories: 102, Carbs: 12.89g, Fat: 5.7g, Fiber: 2.6g, Protein: 2.55g, Sugar: 7.65g

170.   Chia almond butter pudding

Preparation time: 5 minutes | **Cooking time:** 5 minutes | **Servings:** 1

Ingredients:

- ¼ cup chia seeds
- 1 cup unsweetened almond milk
- 1 ½ tablespoon maple syrup
- 2 ½ tablespoon almond butter

Directions:

1. Add almond milk, maple syrup, and almond butter to a bowl and stir well.
2. Add chia seeds and stir to mix.
3. Pour pudding mixture into the mason jar and place in the refrigerator overnight.

4. Serve and enjoy.

Nutrition: Calories: 589, Carbs: 48.9g, Fat: 39.3g, Fiber: 20.54g, Protein: 17.69g, Sugar: 20.3g

171.   Refreshing strawberry popsicles

Preparation time: 5 minutes | **Cooking time:** 5 minutes | **Servings:** 2

Ingredients:

- ½ cup almond milk
- 2 ½ cup fresh strawberries

Directions:

1. Add strawberries and almond milk into the blender and blend until smooth.
2. Pour strawberry mixture into popsicle molds and place in the refrigerator for 4 hours or until set.
3. Serve and enjoy.

Nutrition: Calories: 86, Carbs: 19g, Fat: 1.2g, Fiber: 4.12g, Protein: 1.6g, Sugar: 13.5g

172.   Dark chocolate mousse

Preparation time: 10 minutes | **Cooking time:** 10 minutes | **Servings:** 4

Ingredients:

- oz unsweetened dark chocolate, grated
- ½ teaspoon vanilla
- 1 tablespoon corn syrup
- 2 cups greek yogurt
- ¾ cup unsweetened almond milk

Directions:

1. Add chocolate and almond milk in a saucepan and heat over medium heat until just chocolate melted. Do not boil.
2. Once the chocolate and almond milk are combined, then add vanilla and corn syrup and stir well.
3. Add yogurt to a large mixing bowl.
4. Pour the chocolate mixture on top of yogurt and mix until well combined.
5. Pour chocolate yogurt mixture into the serving bowls and place in the refrigerator for 2 hours.
6. Top with fresh raspberries and serve.

Nutrition: Calories: 287, Carbs: 15g, Fat: 18.77g, Fiber: 3.31g, Protein: 12.61g, Sugar: 8.38g

173. Warm & soft-baked pears

Preparation time: 10 minutes | **Cooking time:** 25 minutes | **Servings:** 4

Ingredients:

- 4 pears, cut in half, and core
- ½ teaspoon vanilla
- ¼ teaspoon cinnamon
- ½ cup maple syrup

Directions:

1. Preheat the oven to 375 degrees.
2. Spray a baking tray with cooking spray.
3. Arrange pears, cut side up on a prepared baking tray, and sprinkle with cinnamon.
4. In a small bowl, whisk vanilla and maple syrup and drizzle over pears.
5. Bake pears in a preheated oven for 25 minutes.
6. Serve and enjoy.

Nutrition: Calories: 181, Carbs: 47.21g, Fat: 0.22g, Fiber: 4.28g, Protein: 0.5g, Sugar: 37g

174. Healthy & quick energy bites

Preparation time: 10 minutes | **Cooking time:** 0 minutes | **Servings:** 20

Ingredients:

- 2 cups cashew nuts
- ¼ teaspoon cinnamon
- 1 teaspoon lemon zest
- 4 tablespoon dates, chopped
- 1/3 cup unsweetened shredded coconut
- ¾ cup dried apricots

Directions:

1. Line the baking tray with parchment paper and set aside.
2. Add all ingredients to a food processor and process until the mixture is crumbly and well combined.
3. Make small balls from the mixture and place them on a prepared baking tray.

4. Place in the refrigerator for 1 hour.
5. Serve and enjoy.

Nutrition: Calories: 109, Carbs: 9.51g, Fat: 7.71g, Fiber: 1.19g, Protein: 2.4g, Sugar: 4.67g

175. Creamy yogurt banana bowls

Preparation time: 10 minutes | **Cooking time:** 0 minutes | Servings: 4

Ingredients:

- 2 bananas, sliced
- ½ teaspoon ground nutmeg
- 3 tablespoon flaxseed meal
- ¼ cup creamy peanut butter
- 4 cups greek yogurt

Directions:

1. Divide greek yogurt between 4 serving bowls and top with sliced bananas.
2. Add peanut butter to a microwave-safe bowl and microwave for 30 seconds.
3. Drizzle 1 tablespoon of melted peanut butter on each bowl on top of the sliced bananas.
4. Sprinkle cinnamon and flax meal on top and serve.

Nutrition: Calories: 368, Carbs 25.41g, Fat: 20.7g, Fiber: 3.63g, Protein: 23.56g, Sugar: 15.8g

176. Chicken wings platter

Preparation time: 10 minutes | **Cooking time:** 20 minutes | **Serves:** 4

Ingredients:

- 2 pounds chicken wings
- ½ cup tomato sauce
- A pinch of salt and black pepper
- 1 teaspoon smoked paprika
- 1 tablespoon cilantro, chopped
- 1 tablespoon chives, chopped

Directions:

1. In your instant pot, combine the chicken wings with the sauce and the rest of the ingredients, stir, put the lid on and cook on high for 20 minutes.

2. Release the pressure naturally for 10 minutes, arrange the chicken wings on a platter and serve as an appetizer.

Nutrition: Calories: 282, Carbs: 2g, Fat: 18g, Fiber: 0.59g, Protein: 25.55g

177. Carrot spread

Preparation time: 10 minutes | **Cooking time:** 10 minutes | **Serves:** 4
Ingredients:
- ¼ cup veggie stock
- A pinch of salt and black pepper
- ½ teaspoon oregano, dried
- 1 pound carrots, sliced
- ½ cup coconut cream

Directions:
1. In your instant pot, combine all the ingredients except the cream, put the lid on, and cook high for 10 minutes.
2. Release the pressure naturally for 10 minutes, transfer the carrots mix to a food processor, add the cream, pulse well, divide into bowls and serve cold.

Nutrition: Calories: 153, Carbs: 26.8g, Fat: 5.17g, Fiber: 3.15g, Protein: 1.49g

178. Chocolate mousse

Preparation time: 10 minutes | **Cooking time:** 6 minutes | **Servings:** 5
Ingredients:
- 4 egg yolks
- ½ teaspoon vanilla
- ½ cup unsweetened almond milk
- 1 cup whipping cream
- ¼ cup cocoa powder
- ¼ cup water
- ½ cup swerve
- 1/8 teaspoon salt

Directions:
1. Add egg yolks to a large bowl and whisk until well beaten.
2. In a saucepan, add swerve, cocoa powder, and water and whisk until well combined.

3. Add almond milk and cream to the saucepan and whisk until mixed well.
4. Once saucepan mixtures are heated up, then turn off the heat.
5. Add vanilla and salt and stir well.
6. Add a tablespoon of chocolate mixture into the eggs and whisk until well combined.
7. Slowly pour the remaining chocolate into the eggs and whisk until well combined.
8. Pour batter into the ramekins.
9. Pour 1 ½ cups of water into the instant pot, then place a trivet in the pot.
10. Place ramekins on a trivet.
11. Seal pot with lid and select manual, and set timer for 6 minutes.
12. Release pressure using the quick-release method, then open the lid.
13. Carefully remove ramekins from the instant pot and let them cool completely.
14. Serve and enjoy.

Nutrition: Calories: 217, Carbs: 23g, Fat: 21.44g, Fiber: 1.28g, Protein: 4.21g

179. Pistachio arugula salad

Preparation time: 10 minutes | **Cooking time:** 20 minutes | **Servings:** 6
Ingredients:
- 6 cups kale, chopped
- ¼ cup olive oil
- 2 tablespoons lemon juice, fresh
- ½ teaspoon smoked paprika
- 2 cups arugula
- 1/3 cup pistachios, unsalted & shelled
- 6 tablespoons parmesan cheese, grated

Directions:
1. Get out a salad bowl and combine your oil, lemon, smoked paprika, and kale. Gently massage the leaves for half a minute. Your kale should be coated well.
2. Gently mix your arugula and pistachios when ready to serve.

Nutrition: Calories: 176, Carbs: 8.24g, Fat: 14.52g, Fiber: 3.15g, Protein: 6.12g

180. Asparagus couscous

Preparation time: 15 minutes | **Cooking time:** 30 minutes | **Servings:** 6

Ingredients:

- 1 cup goat cheese, herb flavored
- 1½ lbs. Asparagus, trimmed & chopped into 1-inch pieces
- 1 tablespoon olive oil
- ¼ teaspoon black pepper
- 1 ¾ cup water
- 8 ounces whole-wheat couscous, uncooked
- ¼ teaspoon sea salt, fine

Directions:

1. Start by heating your oven to 425 °f, and then put your goat cheese on the counter. It needs to come to room temperature.
2. Get out a bowl and mix your oil, pepper, and asparagus. Spread the asparagus on a baking sheet and roast for ten minutes. Make sure to stir at least once.
3. Remove it from the pan, and place your asparagus in a serving bowl.
4. Get out a medium saucepan, and bring your water to a boil. Add in your salt and couscous. Reduce the heat to medium-low, and then cover your saucepan. Cook for twelve minutes. All your water should be absorbed.
5. Pour the couscous in a bowl with asparagus, and add in your goat cheese. Stir until melted, and serve warm.

Nutrition: Calories: 236, Carbs: 30.75g, Fat: 8.3g, Fiber: 3.75g, Protein: 11.76g

181.   Easy salad wraps

Preparation time: 10 minutes | **Cooking time:** 20 minutes | **Servings:** 4

Ingredients:

- 1 ½ cups cucumber, seedless, peeled & chopped
- 1 cup tomato, chopped
- ½ cup mint, fresh & chopped fine
- Ounce can black olives, sliced & drained
- 2 tablespoons olive oil
- Sea salt & black pepper to taste

- 1 tablespoon red wine vinegar
- ½ cup goat cheese, crumbled
- 4 flatbread wraps, whole wheat

Directions:

1. Get out a bowl and mix your tomato, mint, cucumber, and olives together.
2. Get out another bowl and whisk your vinegar, oil, pepper, and salt. Drizzle this over your salad, and mix well.
3. Spread your goat cheese over the four wraps, and then spoon your salad filling in each one. Fold up to serve.

Nutrition: Calories: 263, Carbs: 19g, Fat: 15.9g, Fiber: 9.4g, Protein: 15.51g

182.   Margherita slices

Preparation time: 5 minutes | **Cooking time:** 15 minutes | **Servings:** 4

Ingredients:

- 1 tomato, cut into 8 slices
- 1 tablespoon olive oil
- ¼ teaspoon oregano
- 1 cup mozzarella, fresh & sliced
- ¼ cup basil leaves, fresh, Tron & lightly packed
- Sea salt & black pepper to taste
- 2 hoagie rolls, 6 inches each

Directions:

1. Start by heating your oven broiler to high. Your rack should be four inches under the heating element.
2. Place the sliced bread on a rimmed baking sheet. Broil for a minute. Your bread should be toasted lightly. Brush each one down with oil.
3. Place the bread back on your baking sheet. Distribute the tomato slices on each one, and then sprinkle with oregano and cheese.
4. Bake for one to two minutes, but check it after a minute. Your cheese should be melted.
5. Top with basil and pepper before serving.

Nutrition: Calories: 231, Carbs: 23.14g, Fat: 11g, Fiber: 1.38g, Protein: 10.23g

183. Baked Brie With Cranberry Chutney and Caramelized Pecans

Preparation time: 10 minutes | **Cooking time:** 25 minutes | **Servings:** 8

Ingredients

- 230g Brie cheese, ground, with the rind on
- ¼ cranberry chutney
- 2 tbsp. agave syrup
- 2 tbsp. pecans, chopped
- 2 tsp. dairy-free butter

Directions

1. Preheat oven to 350°F.
2. Grease a small oven dish with cooking spray.
3. Remove the top from the brie, if you want a straight cut, use a piece of fishing line, or you can use a sharp knife.
4. Spread the chutney over the top of the brie and sprinkle pecans over the top.
5. Sprinkle agave syrup over the top of the pecans and dot the butter over the top.
6. Place the brie in the oven and bake for about 15–18 minutes or until the cheese is soft.
7. Turn the heat up to 425°F and bake for another 5 minutes.
8. The brie should be starting to melt at the base, and the syrup will be bubbling.
9. Serve hot on its own or with graham crackers.

Nutrition: Calories: 333, Fat: 1, Fiber: 1g, Carbs: 6g, Protein: 2g

184. Sausage Cheese Balls

Preparation time: 10 minutes | **Cooking time:** 15 minutes | **Servings:** 6–8

Ingredients

- 450 g pork sausage
- 200 g Fontina cheese, grated
- 250 g gluten-free bisquick

- 120 ml lactaid milk (use more if the dough is too dry)

Directions:

1. Put all the ingredients into a bowl and mix together into a sticky dough.
2. Form into balls about 1-inch in diameter.
3. Lace each ball on a baking sheet, around 1-inch apart from each other.
4. Bake for about 15 minutes or until they have turned a golden-brown color.
5. Serve hot.

Nutrition: Calories: 200, Fat: 8g, Fiber: 2g, Carbs: 8g, Protein: 6g

185. Candied Pumpkin Seeds

Preparation time: 5 minutes | **Cooking time:** 45 minutes | **Servings:** 1

Ingredients:

- 1 egg white
- 130 g fresh pumpkin seeds
- 56 g corn syrup
- ¼ tsp. ginger, ground
- ⅛ tsp. cloves, ground
- ⅛ tsp. nutmeg
- ¼ tsp. cinnamon
- ⅛ tsp. salt

Directions:

1. Preheat oven to 250°F.
2. Mix the syrup and the spices together in a bowl.
3. Beat the egg white until soft peaks form- use an electric mixer if necessary.
4. Add the pumpkin seeds to the egg white and stir in until evenly coated.
5. Now toss the seeds in the spice and corn syrup mix.
6. Line a baking tray with foil sprayed with cooking spray.
7. Spread the seeds evenly over the tray, in a single layer.
8. Bake for about 45–50 minutes.
9. Leave to cool and then break into chunks for serving.

Nutrition: Calories: 260, Fat: 25g, Fiber: 2g, Carbs: 8g, Protein: 2g

186. Coated Pecans

Preparation time: 10 minutes | **Cooking time:** 60 minutes | **Servings:** 4

Ingredients:

- 450 g pecan halves
- 1 egg white
- 1 tsp. water
- 225 ml corn syrup
- ¾ tsp. salt
- ½ tsp. cinnamon, ground

Directions:

1. Preheat oven to 250°F.
2. Grease a baking sheet with cooking spray—non-stick is best.
3. Using an electric mixer, beat the egg white and the water until the mixture is frothy.
4. In another bowl, mix together the cinnamon, salt, and corn syrup.
5. Add the pecan halves to the egg white mix and stir to coat them thoroughly.
6. Remove the nuts and then toss them in the corn syrup and cinnamon mix until well coated.
7. Spread the nuts over the tray in a single even layer.
8. Bake for 60 minutes.
9. Stir them around every 15 minutes.

Nutrition: Calories: 260, Fat: 25g, Fiber: 2g, Carbs: 8g, Protein: 2g

187. Baked Tortilla Chips

Preparation time: 5 minutes | **Cooking time:** 20 minutes | **Servings:** 4

Ingredients:

- 1 tbsp. canola or sunflower oil
- 4 medium whole-wheat tortillas
- ⅛ tsp. coarse salt

Directions:

1. Preheat the oven to 350°F. Brush the oil onto both sides of each tortilla.
2. Stack them on a large cutting board, and cut the entire stack at once, cutting the stack into 8 wedges of each tortilla.
3. Transfer the tortilla pieces to a rimmed baking sheet.
4. Sprinkle a little salt over each chip.
5. Bake for 10 minutes, and then flip the chips.
6. Bake for another 3–5 minutes, until they're just starting to brown.
7. Flavor boost: Mix the salt with ½ tsp. each ground cumin and chili powder before sprinkling it onto the chips.
8. Watch that you don't overcook because they'll look brown from the start.

Nutrition: Calories: 260, Fat: 8g, Fiber: 2g, Carbs: 8g, Protein: 45g

188. Tapenade

Preparation time: 10 minutes | **Cooking time:** 20 minutes | **Servings:** 4

Ingredients:

- ½ C. Kalamata olives
- 1 tsp. capers
- ½ C. olive oil
- 1 tbsp. balsamic vinegar

Directions

1. In a bowl, chop olive with balsamic vinegar
2. Add the rest of the ingredients and mix well.
3. Chill for 1–2 hours serve with asparagus or vegetables.

Nutrition: Calories: 200, Fat: 8g, Fiber: 2g, Carbs: 8g, Protein: 6g

189. Carrot Cake Bites

Preparation time: 10 minutes | **Cooking time:** 0 minutes | **Servings:** 4

Ingredients:

- 4 baby carrots, peeled and chopped
- ⅛ tsp. pure vanilla extract, sugar-free
- ⅓ C. coconut, shredded and unsweetened
- 2 tbsp. almond butter, unsalted
- ⅛ tsp. cinnamon, ground
- 1 tbsp. pure maple syrup
- ⅓ C. gluten-free oats, rolled

- ⅛ tsp. salt, iodized

Directions:
1. Thoroughly clean carrots and remove the skins.
2. Pulse for approximately 2 minutes until consistency is slightly chunky. Transfer to a glass dish.
3. Combine coconut and oats in a food blender and pulse for an additional 2 minutes.
4. Empty carrots, almond butter, maple syrup, salt, vanilla extract, and cinnamon in a food blender and pulse for a total of 2 minutes until the batter thickens. Section into 4 pieces and hand roll into spheres.
5. Serve immediately and enjoy!

Nutrition: Calories: 160, Fat: 8g, Fiber: 2g, Carbs: 8g, Protein: 5g

190.   Pumpkin Peanut Pudding

Preparation time: 10 minutes | **Cooking time:** 0 minutes | **Servings:** 4

Ingredients:
- ⅛ tsp. nutmeg, ground
- ½ C. peanuts, raw and unsalted
- ⅛ tsp. salt, iodized
- ⅓ C. pumpkin puree
- ¼ tsp. cinnamon, ground
- ⅛ C. pure maple syrup
- ¼ C. almond milk, unsweetened
- ½ tbsp. coconut oil, melted
- ⅛ cloves, ground

Directions:
1. Pulse nutmeg, peanuts, salt, pumpkin puree, cinnamon, maple syrup, almond milk, coconut oil, and cloves for 3 mins.
2. Make sure all ingredients are incorporated. Divide equally into individual glasses or a dish.
3. Serve immediately and enjoy!

Nutrition: Calories: 140, Fat: 1g, Fiber: 2g, Carbs: 8g, Protein: 2g

191.   Rice Pudding

Preparation time: 5 minutes | **Cooking time:** 20 minutes | **Servings:** 4

Ingredients:
- 4 ⅓ C. almond milk, unsweetened
- 3½ oz. brown rice
- 1 tbsp. corn syrup
- 2 tbsp. pure maple syrup, separated

Directions:
1. Empty milk in a saucepan on the highest heat setting. As it starts to bubble, turn heat to medium/low, then transfer the rice into the pot.
2. Toss to cover the rice completely. Blend corn syrup and integrate fully. Toss frequently for 20 minutes or until it reaches the desired thickness.
3. Transfer to serving dishes and drizzle with ½ tbsp. each with maple syrup.

Nutrition: Calories: 100, Fat: 7g, Fiber: 2g, Carbs: 8g, Protein: 6g,

192.   Creamy Butternut Porridge

Preparation time: 10 minutes | **Cooking time:** 25 minutes | **Servings:** 3

Ingredients:
- 2 C. butternut squash, peeled and cubed
- 4 tbsp. coconut kefir
- ¼ tsp. sea salt

Directions:
1. Cook butternut squash in water until tender.
2. Add cooked butternut squash, salt and kefir in a blender and blend until creamy.
3. Serve and enjoy.

Nutrition: Calories: 270, Fat: 18g, Carbs: 3g

193.   Avocado and Sauerkraut

Preparation time: 5 minutes | **Cooking time:** 0 minutes | **Servings:** 1

Ingredients:
- ¼ avocado, pitted and mashed
- 1 tsp. homemade sauerkraut
- 1 pinch Celtic Sea salt

Directions:
1. Slice the avocado and mash with the sauerkraut.

2. Season with salt and enjoy right away.
3. Tip: The recipe for homemade sauerkraut can be found in the base recipes section.

Nutrition: Calories: 298, Fat: 12g, Fiber: 2g, Carbs: 20g, Protein: 5g

Dinner

194. Ginger and Spring Egg Drop Soup

Preparation time: 5 minutes | **Cooking time:** 10 minutes | **Serving:** 4
Ingredients:
- Chicken stock – four cups
- Corn starch – 1 tbsp, mixed with ¼ cup of water
- Ginger – 1 tbsp, minced
- Ground black pepper – ½ tsp
- Eggs – 2, whisked
- Sesame oil – 1 tbsp

Directions
1. Combine 1 tbsp cornstarch and ¼ cup water into the bowl. Whisk to combine. Keep it aside.
2. Add stock, black pepper, and ginger into the pot and bring to a boil. When boiled, add cornstarch mixture and chicken stock and cook for one to two minutes.
3. Whisk the eggs and then pour them into the soup. Keep stirring for a half minute.
4. Sprinkle with salt and black pepper. Drizzle with sesame oil.

Nutrition: Calories; 116kcal, Carbs; 6g, protein; 8g, fat; 1g

195. Turkey Burgers with Spinach

Preparation time: 15 minutes | **Cooking time:** 30 minutes | **Serving:** 4
Ingredients:
- Ground turkey, 1lb
- Ground black pepper – 1 tsp
- Sea salt – ¾ tsp
- 1 cup spinach – 1 cup, chopped
- Coconut aminos – 1 tbsp
- Egg – 1
- Tapioca flour – ¼ cup
- Oil, for frying

Directions
1. Add egg, coconut aminos, spinach, salt, pepper, and ground turkey into the bowl.
2. Combine in tapioca flour.
3. Divide the meat into four portions. Shape mixture into round patties.
4. Add oil into the frying pan. Place patties in the pan and cook for ten to fifteen minutes.
5. Serve in lettuce wraps and top with fresh cilantro leaves.

Nutrition: Calories; 176kcal, Carbs; 8g, protein; 28g, cholesterol; 103mg

196. Carrot Tomato Soup

Preparation time: 5 minutes | **Cooking time:** 20 minutes | **Serving:** 6
Ingredients:
- Olive oil – 2 tbsp
- Ginger – 2 tsp
- Carrots, 1lb, peeled and chopped into 1 inch slices
- Tomatoes – 1 ½ lbs
- Oregano – 1 tsp
- Salt – 1 tsp
- Vegetable stock -2 cups, low fodmap
- Bay leaf – 1
- Nutritional yeast – 2 tbsp

Directions:
1. Add olive oil into the cooking pot and place it over medium flame.
2. Add ginger and carrot and sauté for one minute.
3. Add salt, oregano, and tomatoes and stir it well.
4. Add nutritional yeast, bay leaf, and vegetable stock and stir well.
5. Bring to a boil. Lower the heat to low and simmer for 15 to 20 minutes.
6. Remove the pot from the flame.

7. Discard the bay leaf.
8. Add soup into the blender and blend until smooth.
9. Sprinkle with pepper and salt.

Nutrition: Calories; 104kcal, Carbs; 13g, protein; 2g, fiber; 4g

197. Lemony Feta and Sweet Potato Mash

Preparation time: 5 minutes | **Cooking time:** 15 minutes | **Serving:** 4
Ingredients:
- Sweet potatoes – 3 to 4, cut into chunks
- Lemon – half
- Salt – ½ tsp
- Olive oil – 1 tbsp
- Cilantro leaves – ½ cup
- Feta – 3 ½ ounces, crumbled
- Jalapeno – 1 green, deseeded and chopped

Directions:
1. Add sliced sweet potatoes and half lemon into the saucepan and cover with water.
2. Then, add salt and elevate the heat to high. Then, bring to a boil.
3. When boiled, lower the heat to medium and simmer for fifteen minutes.
4. Drain out the water.
5. Transfer the potatoes to the bowl. Mash it with a fork.
6. Add feta, pepper, olive oil, and cilantro and continue mashing it until combined.
7. Sprinkle with salt.

Nutrition: Calories; 144kcal, Carbs; 19g, protein; 5g, fiber; 2g

198. Salmon Cakes and Lemony Herb Aioli

Preparation time: 15 minutes | **Cooking time:** 30 minutes | **Serving:** 10
Ingredients:
- Cooked salmon – 2 ¼ cups
- flaked Sweet potato – ¼ cup, pureed
- Parsley – 1 tbsp, chopped
- Dijon mustard
- 1 tbsp Lemon zest – 1 tsp
- Lemon juice – 1 tbsp
- Capers – 3 tbsp, liquid drained
- Egg – 1, beaten
- Sea salt – ¾ tsp
- Ground black pepper – ½ tsp

Directions:
1. Preheat the oven to 350°/180°C
2. In a large mixing bowl, add all of the salmon cake ingredients.
3. Mix everything together with a fork util combined.
4. Form mini patties, about 3 inches in diameter and place on the baking tray. Bake for 25-30 minutes or until firm and browned on the sides.
5. Make sure to flip the patties over in the oven halfway through cook time.

Lemon Herb Aioli
1. While the salmon cakes are baking make the aioli.
2. The easiest way to make this is with an immersion blender but you can also make this in a food processor, blender, or using an electric mixer.
3. Place the egg yolk, 1/2 of the lemon juice, and mustard in a small bowl or blender/processor.
4. Start whisking/blending everything together until the mixture thickens.
5. Then gradually pour in the olive oil. It's important to add the oil slowly because adding too much too soon will result in a runny or cuddled aioli. As the mixture thickens, add more oil until you have a thick, creamy mayo.
6. Add the remaining lemon juice along, parsley, and dill and mix in by hand.
7. Taste and season with salt if needed. Transfer the aioli to a small bowl and serve with the salmon cakes. Store

leftovers in an airtight container in the fridge for up to a week.

Nutrition: Calories 61, Carbs 1g, Protein 7g, Cholesterol 35 mg, Sodium 281 mg

199. Chicken Avocado and Raspberry Salad

Preparation time: 10 minutes | **Cooking time:** 5 minutes | **Serving:** 4
Ingredients:
Salad:
- Head of gem lettuce – three cup
- Chicken breasts – 2, cooked, skinless, chopped
- Pancetta – six slices
- Raspberries – one cup
- Avocado – one, sliced
- Almonds – ¼ cup, chopped
Dressing:
- Lemon juice – 3 tbsp
- Maple syrup – 2 tbsp
- Dijon mustard – 2 tsp
- Whole grain mustard – 1 tsp
- Olive oil – ¼ cup
- Salt and pepper, to taste

Directions:
1. Add pancetta into the frying pan and fry over medium flame for two minutes per side.
2. When cooked, remove from the flame. Let cool it.
3. Add remaining ingredients into the bowl.
4. Add pancetta slices over the salad.
5. To prepare the dressing: Add all ingredients into the jar and close it. Shake it well.
6. Drizzle the dressing over the salad.

Nutrition: Calories; 441kcal, Carbs; 16g, protein; 21g, cholesterol; 61mg

200. Cucumber Sesame Salad

Preparation time: 25 minutes | **Serving:** 4

Ingredients:
Salad:

- Cucumbers – 2, seedless
- Carrots – 2
- Sweet pepper – 1, chopped
- Kosher salt – 1 tsp
- Sesame seeds – 1 tbsp, white or black
- Cilantro – 2 tbsp, chopped
Dressing:
- Rice vinegar – 2 tbsp
- Freshly squeezed lime juice – 1 tbsp
- Coconut aminos – 1 tbsp
- Maple syrup – 1 tbsp
- Ginger – 1 tsp, grated
- Sesame oil – 1 tbsp
- Red pepper flakes – 1 pinch
- Salt – to taste

Directions:
1. Trim the ends of the cucumber and spiralize the cucumber. Place sliced cucumber into the colander and toss with one tsp of salt. Let rest for five minutes.
2. Peel or spiralize the carrots and chop the sweet peppers.
3. Spread drained cucumber onto the paper towel.
4. Add pepper, carrots, and cucumber noodles into the mixing bowl.
5. Add 2 to 3 tbsp of dressing and toss to combine.
6. Top with fresh cilantro leaves and sesame seeds.

Nutrition: Calories; 102kcal, Carbs; 12g, protein; 1g, fiber; 2g

201. Vegetable Noodle Miso Soup

Preparation time: 25 minutes | **Cooking time:** 10 minutes | **Serving:** 4
Ingredients:
- Vegetable broth or chicken broth – four cups
- Miso paste – 2 tbsp
- Ginger root – 1 tbsp, grated
- Zucchini – 2, spiralized

- Carrot – 1, spiralized
- Coriander – 2 tbsp, chopped
- Salt and pepper, to taste

Miso soup:
- Nori, one sheet, cut into rectangles, dried seaweed
- Tofu – four ounces

Directions:
1. Add ginger and stock into the saucepan and bring to a boil. Then, lower the heat and simmer for three to four minutes.
2. Add miso paste to the bowl. Add half a cup of broth over the miso paste and combine it well.
3. Add spiralized zucchini, cilantro, and shred carrot to the soup and simmer for two to three minutes.
4. Remove the soup from the flame. Place miso broth back in the pot with the remaining soup and sprinkle with pepper and salt.
5. Garnish with fresh coriander leaves.

Nutrition:
Calories 82, Carbs 10g, Protein 7g, Fiber 2g

202. Eggs in Squash Rings

Preparation time: 5 minutes | **Cooking time:** 25 minutes | **Serving:** 4
Ingredients:
- Carnival or acorn squash – one
- Extra virgin olive oil – 1 tbsp
- Eggs – 2 to 4 Bacon – 2 to 4 slices
- Crushed red pepper – to taste
- Dried oregano – to taste
- Thyme – 2 sprigs
- Salt – to taste

Directions:
1. Preheat the oven to 425 degrees Fahrenheit.
2. Cut off both ends of the squash and discard. Cut the remaining middle part of the squash into slices. Scoop out the seeds.
3. Brush squash with olive oil on each side and sprinkle with salt.
4. Place squash onto the baking sheet and put it into the oven, and cook for fifteen minutes.
5. Remove the squash from the oven and break an egg in the middle of each ring. Sprinkle with crushed red pepper, thyme, and oregano.
6. Lower the oven heat to 350 degrees Fahrenheit. Bake for ten minutes more.
7. When eggs are baking and cook the bacon until crispy.
8. Remove the eggs from the oven and crumble one slice of bacon over each ring.
9. Sprinkle with thyme and oregano.

Nutrition:
Calories; 139, Carbs; 11g, protein; 4g, fat; 2g

203. Pot beef stew

Preparation time: 10 minutes | **Cooking time:** 1 hour 45 minutes | **Serving:** 8
Ingredients:
- Beef stew meat – 2 ½ pounds – cut into large chunks, trimmed excess fat
- Scallions – one cup, chopped, green parts only
- Tomato paste – two tbsp
- Worcestershire sauce – one tbsp
- Dried rosemary – one tsp
- Dried thyme – one tsp
- Beef stock or water – 1 ½ cups, low fodmap
- Dry red wine – one cup
- Kosher salt and ground black pepper – to taste
- Carrots – one pound, trimmed, peeled and cut into big bite-sized pieces
- Parsnips – one pound, trimmed, peeled and cut into big bite-sized pieces
- Fresh flat-leaf parsley – to garnish

Directions:
1. Adjust the instant pot for sauté mode. Adjust the temperature to 300 degrees

Fahrenheit. Set time for twenty-five minutes.
2. Place oil and then add meat and stir well.
3. Cook for ten minutes until browned.
4. Add scallions and cook for a few minutes more.
5. Add thyme, rosemary, Worcestershire sauce, and tomato paste and stir well. Then, add wine and stock and mix well.
6. Sprinkle with pepper and salt.
7. Turn off the sauté function and lock the lid.
8. Adjust the instant pot for pressure cook on maximum setting for forty minutes—press start button.
9. When done, allow the pressure to return to normal for twenty to thirty minutes. Unlock the lid. Add parsnips and carrots and lock the lid. Adjust the instant pot to pressure cook on maximum for five minutes—press the start button.
10. Use a quick method to release the pressure. Stir well.
11.   Garnish with fresh parsley leaves.

Nutrition: Calories; 485,   Carbs; 11g, Protein;29g, Fat; 32g

204.   Chicken ratatouille

Preparation time: 15 minutes | **Cooking time:** 40 minutes | Serving: 8
Ingredients:
- Chicken thighs – eight, patted dry
- Kosher salt and ground black pepper – to taste
- Scallions – ¾ cup, chopped, green parts only
- Eggplant – one pound, trimmed, peeled and cut into cubes
- Beefsteak tomatoes – two pounds, cut into dice
- Zucchini – two, cut into half-inch dice
- Red bell pepper – one, trimmed, cored and chopped
- Tomato paste – three tbsp
- Fresh thyme – one tbsp, chopped

- Fresh basil leaves and fresh thyme – to taste

Directions:
1. Firstly, season the chicken with pepper and salt.
2. Add half of the oil into the Dutch oven and heat over medium flame.
3. Then, add chicken and cook until golden brown and crispy.
4. Flip over and cook for eight minutes. Remove chicken from the pan and keep it aside.
5. Add scallion greens and remaining oil and cook on medium-low flame until softened. Then, add eggplant and cook for five minutes until softened.
6. Add thyme, tomato paste, red bell pepper, tomatoes and zucchini and cook over medium flame for ten minutes until thickened.
7. After that, nestle the chicken down into ratatouille and cover it with a lid. Let cook for ten minutes more.
8. Slice the thyme or basil and place it over the chicken.
9. Serve with low fodmap crusty bread and green salad.

Nutrition: Calories; 24,   Carbs; 12g, Protein; 28g, fat; 9g

205.   Low FODMAP scampi

Preparation time: 10 minutes | **Cooking time:** 10 minutes | **Serving:** 4
Ingredients:
- Dry white wine – half cup
- FreeFod Garlic Replacer – one tsp
- Unsalted butter – two tbsp
- Kosher salt and ground black pepper – half tsp
- Pinch red pepper flakes – it is an optional
- Shrimp – 1 ½ pounds, deveined, peeled or shells intact
- Flat-leaf parsley – ¼ cup, chopped

- Whole lemon – half, cut into wedges
- Baguette – low Fodmap

Directions:
1. Firstly, whisk the Freefod garlic replacer and wine into the cup and keep it aside.
2. Add butter and oil into the skillet and melt over medium-low flame.
3. Whisk the red pepper, black pepper, and salt and cook for few seconds.
4. Then, add wine and cook for two minutes.
5. Add shrimp and toss until it turns pink, and it will take two to three minutes.
6. Remove from the flame. Squeeze lemon juice over it.
7. Top with fresh parsley leaves.
8. Serve with a low FODMAP baguette.

Nutrition: Calories; 315, Carbs; 1g, Protein; 35g, fat; 15g

206. Salmon with basil-caper pesto

Preparation time: 5 minutes | **Cooking time:** 10 minutes | **Serving:** 2
Ingredients:
- Extra-virgin olive oil – three tbsp
- Salmon fillets – 4-6 ounces
- Cherry tomato – 1 ½ cups, halved
- Pinch of salt and ground black pepper – to taste
- Basil leaves – ¼ cup
- Capers – two tbsp

Directions:
1. Add one tbsp oil into the skillet and heat over medium flame.
2. Then, add tomatoes and salmon and sprinkle with pepper and salt.
3. Cook for three to four minutes. Flip over and cook for three to four minutes more.
4. After that, mince the capers and basil and add them to the small bowl.
5. Add two tbsp oil into the bowl and stir well. Mash with a fork.
6. Place salmon, basil-caper mixture, and tomatoes onto the serving plates.
7. Serve and enjoy!

Nutrition: Calories; 408, Carbs; 5g, Protein; 24g, fat; 33g

207. Orange chicken and broccoli bowl

Preparation time: 20 minutes | **Cooking time:** 15 minutes | **Serving:** 4
Ingredients:
- Sesame oil – one tbsp
- Chicken thighs – 1 ½ pounds, cut into bite-size pieces
- Low fodmap vegetable broth – half cup
- Grated zest and juice of one orange
- Glucose syrup – ¼ cup
- Soy sauce – ¼ cup
- Broccoli florets – three cup, cut into bite-size pieces
- Carrots – three cup, sliced and peeled
- Scallions – ¼ cup, chopped, green parts only
- Sesame seeds – two tbsp

Directions:
1. Add oil into the skillet and cook over medium flame.
2. Then, add chicken and cook for five to seven minutes until browned.
3. Remove from the flame. Add soy sauce, glucose syrup, broth, and orange zest and juice and stir well.
4. Lower the heat and cook for eight to ten minutes until thickened.
5. Add mixture over the chicken into the skillet and combine well.
6. Mix the water, carrots, and broccoli into the pot, heat over a medium-high flame, and cook for five minutes until tender.
7. Place between four bowls.
8. Top with sesame seeds, scallions, and chicken.

Nutrition: Calories; 531, Carbs; 24g, Protein; 32g, fat; 34g

208. Low fodmap chili mac

Preparation time: 15 minutes | **Cooking time:** 30 minutes | **Serving:** 8

Ingredients:
1. Macaroni – eight ounces, low fodmap
2. Scallions – one cup, green parts only Green bell pepper – one, cored, diced
3. Lean ground beef – one pound Cumin – two tbsp
4. Dried oregano – half tsp Smoked paprika – half tsp
5. Cayenne – ¼ tsp Chipotle powder – ¼ tsp
6. Kosher salt – half tsp Ground black pepper – to taste
7. Low fodmap beef stock – one cup Tomatoes – one cup, diced, with juice
8. Tomato purée – one cup Black beans – half cup, drained
9. Pinto beans – half cup, drained Cheddar cheese – three ounces, shredded
10. Mozzarella cheese – three ounces, shredde

Directions:
1. Firstly, add macaroni into the pot of salted boiling water and cook until firm. Then, drain it and keep it aside.
2. Add chopped scallion greens and cook until softened. Then, add green pepper and cook for two minutes more.
3. Add ground beef and cook over medium flame. Then, add black pepper, half tsp salt, chipotle powder, cayenne, paprika, oregano, and cumin and cook until meat is no longer pink.
4. Then, add pinto beans, black beans, tomato puree, beef stock, and diced tomatoes and stir well.
5. Cover with a lid and simmer for fifteen minutes.
6. During this, preheat the broiler over high heat. Fold reserved macaroni into the chili and top with both kinds of cheese. Place under broiler.
7. Serve and enjoy!

Nutrition: Calories; 316kcal, Carbs; 32g, Protein; 23g, fat; 11g

209. Turkey burgers

Preparation time: 10 minutes | **Cooking time:** 10 minutes | **Serving:** 4

Ingredients:
- Egg – one
- Lean ground turkey – one pound
- Scallions – two tbsp, chopped, green parts only
- Worcestershire sauce – one tsp
- Bell's seasoning – half tsp
- Kosher salt and ground black pepper – to taste
- Unsalted butter – two tbsp
- Low fodmap rolls – four
- Low fodmap condiments – your choice
- Sliced tomato and lettuce – these are an optional ingredients

Directions:
1. Firstly, add an egg into the mixing bowl. Then, beat it well.
2. Add pepper, salt, Worcestershire sauce, turkey, bell's seasoning, and scallions and combine well.
3. Let stand mixture for five minutes. Next, prepare four patties.
4. Cook the butter into the skillet and over medium flame. Then, place patties and cook for four minutes.
5. Flip over and cook it well.
6. Top with your favorite condiments.
7. Serve over rolls.

Nutrition: Calories; 270, Carbs; 1g, protein; 21g, fat; 20g

210. Sticky pork ribs

Preparation time: 30 minutes | **Cooking time:** 2 hours 30 minutes | **Serving:** 6

Ingredients:
Ribs:
- Pork spareribs – 3 ½ pounds
- Leeks – one cup, chopped, green leaves only

Spice Rub:
- Paprika – three tsp

- Glucose syrup – one tbsp
- Ground cumin – two tsp
- Salt – half tsp
- Black pepper – half tsp
- Pinch of crushed red pepper – it is an optional ingredient

Sauce:
- Chicken stock – one cup, low Fodmap
- Orange juice – one cup, squeezed
- Tomato paste – five ounces
- Soy sauce – two tbsp
- Rice wine vinegar – two tbsp
- Yellow mustard powder – two tsp
- Worcestershire sauce – two tsp

Directions:
1. Preheat the oven to 325 degrees Fahrenheit.
2. Remove the white membrane from the ribs.
3. Cut the membrane with a knife.
4. Cut the strips and peel them with your hands.
5. Mix the spice rubs ingredients into a bowl. Rub the meat with a spice mixture and let stand for thirty minutes.
6. Add oil into the frying pan and cook over medium-high flame.
7. Then, add ribs and leeks and cook for three to four minutes.
8. Transfer it to the roasting pan.
9. During this, prepare the sauce: Combine the sauce ingredients into the saucepan and cook for three to four minutes.
10. Place the sauce over the pork and cover with a foil and bake for one and half hours. If it is not tender, cook for thirty minutes more.
11. Transfer the pork onto the chopping board.
12. Strain sauce into the saucepan through a strainer. Boil over medium-high flame for ten to fifteen minutes.
13. Elevate the oven temperature to 425 degrees Fahrenheit.
14. Line a baking sheet with parchment paper.
15. Next, slice ribs into a single portion, place them onto the baking sheet and coat them with sauce. Place it into the oven and bake for ten to fifteen minutes.
16. Baste the ribs with sauce and cook on BBQ for few minutes.
17. Serve!

Nutrition: Calories; 827,   Caarbs; 15g, Protein; 44g, fat; 65g

211.   Whole roast fish
Preparation time: 5 minutes | **Cooking time:** 20 minutes | **Serving:** 4
Ingredients:
- Whole fish – 2 pounds, cleaned and scaled
- Kosher salt and ground black pepper – to taste
- Fresh flat leaf parsley – ¼ cup, chopped
- Fresh herbs – ¼ cup, like thyme, rosemary, dill, marjoram, and basil
- Scallions – ¼ cup, chopped, green parts only
- Lemon – one, thinly sliced crosswise

Directions:
1. Preheat the oven to 450 degrees Fahrenheit.
2. Rimmed roasting pan or baking sheet. Let stand the fish for fifteen minutes at room temperature.
3. Place fish into the pan and rub the whole fish. Sprinkle with pepper and salt. Place scallions and fresh herbs and toss to combine. Press lime slice and herb mixture into each piece, stuff the fish with herbs and lemon, and cook for twenty minutes.
4. Serve!

Nutrition: Calories; 222,   Carbs; 4g, Protein; 26g, Fat; 11g

212.   Potato eggplant curry
Preparation time: 10 minutes | **Cooking time:** 40 minutes | **Serving:** 20
Ingredients:
- Eggplant – three pounds

- Kosher salt – to taste
- Mustard seed – one tsp
- Ghee – ¼ cup
- Fresh ginger root – one tbsp, grated
- Ground coriander – two tsp
- Ground cumin – one tsp
- Cayenne – half tsp
- Fresh beefsteak tomatoes – six, cored, seeded and chopped
- Yukon gold potatoes – three pounds, cubed Water – one cup
- Lime juice – two tbsp
- Fresh cilantro – it is an optional ingredient

Directions:
1. Firstly, cube the eggplant with a sharp knife.
2. Then, place the colander into the sink. Then, rub the eggplant with salt and toss to combine. Let stand for one hour.
3. During this, add oil into the Dutch oven and cook over medium-low flame. Then, add mustard seeds and cook them well.
4. Add cayenne, cumin, coriander, ginger, root, and ghee and stir well.
5. Let cook it for thirty seconds to one minute.
6. Add pepper, salt, eggplant, potatoes, and tomatoes and mix well.
7. Cover the pot with a lid and simmer over medium-low flame for thirty minutes until tender.
8. Sprinkle with pepper and salt if desired.
9. Add cayenne if desired. Then, add lime juice and garnish with chopped cilantro.
10. Serve and enjoy!

Nutrition: Calories; 97k, Carbs; 14g, Protein; 3g, fat; 4g

213. Thai curry tofu and green beans

Preparation time: 10 minutes | **Cooking time:** 15 minutes | **Serving:** 6
Ingredients:
- Extra-firm tofu – 14-16 ounces

- Scallions – ¼ cup, chopped, green parts only
- Thai Curry Seasoning – one tbsp
- Beefsteak tomatoes – two, cored and chopped
- Fresh green beans – eight ounces, trimmed
- Coconut milk – 14.5 ounces
- Kosher salt and ground black pepper – to taste
- Fresh cilantro – to garnish, optional

Directions:
1. Firstly, slice the tofu in half lengthwise.
2. Place a triple layer of paper towel onto the cutting board.
3. Then, place tofu on it. Cover with another triple-layered paper towel.
4. Next, place a heavy cutting board on the top of it. Let stand for ten minutes.
5. When tofu has drained, remove paper towels and slice tofu into the cubes.
6. Add one tbsp oil or ghee into the skillet and cook over medium flame.
7. Then, add tofu and elevate the flame to medium-high speed and cook for few minutes until browned.
8. Remove it from the pan and keep it aside.
9. Then, add the remaining oil or ghee into the pan and cook over medium flame. Then, add scallions and cook for two minutes until softened.
10. Then, add Thai curry powder and stir for thirty seconds.
11. Add green beans and tomatoes and toss to combine.
12. Add coconut milk and stir well. Let simmer for three minutes.
13. Add tofu and stir until coated with sauce. Simmer for five minutes more.
14. Sprinkle with pepper and salt.
15. Garnish with fresh cilantro leaves.

Nutrition: Calories; 260, Carbs; 8g, Protein; 9g, Fat; 23g

214. Roast beef hash

Preparation time: 5 minutes | **Cooking time:** 8 minutes | **Serving:** 4

Ingredients:

- Unsalted butter – one tbsp
- Scallions – half cup, chopped, green parts only
- Green bell pepper – half, cored and diced
- Yukon gold potatoes – one pound, cooked, cooled, cubed
- Roast beef – ten ounces, cut into the cubes
- Kosher salt and ground black pepper – to taste
- Paprika – to taste
- Poached or fried eggs – if desired

Directions:

1. Add one tbsp oil and one tbsp butter into the skillet and cook over medium-low flame. Then, add scallion greens and cook for two minutes until softened. Add bell pepper and cook for two minutes more.
2. Then, add one tbsp oil and cook over medium flame. Then, add roast beef and potatoes and sprinkle with paprika, pepper and salt.
3. Let stand the mixture for few minutes.
4. Serve with eggs.

Nutrition: Calories; 387, Carbs; 24g, Protein; 13g, fat; 10g

215. Grilled swordfish with tomato olive salsa

Preparation time: 5 minutes | **Cooking time:** 10 minutes | **Serving:** 6

Ingredients:

Tomato olive salsa:

- Plum tomatoes – 12 ounces, cored, seeded and diced
- Kalamata olives – ¼ cup, pitted, chopped
- Green olives – ¼ cup, pitted, chopped
- Fresh basil – two tbsp, chopped
- Parsley – two tbsp, chopped
- Capers – two tbsp, drained, brined

- Balsamic vinegar or red wine vinegar – one tbsp
- Kosher salt – to taste
- Ground black pepper – to taste

Fish:

- Lemon juice – one tbsp, squeezed
- Dried basil – half tsp
- Kosher salt – 1/8 tsp
- Ground black pepper – to taste
- Swordfish steaks – 4-5 ounces, ¾ inch to 1-inch thick
- Vegetable oil

Directions:

To prepare the salsa:

1. Mix the vinegar, capers, parsley, basil, green olives, Kalamata olives, oil, and chopped tomatoes into the bowl. Sprinkle with pepper and salt. Prepare this an hour before cooking the fish.

To prepare the fish:

2. Whisk the salt, basil, oil, and lemon juice into the bowl and sprinkle with black pepper. Place fish and coat it well. Let marinate for ten minutes.
3. During this, preheat the grill over high heat. Brush it with vegetable oil. Take out the swordfish from the marinade.
4. Place swordfish onto the grill and cook for three to four minutes.
5. Serve with salsa.

Nutrition: Calories; 331, Carbs; 2g, Protein; 23g, fat; 25g

216. Turkey shepherd's pie

Preparation time: 30 minutes | **Cooking time:** 1 hour | **Serving:** 10

Ingredients:

Turkey shepherd's pie filling:

- Leeks – ¾ cup, chopped, green parts only
- Scallions – ¼ cup, chopped, green parts only
- Carrots – two, peeled, root end removed, slice crosswise into half-inch rounds
- Slender green beans – four ounces, trimmed, cut crosswise into thirds

- Zucchini – one, ends trimmed, quartered lengthwise and slice crosswise into half-inch rounds
- Ground turkey – two pounds
- Tomato paste – two tbsp
- Worcestershire sauce – two tbsp
- Rosemary – ¼ tsp
- Sage – ¼ tsp
- Thyme – ¼ tsp
- Flour – two tbsp, low fodmap
- Unsweetened almond milk – 1 ½ cups
- Kosher salt and ground black pepper – to taste

Mashed potato topping:
- Russet potatoes – three pound, peeled, slice into pieces
- Unsalted butter – two tbsp
- Unsweetened almond milk – ½ to ¾ cup
- Kosher salt and ground black pepper – to taste
- Paprika – to taste

Directions:

To prepare the filling:
1. Preheat the oven to 375 degrees Fahrenheit.
2. Let coat the casserole dish with non-stick spray and keep it aside.
3. Add green beans, carrots, scallions, and leeks and cook for ten minutes until tender.
4. Add zucchini and stir well. Cook for two minutes more until tender.
5. Then, add sliced turkey to the skillet and cook over medium flame and cook until browned.
6. Add thyme, sage, rosemary, Worcestershire sauce, and tomato sauce and cook it well.
7. Then, add flour and stir well. Add almond milk and cook it well.
8. Sprinkle with pepper and salt. Place mixture into the prepared pan.

To prepare the topping:

9. Add salt and water into the pot and boil it. Then, add potatoes and cook for fifteen to twenty minutes until tender.
10. Then, drain well and place potatoes back to the pot.
11. Add butter and mash the potatoes with a potato masher. Then, add almond milk to make a smooth texture. Sprinkle with pepper and salt.
12. Place mashed potatoes over the filling and bake for thirty minutes.
13. Sprinkle with paprika.
14. Serve with a green salad.

Nutrition: Calories; 310,   Carbs; 30g, Protein; 25g, fat; 10g

217.   Coconut tofu curry

Preparation time: 10 minutes | **Cooking time:** 15 minutes | **Serving:** 4

Ingredients:
- Extra-firm tofu – 14-16 ounces
- Baby bok choy – five ounces
- Curry powder – one tbsp, low fodmap Fresh ginger – one tbsp, grated, peeled
- Beefsteak tomatoes – two,
- cored and diced Carrots – three, peeled, stem end removed, slice into big bite-size pieces on the diagonal
- Coconut milk – 14.5 ounces
- Basil leaves – half cup, torn
- Fish sauce – one tbsp
- Lime juice – one tbsp
- Low-sodium soy sauce – one tbsp
- Agave syrup – two tsp

Directions:
1. Firstly, slice the tofu in half lengthwise.
2. Place a triple layer of paper towel onto the cutting board.
3. Then, place tofu on it. Cover with another triple-layered paper towel.
4. Next, place a heavy cutting board on the top of it. Let stand for ten minutes.
5. When tofu is draining, prepare the baby bok choy.

6. Trim and remove the root ends. Let soak each baby bok choy into the cold water.
7. Let pat dry it with a clean paper towel.
8. Cut the baby bok choy in half lengthwise and keep it aside.
9. Slice tofu into the cubes.
10. Add 1 and ½ tbsp oil into the skillet and heat over medium flame.
11. Then, add tofu and elevate the heat to medium-high and cook for few minutes.
12. Remove from the pan and keep it aside.
13. Then, add two tsp oil into the pan and cook over medium flame.
14. Add scallions and cook for two minutes. Add ginger and curry powder and stir well for thirty seconds.
15. Add agave syrup, soy sauce, lime juice, fish sauce, basil, coconut milk, carrots, tomatoes, and bok choy and stir well.
16. Let simmer for three minutes. Add tofu and coat it well with the sauce. Let simmer for five minutes more.
17. Serve!

Nutrition: Calories; 268,   Carbs; 18g, Protein; 14g, fat; 15g

218.   Lamb curry

Preparation time: 5 minutes | **Cooking time:** 20 minutes | **Serving:** 8

Ingredients:

- Fresh ginger – one tbsp, grated
- Leeks – half cup, chopped, green parts only
- Scallions – half cup, chopped, green parts only
- Curry powder – two tsp, low fodmap Garam masala – half tsp
- Turmeric – half tsp
- Cayenne – ¼ to ½ tsp
- Lamb – one pound, diced
- Tomatoes – 28 ounces, diced
- Bay leaf – one
- Lactose-free yogurt – half cup
- Water – half cup
- Kosher salt – to taste

- Cilantro – optional

Directions:

1. Add oil into the skillet and cook over medium-low flame.
2. Then, add scallions, leeks, and ginger and cook for few minutes.
3. Then, add cayenne, turmeric, garam masala, and curry powder and stir well for thirty seconds.
4. After that, add lamb and mix well and cook for five minutes.
5. Add water, yogurt, bay leaf, and tomatoes with their juice and stir well.
6. Cover with a lid and simmer for five minutes more.
7. Serve!

Nutrition: Calories; 142,   Carbs; 6g, Protein; 10g, Fat; 8g

219.   Parmesan crusted flounder

Preparation time: 5 minutes | **Cooking time:** 25 minutes | **Serving:** 2

Ingredients:

- White bread – two slices, low fodmap Flounder fillets – one pound
- Kosher salt and ground black pepper – to taste
- Parmigiano reggiano – half cup, shredded
- Unsalted butter – two tbsp, melted
- Lemon wedges – to garnish

Directions:

1. Preheat the oven to 300 degrees Fahrenheit.
2. Grate the two bread slices on the box grater or food processor.
3. Place breadcrumbs onto the rimmed baking sheet pan, place it into the oven, and bake for five to nine minutes.
4. Let cool it.
5. Elevate the temperature of the oven to 400 degrees Fahrenheit.
6. Place fish fillets into the casserole dish and sprinkle with pepper and salt.
7. Add oil, melted butter, cooled breadcrumbs, and Parmigiano into the

bowl and combine well. Sprinkle with pepper and salt.

8. Place breadcrumb over the fish and bake for twenty to twenty-five minutes until golden.

9. Top with lemon wedges.

Nutrition: Calories; 518, Carbs; 13g, Protein; 51g, fat; 27g

220. Four cheese baked penne with greens and tomatoes

Preparation time: 10 minutes | **Cooking time:** 50 minutes | **Serving:** 8

Ingredients:

- Unsalted butter – ¼ + one tbsp – softene
- All-purpose flour – ¼ cup, low fodmap
- Whole milk – four cup, lactose-free
- Havarti – three ounces, shredded
- Egg – one
- Kosher salt and ground black pepper – to taste
- Penne – one pound, gluten-free
- Fresh baby arugula or baby spinach leaves – one cup
- Parsley – half cup, chopped
- Cheese – one cup, lactose-free
- Crumbled feta – 2/3 cup
- Grape tomatoes – ¾, halved

Directions:

1. Firstly, add one tbsp butter into the pan and then add half a cup of Parmigiano cheese. Heat it over medium flame.

2. Whisk in flour to make a roux and cook for two minutes. Then, add milk and whisk it slowly. Let simmer for ten minutes.

3. Add one cup Parmigiano and Havarti and whisk it well.

4. Add egg and whisk it well. Sprinkle with pepper and salt.

5. Remove from the flame.

6. Preheat the oven to 375 degrees Fahrenheit.

7. Add salt and water into the pot and boil it. Then, add pasta and cook until al dente.

Then, drain it and transfer it to the mixing bowl.

8. Add ¼ cup parsley, cheese sauce, and baby spinach or arugula to the pasta and stir well. Then, add fodmap cheese, tomatoes, and feta.

9. Place mixture into the pan and season with a remaining half cup of Parmigiano.

10. Place pasta into the oven and bake for thirty to thirty-five minutes until golden brown. Let stand for twenty minutes.

11. Garnish with fresh parsley leaves.

Nutrition: Calories; 574, Carbs; 56g, Protein; 29g, fat; 27g
Parmigiano reggiano cheese – two cups, grated

221. Baked rice with olives, feta and pomegranate

Preparation time: 10 minutes | **Cooking time:** 45 minutes | **Serving:** 12

Ingredients:

Rice:

- Water – 3 ½ cups
- Basmati rice – two cups
- Kosher salt – ¾ tsp
- Unsalted butter – four tbsp, cut into pieces
- Pomegranate olive relish and feta: Castelvetrano olives – ¾ cup, pitted, and chopped
- Pomegranate seeds – ¾ cup
- Walnuts – half cup, toasted, chopped
- Fresh mint – ¼ cup, chopped
- Parsley – ¼ cup
- Kosher salt and ground pepper – to taste
- Sheep's milk feta – eight ounces, sliced into ¼-inch slabs

Directions:

For the rice:

1. Preheat the oven to 450 degrees Fahrenheit.

2. Add salt, rice, and water into the casserole dish and drizzle with butter.

3. Seal with aluminum foil and bake it for thirty minutes.

For the Relish:

1. Add mint, parsley, walnuts, pomegranate seeds, and olives into the bowl and stir well.
2. Sprinkle with pepper and salt. Keep it aside.
3. Check the rice and again cover it and cook for five to ten minutes more.
4. Remove from the oven. Fluff the rice using a fork.
5. Set the oven rack from the heat and adjust the broil to high.
6. Place feta over rice
7. Let broil it for six to eight minutes.
8. Top with pomegranate olive relish.

Nutrition: Calories; 339kcal,   Carbs;36g, Protein; 6g, Fat; 20g

222. Stuffed red peppers with quinoa and zucchini

 Preparation time: 10 minutes | Cooking time: 30 minutes | Serving: 4
Ingredients:
- Extra-virgin olive oil – one tsp
- Zucchini – one, diced
- Quinoa – two cup, cooked
- Pinch sea salt and ground black pepper
- Red bell peppers – four
- Feta cheese crumbles – half cup

Directions:
1. Preheat the oven to 375 degrees Fahrenheit.
2. Add olive oil into the skillet and cook over medium-high flame.
3. Then, add zucchini and cook for two to three minutes until tender.
4. Transfer the zucchini to the bowl.
5. Add quinoa to the bowl of zucchini and sprinkle with salt and stir well. Keep it aside.
6. After that, discard the tops, ribs, seeds of bell pepper from the inner side.
7. Stuff the quinoa mixture into peppers.
8. Place onto the baking dish and cover with aluminum foil and bake for twenty minutes.

9. Remove peppers from the oven. Place feta on each pepper.
10. Cover with foil again and bake for five minutes more.

Nutrition: Calories; 230,   Carbs; 33g, Protein; 9g, fat; 8g

223. Cilantro lime rice

Preparation time: 10 minutes | Cooking time: 10 minutes | Serving: 8
Ingredients:
- Rice white or brown rice – four cups, cooked
- Cilantro or parsley leaves – one cup
- Scallions – half cup, chopped, greens part only
- Lime juice – two tbsp, squeezed
- Kosher salt – one tsp
- Ground black pepper – plenty
- Zest of lime – one, optional

Directions:
1. Keep warm the rice and keep it aside.
2. Add salt, lime juice, oil, scallions, and cilantro or parsley into the blender and sprinkle with pepper and lime zest.
3. Blend until smooth.
4. Then, fold the herb mixture into the rice and serve!

Nutrition: Calories; 183,   Carbs; 27g, protein; 2g, fat; 7g

224. Spanakopita spinach pie

Preparation time: 15 minutes | Cooking time: 30 minutes | Serving: 6
Ingredients:
- Unsalted butter – three tbsp
- Scallions – half cup, chopped, green parts only
- Eggs – three
- Cottage cheese – one cup, lactose-free
- Feta cheese – two ounces, crumbled
- Dried dill – one tbsp

- Kosher salt and ground black pepper – to taste
- Spinach – 16 ounces, defrosted, drained and squeezed dry

Directions:
1. Preheat the oven to 350 degrees Fahrenheit.
2. Add butter into the skillet and cook over medium flame.
3. Keep two tbsp of butter aside.
4. Add remaining butter and scallions to the pan and cook for one to two minutes. Remove from the flame.
5. During this, whisk the dill, feta, cottage cheese, and eggs into the mixing bowl.
6. Sprinkle with pepper and salt. Then, add spinach and place mixture into the pan and stir it with cooked scallions.
7. Place one sheet of filo over the spinach filling and brush with reserved butter. Place another sheet over it. Brush with butter.
8. Place it into the oven and bake for thirty to forty minutes until golden brown.
9. Let cool it for five minutes.
10. Top with lemon wedges.

Nutrition: Calories; 210, Carbs; 13g, Protein;13g, Fat; 12g

225. Low fodmap cioppino

Preparation time: 20 minutes | **Cooking time:** 40 minutes | **Serving:** 8
Ingredients:
- Leeks – one cup, chopped, green parts only
- Scallions – one cup, chopped, green parts only
- Green bell pepper – one, cored and diced
- Marjoram – one tsp, chopped
- Red pepper flakes – one tsp
- Tomato paste – two tbsp
- Whole tomatoes – 28 ounces, chopped, peeled
- Dry red or white wine – 1 ½ cups
- Chicken stock – one cup, low fodmap

- Fish stock or clam juice – one cup, low fodmap
- Kosher salt and ground black pepper
- Basil – one cup, torn into pieces
- Lobster tails – four ounce
- Mussels or clams – twenty-four, scrubbed and cleaned
- Fish fillets – one pound, cut into bite-sized pieces
- Shrimp – one pound, deveined, tail-on
- Baguette or sourdough – crusty, low fodmap

Directions:
1. Add oil into the stockpot and heat it over medium-low flame.
2. Then, add marjoram, thyme, scallions, and leek and cook until softened.
3. Whisk in tomatoes with their juices and tomato paste.
4. Break the tomatoes with a potato masher into the pot.
5. Then, add clam juice, chicken stock, and wine and cover with a lid.
6. Let simmer for twenty minutes.
7. Sprinkle with pepper and salt. Then, add half of the basil leaves.
8. Insert a bamboo skewer in each lobster tail and add to the pot.
9. Cover the pot with a lid and simmer for four minutes.
10. Add clams or mussels to the pot and cover with a lid and cook for eight minutes.
11. Then, add shrimp and fish and cover with a lid and simmer it.
12. Garnish with reserved basil.

Nutrition: Calories; 313, Carbs; 8g, protein; 43g, fat; 9g

226. Carrot and fennel soup

Preparation time: 10 minutes | **Cooking time:** 50 minutes | **Serving:** 4
Ingredients:
- Carrots – two, big
- Potatoes – 340g

- Sweet potato or parsnip – 200g
- Leek – half cup, green tips only
- Olive oil – one tbsp
- Chicken stock or vegetable stock – three cups, low fodmap
- Butter or olive oil – one tbsp
- Fennel seeds – two teaspoon
- Fresh coriander – 1 ½ tbsp
- Milk – half cup, low fodmap
- Salt and pepper – to taste
- Bread – eight slices, low fodmap

Directions:
1. First, thinly slice the green tips of the leeks. Then, peel the sweet potato, carrot, and potato into small slices.
2. After that, chop the fresh coriander. Add olive oil into the saucepan and cook over a low flame—Cook the leeks tip for one to two minutes.
3. Add sweet potato or parsnip, carrot, and potato into the saucepan and cook over low flame for five minutes.
4. Add vegetable or chicken stock to the saucepan and elevate the flame to medium-high flame. Let boil it for ten to fifteen minutes and cover the pot with a lid.
5. During this, add butter or olive oil into the frying pan.
6. Then, add fennel seeds and cook for one minute.
7. Add coriander and cook for one minute more.
8. Remove from the flame. Add fennel seed mixture and coriander to the soup.
9. Remove soup from the flame. Let cool it for ten minutes.
10. Transfer the soup to the food processor and blend until smooth.
11. Wash the soup pot and place soup back to the pot.
12. Add low fodmap milk and sprinkle with pepper and salt.
13. Garnish with fresh coriander.

Nutrition: Calories; 416, Fat; 12.4g, Protein; 10.5g, carbs; 67.3g

227. Beef Bourguignon

Preparation Time: 10 minutes | **Cooking Time:** 6 hours | **Servings:** 4

Ingredients:
- ¼ cup tapioca flour
- 1 teaspoon cumin powder
- 18 oz chuck steak, sliced into strips
- 2 tablespoons olive oil
- 2 cups dry red wine
- 1 tablespoon tomato paste
- 2 carrots, peeled and chopped
- 2 zucchinis, chopped
- 1 bay leaf
- 1 teaspoon dried rosemary
- Salt and pepper to taste

Directions:
1. In a bowl, mix together the flour, salt, pepper, and cumin powder.
2. Toss in the beef slices into the flour mixture.
3. Heat the olive oil in a large skillet over medium flame and sauté the beef slices until brown.
4. Continue cooking for 6 minutes and remove the meat from the pan.
5. Using the same pan, add wine to the pan and scrape the beef residue while heating.
6. Place the contents in the pan on a slow cooker and add in the rest of the ingredients including the beef.
7. Close the slow cooker and cook for 6 hours on low.

Nutrition: Calories: 314, Total Fat: 15.2g, Saturated Fat: 4.5g, Cholesterol: 0 mg, Sodium: 120 mg, Total Carbs: 11.8g, Fiber: 1.1g, Sugar: 1.6g, Protein: 27.8g

228. Steak And Potatoes Sheet Pan Meal

Preparation Time: 10 minutes | **Cooking Time:** 30 minutes | **Servings:** 4
Ingredients:
- 680 grams baby potatoes, quartered
- 1 red bell pepper, seeded and cubed
- 1 green bell pepper, seeded and cubed
- 1 ½ lb. top sirloin steak,
- What you'll need from the store cupboard:
- Salt and pepper to taste

Directions:
1. Preheat the oven to 400°F and line a baking sheet with aluminum foil.
2. In a bowl, mix the potatoes, peppers, steak, and olive oil.
3. Season with salt and pepper to taste.
4. Bake for 30 minutes until the steaks and potatoes are done.

Nutrition: Calories: 461, Total Fat: 19.2g, Saturated Fat: 7.6g, Cholesterol: 0 mg, Sodium: 102 mg, Total Carbs: 31.8g, Fiber: 4.1g, Sugar: 2.5g, Protein: 39.1g

229. French Oven Beef

Preparation Time: 5 minutes | **Cooking Time:** 3 hours | **Servings:** 4
Ingredients:
- 1 lb. beef chuck, sliced
- 1 cup fennel bulb, diced
- 1 medium celery stalk, diced
- 6 medium carrots,
- 4 medium parsnips
- 4 medium potatoes
- ¼ cup tapioca starch
- 1 cup tomato juice
- 1 tablespoon maple syrup
- Salt and pepper to taste

Directions:
1. Preheat the oven to 300°F.
2. Place all ingredients in a heat-proof deep dish and mix until well combined.
3. Bake the dish for 3 hours on medium heat.
Nutrition: Calories: 548, Total Fat: 7.3g, Saturated Fat: 2.1g, Cholesterol: 0 mg,

Sodium: 288 mg, Total Carbs: 91.2g, Fiber: 13.8g, Sugar: 14.4g, Protein: 32.g

230. Beef Stroganoff

Preparation Time: 5 minutes | **Cooking Time:** 20 minutes | **Servings:** 4
Ingredients:
- 2 teaspoons olive oil
- ½ lb. beef strips
- 1 tablespoon tapioca flour
- 1 cup white cabbage, thinly sliced
- 1 teaspoon sweet paprika
- 2 tablespoon tomato paste
- 2 teaspoon Dijon mustard
- 2 tablespoons coconut yoghurt
- 1 can sliced champignon mushrooms, drained and rinsed well
- 1 ¼ cups water
- Salt and pepper to taste

Directions:
1. Heat oil in a large pan on medium flame. Stir in the cabbages and cook for 4 minutes or until wilted.
2. Sliced mushrooms.
3. Cook for another 2 minutes while stirring constantly.
4. Set aside. Using the same pan, increase the heat to medium high and stir in the beef strips and cook until brown.
5. While the beef strips are cooking, mix together the tapioca starch and paprika.
6. Add the flour mixture into the beef and reduce the heat to medium.
7. Stir until the beef strips are coated.
8. Cook for another minute while stirring constantly.
9. Add in the tomato paste, Dijon mustard, and water.
10. Season with salt and pepper to taste.
11. Close the lid and allow to boil. Once boiling, lower the heat and add in the cabbage and mushroom mixture.
12. Allow to simmer for 10 minutes before adding the coconut yoghurt last.

Nutrition: Calories: 122, Total Fat: 4.2g, Saturated Fat: 0.8g, Cholesterol: 0 mg, Sodium: 82 mg, Total Carbs: 8.2g, Fiber: 1.8g, Sugar: 3.4g, Protein: 14.3g

231.   Lamb Casserole

Preparation Time: 10 minutes | **Cooking Time:** 2 hours and 10 minutes | **Servings:** 4
Ingredients:

- 1 tablespoon coconut oil
- 900 grams lamb meat, cut into chunks
- 1 tablespoon coriander
- 1 teaspoon ground cardamom
- 1 tablespoon ground cumin
- ½ cup red wine
- ½ cup tomato paste
- 3 large carrots, chopped
- 1 can of lentils, rinsed and drained thoroughly
- Salt and pepper to taste
- 2 cups water

Directions:

1. In a large pan, heat the oil over medium flame.
2. Cook the lamb while stirring constantly until all sides turn brown.
3. Add the coriander, cardamom, and cumin. Season with salt and pepper to taste.
4. Stir in the red wine, tomato paste, lentils, and carrots.
5. Pour in water and bring to a boil.
6. Cook the lamb for 2 hours on medium meat or until the meat is tender.

Nutrition: Calories: 407, Total Fat: 15.4g, Saturated Fat: 7.4g, Cholesterol: 0 mg, Sodium: 221 mg, Total Carbs: 16.7g, Fiber: 3.2g, Sugar: 6.6g, Protein: 48.9g

232.   Maple Mustard Chicken With Rosemary

Preparation Time: 5 minutes | **Cooking Time:** 35 minutes | **Servings:** 6
Ingredients:

- 1 tablespoon olive oil
- 6 bone-in chicken thighs
- 2 tablespoons Dijon mustard
- 2 tablespoons whole grain mustard seed
- 3 tablespoons maple syrup
- 1 tablespoon lemon juice
- 1 tablespoon fresh rosemary
- Salt and pepper to taste

Directions:

1. Preheat the oven to 375°F and grease a baking dish. Season the chicken thighs with salt and pepper to taste.
2. Heat the oil in a large skillet over medium flame and put the chicken thighs skin side down and cook for 4 minutes on each side or until the skin turns golden brown.
3. While the chicken is cooking on the stovetop, prepare the mustard glaze by mixing the rest of the ingredients in a bowl.
4. Once the chicken has turned golden, transfer into the prepared baking dish.
5. Brush each thigh with the prepared mustard sauce.
6. Place inside the oven and bake for 30 minutes or until the chicken is cooked through.

Nutrition: Calories: 487, Total Fat: 35.2g, Saturated Fat: 9.1g, Cholesterol: 0 mg, Sodium: 215 mg, Total Carbs: 8.3g, Fiber: 0.5g, Sugar: 6.3g, Protein: 32.6g

233.   Baked Potato And Chicken Casserole

Preparation Time: 10 minutes | **Cooking Time:** 35 minutes | **Servings:** 4
Ingredients:

- ½ cup coconut cream
- 1 ½ cups cheddar cheese, grated
- 4 slices of bacon, cooked crisp and crumbled
- 4 medium russet potatoes, scrubbed and diced

- 1 lb. boneless chicken breasts, skin removed and diced
- What you'll need from the store cupboard:
- salt and pepper to taste

Directions:
1. Heat the oven to 350°F and grease a casserole pan.
2. Spread the potatoes in the bottom of the pan.
3. Place the chicken on top and season with salt and pepper to taste.
4. Sprinkle with bacon crumbles.
5. Pour in the coconut cream and top with cheddar cheese.
6. Place inside the oven and bake for 35 minutes

Nutrition: Calories: 662, Total Fat: 35.4g, Saturated Fat: 14.7g, Cholesterol: 0 mg, Sodium: 685 mg, Total Carbs: 49.3g, Fiber: 4.7g, Sugar: 7.3g, Protein: 38.9g

234. Quick Curry Casserole

Preparation Time: 10 minutes | **Cooking Time:** 20 minutes | **Servings:** 4
Ingredients:
- 2 chicken breasts
- 2 cups broccoli florets
- ½ cup Mayonnaise
- 2 teaspoons curry powder
- 1 teaspoon lemon juice
- 1 bell pepper, seeded and chopped
- 1 cup grated cheese
- Oil for frying
- Salt and pepper to taste

Directions:
1. Heat the oven to 375°F and grease the casserole dish.
2. Heat the oil in a large pan and fry the chicken breasts on each side until golden brown. Set aside.
3. Using the same pan, cook the broccoli florets for 2 minutes. Set aside.
4. In a bowl, combine the mayonnaise, curry powder, and lemon juice.

5. Season with the salt and pepper to taste. Place the chicken in the casserole dish and top with broccoli.
6. Pour over the curry sauce and top with bell pepper and cheese. Bake in the oven for 15 minutes.

Nutrition: Calories: 482, Total Fat: 33.2g, Saturated Fat: 11g, Cholesterol: 0 mg, Sodium: 529 mg, Total Carbs: 3.4g, Fiber: 1.6g, Sugar: 1.1g, Protein: 41.1g

235. One Pan Chicken Cacciatore

Preparation Time: 10 minutes | **Cooking Time:** 25 minutes | **Servings:** 4
Ingredients:
- 2 tablespoons olive oil
- 900 gramsboneless chicken thighs
- 2 small carrots, sliced thinly
- 1 red bell pepper, seeded and diced
- ¼ teaspoon red pepper flakes
- ½ cup dry red wine
- 2 tablespoons pitted Kalamata olives
- 2 cups crushed tomatoes
- 4 sprigs fresh thyme, chopped
- 4 sprigs fresh oregano, chopped
- Salt and pepper to taste

Directions:
1. In a skillet, heat the oil over medium flame.
2. Season the chicken thighs with salt and pepper to taste and cook the chicken until golden brown.
3. Remove from the plate and set aside.
4. On the same skillet, sauté the vegetables and scrape the brown bits at the bottom of the pan.
5. Continue cooking for 5 minutes and season the vegetables with salt and pepper to taste.
6. Pour in the red wine and simmer until reduced by half. Add the olives, tomatoes, thyme, and oregano.
7. Place the chicken on top of the vegetables. Allow to simmer for 15 minutes.

Nutrition: Calories: 591, Total Fat: 45.1g, Saturated Fat: 11.3g, Cholesterol: 0 mg, Sodium: 223 mg, Total Carbs: 5.2g, Fiber: 1.3g, Sugar: 2.8g, Protein: 28.5,

236. Moroccan Chicken

Preparation Time: 8 hours | **Cooking Time:** 16 minutes | **Servings:** 4

Ingredients:

- 2 tablespoons olive oil
- 2 teaspoons ground paprika
- 1 teaspoon ground cumin
- ½ teaspoon ground coriander
- ½ teaspoon ground turmeric
- ¼ teaspoon ground ginger
- 1/8 teaspoon cayenne pepper
- 1 package 20-oz boneless and skinless chicken breasts
- Salt and pepper to taste

Directions:

1. In a bowl, combine all ingredients except for the chicken.
2. Place the chicken breasts in a Ziploc bag and pour in the sauce.
3. Allow to marinate in the fridge for at least 8 hours.
4. Heat the grill to medium and remove the chicken from the marinade.
5. Grill the chicken for 8 minutes on each side until fully cooked.

Nutrition: Calories: 237, Total Fat: 10.2g, Saturated Fat: 1.8g, Cholesterol: 0 mg, Sodium: 66 mg, Total Carbs: 1.2g, Fiber: 0.2g, Sugar: 0.1g, Protein: 32.2g

237. Alfredo Peppered Shrimp

Preparation Time: 5 minutes | **Cooking Time:** 20 minutes | **Servings:** 6

Ingredients:

- 12 kg penne
- 1/4 cup butter
- 2 tablespoons extra virgin olive oil
- 1 red pepper, diced
- 1/2 kg Portobello mushrooms, cubed
- 1 pound shrimp, peeled and thawed
- 1 jar of Alfredo sauce
- 1/2 cup of grated Romano cheese
- 1/2 cup of cream
- 1/4 cup chopped parsley
- 1 teaspoon cayenne pepper
- salt and pepper to taste

Directions:

1. Bring a large pot of lightly salted water to a boil. Put the pasta and cook for 8 to 10 minutes or until al dente; drain.
2. Meanwhile, melt the butter and olive oil in a pan over medium heat. Cook until soft and translucent, about 2 minutes.
3. Stir in red pepper and mushrooms; cook over medium heat until soft, about 2 minutes longer.
4. Stir in the shrimp and fry until firm and pink, then add Alfredo sauce, Romano cheese and cream; bring to a boil, constantly stirring until thick, about 5 minutes. Season with cayenne pepper, salt, and pepper to taste.
5. Add the drained pasta to the sauce and sprinkle with chopped parsley.

Nutrition: 707 calories, 45 g fat, 50.6, Carbs, 28.4 g of protein, 201 mg of cholesterol, 1034 mg of sodium,

238. Sherry and Butter Prawns

Preparation Time: 5 minutes | **Cooking Time:** 5 minutes | **Servings:** 4

Ingredients:

- 1 ½ pounds king prawns, peeled and deveined
- 2 tablespoons dry sherry
- 1 teaspoon dried basil
- 1/2 teaspoon mustard seeds
- 1 ½ tablespoons fresh lemon juice
- 1 teaspoon cayenne pepper, crushed
- 1/2 stick butter, at room temperature

Directions:

1. Whisk the dry sherry with cayenne pepper, basil, mustard seeds, lemon juice

and prawns. Let it marinate for 1 hour in your refrigerator.

2. In a frying pan, melt the butter over medium-high flame, basting with the reserved marinade.

3. Sprinkle with salt and pepper to taste.

Nutrition: 294 Calories, 14.3g Fat, 3.6g Carbs, 34.6g Protein, 1.4g Fiber

239. Fried Codfish with Almonds

Preparation Time: 8 minutes | **Cooking Time:** 18 minutes | **Servings:** 3
Ingredients:
- 16 oz. codfish fillet
- 3 oz. chopped almonds
- ½ tsp chili pepper
- 1 egg
- 1 tbsp. ghee butter
- 1 tsp psyllium
- 3 oz. cream
- 3 tbsp. keto mayo
- 1 tbsp. chopped fresh dill
- ½ tsp chives
- Salt and pepper to taste

Directions:
1. In a small mixing bowl, combine the psyllium, chives, chili, and almonds
2. Beat the eggs in another bowl, mix well
3. Warm the butter in a skillet at medium heat.
4. Cut the fillet into 3 slices
5. Dip into the egg mixture, then into almonds and spices
6. Fry in the skillet for about 7 minutes each side
7. Meanwhile, in another bowl combine the cream, dill, and salt, stir well
8. Serve the fish with this sauce

Nutrition: Carbs: 4,9g, Fats: 63g, Protein: 33,6g, Calories: 709

240. Salmon Balls

Preparation Time: 5 minutes | **Cooking Time:** 13 minutes | **Servings:** 2
Ingredients:

- 1 can of tuna
- 2 tbsp. keto mayo
- 1 avocado
- 1 egg
- ½ cup heavy cream
- 3 tbsp. coconut oil
- ½ tsp ginger powder
- ½ tsp paprika
- ½ tsp dried cilantro
- 2 tbsp. lemon juice
- 2 tbsp. water
- Salt and ground black pepper to taste

Directions:
1. Drain the salmon, chop it
2. Peel the avocado
3. In a bowl, combine the fish, mayo and egg, season with salt, paprika, and ginger, mix well
4. Make 4 balls of it
5. Warm the oil in a skillet at medium heat
6. Put the balls and fry for 4-6 minutes each side
7. Meanwhile, put the heavy cream, avocado, cilantro, lemon juice, and 1 tablespoon of oil in a blender. Pulse well
8. Serve the balls with the sauce

Nutrition: Carbs: 3,9g, Fats: 50g, Protein: 20,1g, Calories: 555

241. Clams with Tomato Sauce

Preparation Time: 5 minutes | **Cooking Time:** 20 minutes | **Servings:** 4
Ingredients:
- 40 littleneck clams
- For the Sauce:
- 2 tomatoes, pureed
- 2 tablespoons olive oil
- 1 shallot, chopped
- Sea salt, to taste
- Freshly ground black pepper, to taste
- 1/2 teaspoon paprika
- 1/3 cup port wine
- 1/2 lemon, cut into wedges

Directions:

1. Grill the clams until they are open, for 5 to 6 minutes.
2. In a frying pan, heat the olive oil over moderate heat. Cook the shallot until tender and fragrant.
3. Stir in the pureed tomatoes, salt, black pepper and paprika and continue to cook an additional 10 to 12 minutes, up to well cooked.
4. Heat off and add in the port wine; stir to combine. Garnish with fresh lemon wedges.

Nutrition: 134 Calories, 7.8g Fat, 5.9g Carbs, 8.3g Protein, 1g Fiber

242. Greek Chicken Bites

Preparation time: 10 minutes | **Cooking time:** 20 minutes | **Servings:** 6

Ingredients
- 1-lb. chicken fillet
- 1 tbsp. Greek seasoning
- 1 tsp. sesame oil
- ½ tsp. salt
- 1 tsp. balsamic vinegar

Directions:
1. Cut the chicken fingers on small tenders (fingers) and sprinkle them with Greek seasoning, salt, and balsamic vinegar. Mix up well with the help of the fingertips.
2. Then sprinkle chicken with sesame oil and shake gently.
3. Line the baking tray with parchment.
4. Place the marinated chicken fingers in the tray in one layer.
5. Bake the chicken fingers for 20 minutes at 355°F. Flip them on another side after 10 minutes of cooking.

Nutrition: Calories: 154, Fat: 6.4g, Fiber: 0g, Carbs: 0.8g, Protein: 22g

243. Turkey Verde With Brown Rice

Preparation time: 15 minutes | **Cooking time:** 30 minutes | **Servings:** 5

Ingredients
- ⅔ C. chicken broth
- 1 ¼ C. brown rice
- 1 ½ lb. turkey tenderloins
- ½ C. salsa Verde

Directions:
1. Add the chicken broth and rice to the Instant Pot.
2. Top with the turkey, and salsa.
3. Cover the pot.
4. Set it to manual.
5. Cook at high pressure for 18 minutes.
6. Release the pressure naturally.
7. Wait for 8 minutes before opening the pot.

Nutrition: Calories: 336, Total Fat: 3.3g, Saturated Fat: 0.3g, Cholesterol: 54 mg, Sodium: 321 mg, Total Carbohydrates: 39, Dietary Fiber: 2.2g, Total Sugar: 1.4g, Protein: 38.5g, Potassium: 187 mg

244. Chicken Tacos

Preparation time: 10 minutes | **Cooking time:** 20 minutes | **Servings:** 4

Ingredients:
- 2 bread tortillas
- 1 tsp. butter
- 2 tsp. olive oil
- 1 tsp. Taco seasoning
- 6 oz. chicken breast, skinless, boneless, sliced
- ⅓ C. Cheddar cheese, shredded
- 1 bell pepper, cut on the wedges

Directions:
1. Pour 1 tsp. of olive oil in the skillet and add chicken.
2. Sprinkle the meat with Taco seasoning and mix up well.
3. Roast chicken for 10 minutes over medium heat. Stir it from time to time.
4. Then transfer the cooked chicken to the plate.
5. Add remaining olive oil to the skillet.
6. Then add bell pepper and roast it for 5 minutes. Stir it all the time.
7. Mix up together bell pepper with chicken.
8. Toss butter in the skillet and melt it.
9. Put 1 tortilla in the skillet.

10. Put Cheddar cheese on the tortilla and flatten it.
11. Then add a chicken-pepper mixture and cover it with the second tortilla.
12. Roast the quesadilla for 2 minutes from each side.
13. Cut the cooked meal on the halves and transfer it to the serving plates.

Nutrition: Calories: 194, Fat: 8.3g, Fiber: 0.6g, Carbs: 16.4g, Protein: 13.2g

245. Chicken and Butter Sauce

Preparation time: 5 minutes | Cooking time: 30 minutes | Servings: 5
Ingredients
- 1-lb. chicken fillet
- ⅓ C. butter, softened
- 1 tbsp. rosemary
- ½ tsp. thyme
- 1 tsp. salt
- ½ lemon

Directions:
1. Churn together thyme, salt, and rosemary.
2. Chop the chicken fillet roughly and mix it up with churned butter mixture.
3. Place the prepared chicken in the baking dish.
4. Squeeze the lemon over the chicken.
5. Chop the squeezed lemon and add it to the baking dish.
6. Cover the chicken with foil and bake it for 20 minutes at 365°F.
7. Then discard the foil and bake the chicken for 10 minutes more.

Nutrition: Calories: 285, Fat: 19.1g, Fiber: 0.5g, Carbs: 1g, Protein: 26.5g

246. Pork and Chestnuts Mix

Preparation time: 30 minutes | Cooking time: 0 minutes | Servings: 6
Ingredients:
- 1 and ½ C. brown rice, already cooked
- 2 C. pork roast, already cooked and shredded
- 3 oz. water chestnuts, drained and sliced
- ½ C. sour cream

- A pinch salt and white pepper

Directions:
1. In a bowl, mix the rice with the roast and the other ingredients, toss and keep in the fridge for 2 hours before serving.

Nutrition: Calories: 294, Fat: 17g, Fiber: 8g, Carbs: 16g, Protein: 23.5g

247. Steak With Olives and Mushrooms

Preparation time: 20 minutes | Cooking time: 9 minutes | Servings: 6

Ingredients
- 1 lb. beef sirloin steak, boneless
- 5–6 white button mushrooms
- ½ C. green olives, coarsely chopped
- 4 tbsp. extra virgin olive oil

Directions:
1. Heat olive oil in a heavy-bottomed skillet over medium-high heat. Brown the steaks on both sides then put aside.
2. Sauté in the mushrooms and olives.
3. Return the steaks to the skillet, cover, cook for 5–6 minutes and serve.

Nutrition: Calories: 299, Fat: 56g, Protein: 16g

248. Greek Pork

Preparation time: 10 minutes | Cooking time: 1 Hour and 10 minutes | Servings: 8
Ingredients:
- 3 lb. pork roast, sliced into cubes
- ¼ C. chicken broth
- ¼ C. lemon juice
- 2 tsp. oregano, dried

Directions:

LOW FODMAP COOKBOOK - SUZANNE SCARRETT

1. Put the pork in the Instant Pot.
2. In a bowl, mix all the remaining ingredients.
3. Pour the mixture over the pork.
4. Toss to coat evenly.
5. Secure the pot.
6. Choose a manual mode.
7. Cook at high pressure for 50 minutes.
8. Release the pressure naturally.

Nutrition: Calories: 478, Total Fat: 21.6g, Saturated Fat: 7.9g, Cholesterol: 195 mg, Sodium: 161 mg, Total Carbohydrates: 1.2g, Dietary Fiber: 0.3g, Total Sugar: 0.5g, Protein: 65.1g

Vegetarian Mains

249. Acorn squash soup

Preparation time: 10 minutes | **Cooking time:** 2 hours | **Servings:** 6

Ingredients:
- Nonstick cooking spray
- 6 cups acorn squash, peeled and cubed
- 2 tablespoons extra-virgin olive oil
- 1 teaspoon of sea salt, and more for seasoning
- 2½ cups vegetable
- 2 tablespoons chopped scallions
- 2 tablespoons unsalted butter (optional)
- Freshly ground black pepper

Directions:
1. Preheat the oven to 350°f. Line a large baking dish with aluminum foil and spray it with the cooking spray.
2. Add the squash, olive oil, and 1 teaspoon of salt to the baking dish, and stir to combine. Pour 1 cup of broth over the squash.
3. Bake for 90 minutes, stirring once after about 45 minutes so the squash doesn't stick to the foil. If there's no broth left in the dish, you can add a little more.
4. Transfer the squash and any leftover broth to a large dutch oven pot.
5. Turn the heat to medium-low and add the remaining 1½ cups of broth. Cook for 25 minutes.
6. Using an immersion blender, blend until the soup is completely smooth. Alternatively, add the soup to a blender, working in batches if necessary, and blend until smooth.
7. Stir in the scallions and butter (if using) until well combined. Season with pepper and additional salt if needed.

Nutrition: Calories: 114, Carbs: 15.9g, Fat: 5.9g, Fiber: 2.19g, Protein: 1.4g, Sodium: 617mg

250. Pasta with basil, tomato & zucchini

Preparation time: 10 minutes | **Cooking time:** 12 minutes | **Servings:** 4

Ingredients:
- 1 (1-pound) package gluten-free pasta
- 1 teaspoon extra-virgin olive oil
- 1 cup cherry tomatoes
- 1 zucchini, diced
- 1 cup fresh basil
- Pinch sea salt
- Freshly ground black pepper

Directions:
1. Cook the pasta according to the package instructions.
2. While the pasta cooks, heat the olive oil in a large pan over medium-high heat.
3. Add the cherry tomatoes and zucchini, then sauté until the tomatoes burst, 6 to 8 minutes.
4. Top the pasta with the vegetables. Add the basil and stir to combine. Season with salt and pepper. Serve immediately.

Nutrition: Calories: 431, Carbs: 93g, Fat: 3.81g, Fiber: 13.5g, Protein: 9.5g, Sodium: 38.87mg

251. Sweet potato chickpea buddha bowl

Preparation time: 15 minutes | **Cooking time:** 10-15 minutes | **Servings:** 2

Ingredients:
Sauce:
- 1 tablespoon tahini
- 2 tablespoons plain greek yogurt
- 2 tablespoons hemp seeds
- Pinch salt
- Freshly ground black pepper, to taste

Bowl:

- 1 small sweet potato, peeled and finely diced
- 1 teaspoon extra-virgin olive oil
- 1 cup from 1 (15-ounce / 425-g) can low-sodium chickpeas, drained and rinsed
- 2 cups baby kale

Directions:

1. Whisk together the tahini and yogurt in a small bowl. Stir in the hemp
2. Season with salt pepper. Add 2 to 3 tablespoons of water to create a creamy yet pourable consistency and set aside.
3. Preheat the oven to 425°F (220°C). Line a baking sheet with parchment paper.
4. Place the sweet potato on the prepared baking sheet and drizzle with olive oil. Toss well
5. Roast in the preheated oven for 10 to 15 minutes, stirring once during cooking, or until fork-tender and browned.
6. In 2 bowls, place ½ cup of chickpeas, 1 cup of baby kale, and half of the cooked sweet potato.
7. Serve drizzled with half of the prepared sauce.

Nutrition: Calories: 336, Carbs: 38.19g, Fat: 15.7g, Fiber: 10g, Protein: 14.72g

252. Easy zucchini patties

Preparation time: 15 minutes | **Cooking time:** 5 minutes | **Servings:** 2
Ingredients:

- 2 medium zucchinis, shredded
- 1 teaspoon salt, divided
- 2 eggs
- 2 tablespoons chickpea flour
- 1 tablespoon chopped fresh mint
- 1 scallion, chopped
- 2 tablespoons extra-virgin olive oil

Directions:

1. Put the shredded zucchini in a fine-mesh strainer and season with ½ teaspoon of salt. Set aside. Beat together the eggs,

chickpea flour, mint, scallion, and remaining ½ teaspoon of salt in a medium bowl.

2. Squash the zucchini to remove of any excess liquid. Now add the zucchini to the egg mixture and stir until well incorporated. In a large skillet over medium-high heat, heat the olive oil.
3. Drop the zucchini mixture by the spoonful into the skillet. Gently flatten the zucchini with the back of a spatula.
4. Now cook for 2 to 3 minutes or until golden brown. Flip and cook for an additional 2 minutes. Remove from the heat and serve on a plate.

Nutrition: Calories: 246, Carbs: 10.21g, Fat: 20.0g, Fiber: 2.76g, Protein: 9.3g

253. Zucchini crisp

Preparation time: 15 minutes | **Cooking time:** 20 minutes | **Servings:** 2
Ingredients:

- 4 zucchinis, sliced into ½-inch rounds
- ½ cup unsweetened almond milk
- 1 teaspoon fresh lemon juice
- 1 teaspoon arrowroot powder
- ½ teaspoon salt, divided
- ½ cup whole wheat bread crumbs
- ¼ cup nutritional yeast
- ¼ cup hemp seeds
- ¼ teaspoon crushed red pepper
- ¼ teaspoon black pepper

Directions:

1. Preheat the oven to 375°F. Set aside two baking sheets lined with parchment paper.
2. Put the zucchini in a medium bowl with the almond milk, lemon juice, arrowroot powder, and ¼ teaspoon of salt. Stir to mix well.
3. In a large bowl with a lid, thoroughly combine the bread crumbs, nutritional yeast, hemp seeds, crushed red pepper, and black pepper. Add the zucchini in batches and shake until the slices are evenly coated.

4. Place the zucchini in a single layer on the prepared baking sheets. Bake in the preheated oven for about 20 minutes or until the zucchini slices are golden brown.
5. Season with the remaining ¼ teaspoon of salt before serving.

Nutrition: Calories: 355, Carbs: 42.37g, Fat: 14.46g, Fiber: 10.6g, Protein: 21.9g

254. Sweet Potato Balls

Preparation time: 15 minutes | **Cooking time:** 10 minutes | **Servings:** 4
Ingredients:
- 1 cup sweet potato, mashed, cooked
- 1 tbsp. fresh cilantro, chopped
- 1 egg, beaten
- 3 tbsp. ground oatmeal
- 1 tsp. ground paprika
- 1/2 tsp. ground turmeric
- 2 tbsp. coconut oil

Directions:
1. Mix mashed sweet potato, fresh cilantro, egg, ground oatmeal, paprika, and turmeric in a bowl.
2. Stir the mixture until smooth and make the small balls.
3. Heat the coconut oil in the saucepan.
4. Put the sweet potato balls, then cook them until golden brown.

Nutrition: Calories: 135, Carbs: 13.1g, Fat: 8.2g, Fiber: 2g, Sodium: 34mg, Protein: 3.26g

255. Chickpea Curry

Preparation time: 15 minutes | **Cooking time:** 10 minutes | **Servings:** 4
Ingredients:
- 1 1/2 cup chickpeas, boiled
- 1 tsp. curry powder
- 1/2 tsp. garam masala
- 1 cup spinach, chopped
- 1 tsp. coconut oil
- 1/4 cup of soy milk
- 1 tbsp. tomato paste

- 1/2 cup of water

Directions:
1. Heat coconut oil in the saucepan. Add curry powder, garam masala, tomato paste, and soy milk.
2. Whisk the mixture until smooth and bring it to a boil.
3. Add water, spinach, and chickpeas.
4. Stir the meal and close the lid.
5. Now cook it for 5 minutes over medium heat.

Nutrition: Calories: 307, Carbs: 49.2g, Fat: 6.1g, Fiber: 10g, Protein: 16.2g, Sodium: 35mg

256. Pan-Fried Salmon With Salad

Preparation time: 15 minutes | **Cooking time:** 20 minutes | **Servings:** 4
Ingredients:
2 Salmon slices
A pinch of salt and pepper
1 tbsp. extra-virgin olive oil
2 tbsp. unsalted butter
1/2 tsp. fresh dill
1 tbsp. fresh lemon juice
100 g. salad leaves, or bag of mixed leaves
Salad dressing:
3 tbsp. olive oil
2 tbsp. balsamic vinaigrette
1/2 tsp. maple syrup
Directions:
1. Pat-dry the salmon fillets with a paper towel and season with a pinch of salt and pepper.
2. In a skillet, warm up oil over medium-high heat and add fillets. Cook each side for 5 to 7 minutes until golden brown.
3. Dissolve butter, dill, and lemon juice in a small saucepan.
4. Put the butter mixture onto the cooked salmon.
5. Lastly, combine all the salad dressing ingredients and drizzle mixed salad leaves in a large bowl.
6. Toss to coat. Serve with fresh salads on the side. Enjoy!

Nutrition: Calories: 221, Carbs: 2.06g, Fat: 22.74g, Protein: 3.16g, Sodium: 217 mg

257. Veggie Variety

Preparation time: 15 minutes | **Cooking time:** 15 minutes | **Servings:** 2
Ingredients:

- 1 tsp. vegetable oil (corn or sunflower oil)
- 200 g. Tofu/ bean curd
- 4 cherry tomatoes, halved
- 30 ml. vegetable milk (soy or oat milk)
- 1/2 tsp curry powder
- 1/4 tsp paprika
- A pinch of salt and pepper
- 2 slices of Vegan protein bread/Whole grain bread
- Chives for garnish

Directions:

1. Add on il the pan. Break the tofu by hand into small pieces and put them in the pan. Sauté 7 to 8 minutes.
2. Season with curry, paprika, salt, pepper, cherry tomatoes, and milk, and cook it all over roast for a few minutes.
3. Serve with bread as desired and sprinkle with chopped chives.

Nutrition: Calories: 317, Carbs: 10.18g, Fat: 17g, Fiber: 13.64g, Protein: 27.29g, Sodium: 470mg

258. Vegetable Pasta

Preparation time: 15 minutes | **Cooking time:** 15 minutes | **Servings:** 4
Ingredients:

- 1 kg. Thin zucchini
- 20 g. fresh ginger
- 350 g. smoked tofu
- 1 lime
- 3 tbsp sunflower oil
- 2 tbsp. sesame seeds
- A pinch of salt and pepper
- Soy sauce

Directions:

1. Wash and clean the zucchini and, using a julienne cutter, cut the pulp around the kernel into long thin strips (noodles). Ginger peel and finely chop. Crumble tofu. Halve lime, squeeze juice.
2. Warm-up 1 tbsp oil in a large pan and fry the tofu for about 5 minutes. After about 3 minutes, add ginger, and sesame. Season with soy sauce. Remove from the pan and keep warm.
3. Wipe out the pan, then warm 2 tbsp of oil in it. Stir fry zucchini strips for about 4 minutes while turning. Season with salt, pepper, and lime juice. Arrange pasta and tofu.

Nutrition: Calories: 275, Carbs: 12.5g, Fat: 19.6g, Fiber: 4g, Protein: 15.5g, Sodium: 825mg

259. Vegetable Noodles With Bolognese

Preparation time: 15 minutes | **Cooking time:** 15 minutes | **Servings:** 4
Ingredients:

- 1.5 kg. small zucchini (e.g., green)
- 600 g. carrots
- 1 tbsp. olive oil
- 250 g. beefsteak
- A pinch of Salt and pepper
- 2 tbsp. tomato paste
- 1 tbsp. flour
- 1 tsp. vegetable broth (instant)
- 40 g. pecorino or parmesan
- 1 stem basil
- 400 ml. water

Directions:

1. Clean and peel zucchini and carrots and wash. Using a sharp, long knife, cut first into thin slices, then into long, fine strips. Clean or peel the soup greens, wash and cut into tiny cubes. Heat the Bolognese oil in a large pan. Fry meat in it crumbly. Season with salt and pepper.
2. Briefly sauté the prepared vegetable. Stir in tomato paste. Dust the flour, sweat

briefly. Pour in 400 ml of water and stir in the vegetable stock. Boil everything, simmer for 7 to 8 minutes.

3. Meanwhile, cook the vegetable strips in plenty of salted water for 3 to 5 minutes. Drain, collect some cooking water. Add the vegetable strips to the pan and mix well. If the sauce is not liquid enough, stir in some vegetable cooking water and season everything again.

4. Slicing cheese into fine shavings. Wash the basil, shake dry, peel off the leaves, and cut roughly. Arrange vegetable noodles, sprinkle with parmesan and basil

Nutrition: Calories: 270, Carbs: 29.31g, Fat: 11.21g, Fiber: 8.16g, Protein: 17.8g, Sodium: 327 mg

260. Harissa With Vegetable Noodles

Preparation time: 15 minutes | **Cooking time:** 30 minutes | **Servings:** 4
Ingredients:
- 3–4 tbsp. oil
- 400 g. ground beef
- A pinch of salt, pepper, cinnamon
- 1 tsp. Harissa (Arabic paste, tube)
- 1 tbsp. tomato paste
- 2 sweet potatoes
- 2 medium Zucchini
- 3 stems/basil
- 100 g. feta
- 200 ml. water

Directions:
1. Warm-up 1 tbsp. Oil in a wide saucepan. Fry meat in it crumbly. Season with salt, pepper, and 1/2 tsp cinnamon. Stir in Harissa and tomato paste.
2. Add tomatoes and 200 ml of water, bring to the boil and simmer for about 15 minutes with occasional stirring. Peel sweet potatoes and zucchini or clean and wash. Cut vegetables into spaghetti with a spiral cutter.

3. Warm up 2–3 tbsp oil in a large pan. Braise sweet potato spaghetti in it for about 3 minutes. Add the zucchini spaghetti and continue to simmer for 3–4 minutes while turning.
4. Season with salt and pepper. Wash the basil, shake dry and peel off the leaves. Garnish vegetable spaghetti and Bolognese on plates. Feta crumbles over. Sprinkle with basil.

Nutrition: Calories: 452, Carbs: 27.6g, Fat: 22.3g, Protein: 37.1g, Sodium: 253 mg

261. Vegetable Noodles With Chicken

Preparation time: 15 minutes | **Cooking time:** 15 minutes | **Servings:** 2
Ingredients:
- 600 g. zucchini
- 500 g. chicken fillet
- A pinch of salt and pepper
- 2 tbsp. oil
- 150 g. red and yellow cherry tomatoes
- 1 tsp. curry powder
- 150 g. fat-free cheese
- 200 ml. vegetable broth
- 4 stalk (s) of fresh basil

Directions:
1. Wash the zucchini, clean it, and cut it into long thin strips with a spiral cutter. Wash meat, pat dry, and season with salt. Heat 1 tbsp. oil in a pan. Roast chicken in it for about 10 minutes until golden brown.
2. Wash cherry tomatoes and cut them in half. Approximately 3 minutes before the end of the cooking time to put the chicken in the pan. Heat 1 tbsp. oil in another pan. Sweat curry powder into it, then stir in cream cheese and broth. Flavor the sauce with salt plus pepper and simmer for about 4 minutes.
3. Wash the basil, shake it dry and pluck the leaves from the stems. Cut small leaves of 3 stems. Remove meat from the pan and cut it into strips. Add tomatoes, basil, and zucchini to the sauce and heat for 2 to 3

minutes. Serve vegetable noodles and meat on plates and garnish with basil.

Nutrition: Calories: 615, Carbs: 19.3g, Fat: 23.12g, Fiber: 4.68g, Protein: 82.8g, Sodium: 1339.33mg

262. Sweet and Sour Vegetable Noodles

Preparation time: 15 minutes | **Cooking time:** 30 minutes | **Servings:** 4

Ingredients:

- 4 chicken fillets (75 g. each)
- 300 g. whole-wheat spaghetti
- 750 g. carrots
- 1/4 liter clear chicken broth (instant)
- 1 tbsp. glucose syrup
- 1 tbsp. green peppercorns
- 2–3 tbsp. balsamic vinegar
- Capuchin flowers
- A pinch of salt
- Water

Directions:

1. Cook spaghetti in boiling water for about 8 minutes. Then drain.
2. In the meantime, peel and wash carrots. Cut into long strips (best with a special grater).
3. Blanch for 2 minutes in boiling salted water, drain. Wash chicken fillets. Add to the boiling chicken soup and cook for about 15 minutes.
4. Melt the glucose syrup until golden brown. Measure 1/4 liter of chicken stock and deglaze the syrup with it.
5. Add peppercorns, cook for 2 minutes. Season with salt and vinegar. Add the fillets, then cut into thin slices.
6. Then turn the pasta and carrots in the sauce and serve garnished with capuchin flowers.
7. Serve and enjoy.

Nutrition: Calories: 454, Carbohydrate: 77.77g, Fat: 5.26g, Protein: 28.5g, Sodium: 448.11mg

263. Farro Cucumber-Mint Salad

Preparation time: 15 minutes | **Cooking time:** 30 minutes | **Servings:** 4–6

Ingredients:

- 1 cup baby arugula
- 1 English cucumber, halved along the length, seeded, and cut into 1/4-inch pieces
- 1 1/2 cups whole farro
- 2 tbsp. lemon juice
- 2 tbsp. minced shallot
- 2 tbsp. plain Greek yogurt
- 3 tbsp. chopped fresh mint
- 3 tbsp. extra-virgin olive oil
- 6 oz. cherry tomatoes, halved
- Salt and pepper
- 4 quarts of water

Directions:

1. In a Dutch oven, boil 4 quarts of water. Return to a boil and simmer for 15 to 30 minutes, or until the grains are soft with a slight chew.
2. Drain farro, spread in a rimmed baking sheet, and allow to cool completely for about 15 minutes.
3. Beat oil, lemon juice, shallot, yogurt, 1/4 tsp. salt, and 1/4 tsp. pepper together in a big container.
4. Put in farro, cucumber, tomatoes, arugula, and mint and toss gently to combine. Sprinkle it with pepper and salt to taste.
5. Serve.

Nutrition: Calories: 232, Carbs: 35.22g, Fat: 8.8g, Fiber: 4.29g, Protein: 6.48g

264. Creamy sweet potatoes and collards

Preparation time: 15 minutes | **Cooking time:** 35 minutes | **Servings:** 2

Ingredients:

- 1 tablespoon avocado oil
- ½ teaspoon crushed red pepper flakes
- 1 large sweet potato, peeled and diced
- 2 bunches collard greens (about 2 pounds/907 g), stemmed, leaves chopped into 1-inch squares
- 1 (14.5-ounce / 411-g) can diced tomatoes with juice
- 1 (15-ounce / 425-g) can red kidney beans or chickpeas, drained and rinsed
- 1½ cups water
- ½ cup unsweetened coconut milk
- Salt and black pepper, to taste

Directions:

1. At first in a large, deep skillet over moderate heat, melt the avocado oil. Add red pepper flakes and cook for 3 minutes.
2. Stir in the sweet potato and collards.
3. Add the tomatoes with their juice, beans, water, and coconut milk, and mix well.
4. Bring the mixture just to a boil.
5. Turn down the heat to moderate, cover, and cook for approximately 30 minutes, or until the vegetables are softened.
6. Season with pepper and salt to taste and serve.

Nutrition: Calories: 569, Carbs: 84.9g, Fat: 20.16g, Fiber: 16.7g, Protein: 18.1g

265. Romaine wedge salad

Preparation time: 15 minutes | **Cooking time:** 0 minutes | **Servings:** 4

Ingredients:

- 1 English cucumber, chopped
- 1 cup quartered cherry tomatoes
- 1 cup chopped fennel
- ½ cup chopped roasted red peppers
- ¼ cup pitted, halved kalamata olives
- 1 scallion both green parts and white, chopped
- ½ cup pesto vinaigrette, divided
- 2 romaine lettuce heads, cut in half lengthwise
- ¼ cup grated asiago cheese

- 2 tablespoons chopped fresh basil

Directions:

1. Stir together the cucumber, tomatoes, fennel, roasted red peppers, olives, scallion, and ¼ cup of pesto vinaigrette in a large bowl.
2. Place each romaine half on a large plate. Evenly divide the vegetable mixture onto each wedge.
3. Drizzle the remaining dressing over the romaine wedges.
4. Serve topped with asiago cheese and basil.

Nutrition: Calories: 236, Carbs: 19g, Fat: 15.8g, Fiber: 8.5g, Protein: 7.6g

266. Roasted brussels sprouts and halloumi salad

Preparation time: 15 minutes | **Cooking time:** 35 minutes | **Servings:** 4

Ingredients:

For the dressing:

- ¼ cup olive oil
- 1/3 cup freshly squeezed lemon juice
- 2 tablespoons corn syrup
- 1 teaspoon mustard
- Sea salt
- Freshly ground black pepper

For the salad:

- 2 pounds brussels sprouts, trimmed
- 2 tablespoons olive oil
- 1 teaspoon sea salt
- 1½ cups baby spinach
- ½ cup baby arugula
- 1 shallot, halved and thinly sliced
- 3 tablespoons dried cranberries
- ½ cup blanched almonds, toasted
- ¼ cup shredded halloumi cheese

Directions:

To make the dressing:

1. At first in a small mixing bowl, combine the lemon juice, olive oil, maple syrup, and mustard.
2. Set aside and season with pepper and salt.

To make the salad:

2. Preheat the oven to 425°f. Put the brussels sprouts in a large mixing bowl.
3. Season with salt and drizzle with olive oil. To mix, toss everything together.
4. On a large baking sheet, lay the brussels sprouts.
5. Roast for 25 to 30 minutes, stirring once halfway through, until crispy on the outside and tender on the inside.
6. While the brussels sprouts are roasting, combine the spinach, arugula, shallot, cranberries, and almonds in a large mixing bowl.
7. Once cooked, add the roasted brussels sprouts to the bowl.
8. Pour the dressing on the salad and toss to combine. Add shredded halloumi cheese and give it another gentle toss. Transfer the salad to a large serving platter.

Nutrition: Calories: 475, Carbs: 41g, Fat: 34g, Protein: 14g

267. Roasted vegetable mélange

Preparation time: 15 minutes | **Cooking time:** 25 minutes | **Servings:** 4
Ingredients:

- ½ cauliflower head, cut into small florets
- ½ broccoli head, cut into small florets
- 2 zucchinis, cut into ½-inch pieces
- 2 cups halved mushrooms
- 2 orange, red, or yellow bell peppers, cut into 1-inch pieces
- 1 sweet potato, cut into 1-inch pieces
-
- 3 tablespoons olive oil
- 1 teaspoon chopped fresh thyme
- Sea salt
- Freshly ground black pepper

Directions:
1. Preheat the oven to 400°F.
2. Line a baking sheet with parchment paper and set it aside.
3. In a large bowl, toss the cauliflower, broccoli, zucchini, mushrooms, bell peppers, sweet potato, olive oil, and thyme until well mixed.
4. Spread the vegetables on the baking sheet and season lightly with salt and pepper.
5. Roast until the vegetables are tender and lightly caramelized, occasionally stirring, 20 to 25 minutes.
6. Serve.

Nutrition: Calories: 195, Carbs: 20.75g, Fat: 11.5g, Fiber: 5.12g, Protein: 5.19g

268. Couscous-avocado salad

Preparation time: 15 minutes | **Cooking time:** 10 minutes | **Servings:** 4
Ingredients:

- For the dressing:
- ¼ cup olive oil
- 2 tablespoons red wine vinegar
- 1 teaspoon chopped fresh oregano
- Pinch red pepper flakes
- Sea salt
- Freshly ground black pepper
- For the salad:
- 1 cup couscous
- 2 cups halved cherry tomatoes
- ½ English cucumber, chopped
- 1 cup chopped marinated artichoke hearts
- 1 avocado, pitted, peeled, and chopped
- ½ cup crumbled feta cheese
- 2 tablespoons pine nuts

Directions:
To make the dressing:
1. In A bowl, whisk together the olive oil, vinegar, oregano, and red pepper flakes.
2. Season with salt and pepper and set aside.
To make the salad:
2. In a pot, bring 1½ cups of water to a boil. Stir the couscous into the boiling water and remove it from the heat.
3. Cover and let sit for 10 minutes. Fluff with a fork.
4. Toss together the couscous, cherry tomatoes, cucumber, artichoke hearts, avocado, feta cheese, and pine nuts in a

large bowl. Add the dressing and toss to combine. Refrigerate for 1 hour and serve.

Nutrition: Calories: 452, Carbs: 42.76g, Fat: 27.15g, Fiber: 7.43g, Protein: 11g

269. Vegetable soup Moroccan style

Preparation time: 10 minutes | **Cooking time:** 10 minutes | **Servings:** 6
Ingredients:

- ½ teaspoon pepper
- 1 teaspoon salt
- 2 oz whole wheat orzo
- 1 large zucchini, peeled and cut into ¼-inch cubes
- 8 sprigs of fresh cilantro, plus more leaves for garnish
- 12 sprigs flat-leaf parsley, plus more for garnish
- A pinch of saffron threads
- 2 stalks celery leaves included, sliced thinly
- 2 carrots, diced
- 2 small turnips, peeled and diced
- 1 14-oz can diced tomatoes
- 6 cups water
- 1 lb. Lamb stew meat, trimmed and cut into ½-inch cubes
- 2 teaspoon ground turmeric
- 2 tablespoon extra virgin olive oil

Directions:

1. On medium-high fire, place a large dutch oven and heat oil.
2. Add turmeric, stir fry for two minutes.
3. Add meat and sauté for 5 minutes.
4. Add saffron, celery, carrots, turnips, tomatoes and juice, and water.
5. With a kitchen string, tie cilantro and parsley sprigs together and into the pot.
6. Cover and bring to a boil. Once boiling, reduce fire to a simmer and continue to cook for 45 to 50 minutes or until meat is tender.
7. Once the meat is tender, stir in zucchini. Cover and cook for 8 minutes.
8. Add orzo; cook for 10 minutes or until soft.
9. Remove and discard cilantro and parsley sprigs.
10. 1 season with pepper and salt.
11. 1 Transfer to a serving bowl and garnish with cilantro and parsley leaves before serving.

Nutrition: Calories: 241, Carbs: 18.37g, Fat: 11.8g, Fiber: 3.69g, Protein: 17.69g

270. Veggie ramen miso soup

Preparation time: 5 minutes | **Cooking time:** 20 minute | **Servings:** 1
Ingredients:

- 2 teaspoon of chives
- A pinch of salt
- ½ teaspoon shoyu
- 2 tablespoon mellow white miso
- 1 cup zucchini, cut into angel hair spirals
- ½ cup thinly sliced cremini mushrooms
- ½ medium carrot, cut into angel hair spirals
- 1/2 cup baby spinach leaves – optional
- 2 ¼ cups water
- ½ box of medium-firm tofu, cut into ¼-inch cubes
- 1 hard boiled egg

Directions:

1. In a small bowl, mix ¼ cup of water and miso. Set aside.
2. In a small saucepan on medium-high fire, bring 2 cups of water, mushrooms, tofu, and carrots to a boil. Add salt, shoyu, and miso mixture. Allow boiling for 5 minutes. Remove from fire and add chives, zucchini, and baby spinach leaves if using.
3. Let soup stand for 5 minutes before transferring to individual bowls. Garnish with ½ of a hard boiled egg per bowl, serve and enjoy.

Nutrition: Calories: 333, Carbs: 22.49g, Fat: 14.9g, Fiber: 7.26g, Protein: 34.67g

271. Yummy cauliflower fritters

Preparation time: 10 minutes | **Cooking time:** 15 minutes | **Servings:** 6

Ingredients:

- 1 large cauliflower head, cut into florets
- 2 eggs, beaten
- ½ teaspoon turmeric
- ½ teaspoon salt
- ¼ teaspoon black pepper
- 6 tablespoons coconut oil

Directions:

1. Place the cauliflower florets in a pot with water.
2. Bring to a boil and drain once cooked.
3. Place the cauliflower, eggs, turmeric, salt, and pepper into the food processor.
4. Pulse until the mixture becomes coarse.
5. Transfer into a bowl. Using your hands, form six small flattened balls and place them in the fridge for at least 1 hour until the mixture hardens.
6. Heat the oil in a skillet and fry the cauliflower patties for 3 minutes on each side
7. Place in individual containers.
8. Put a label and store it in the fridge.
9. Allow thawing at room temperature before heating in the microwave oven.

Nutrition: Calories: 152, Carbs: 2.53g, Fat: 15.03g, Fiber: 0.9g, Protein: 2.72g

272. Zucchini fries

Preparation time: 15 minutes | **Cooking time:** 20 minute | **Servings:** 6

Ingredients:

- ½ cup almond flour
- 2 large egg whites, beaten
- 3 medium zucchinis, sliced into fry sticks
- Salt and pepper to taste

Directions:

1. Preheat the oven to 400°F.
2. Mix all ingredients in a bowl until the zucchini fries are well coated.
3. Place fries on the cookie sheet and spread evenly.

4. Put in the oven and cook for 20 minutes.
5. Halfway through cooking time, stir-fries.

Nutrition: Calories: 70, Carbs: 4.9g, Fat: 4.36g, Fiber: 1.99g, Protein: 4.1g

273. Zucchini pasta with mango-kiwi sauce

Preparation time: 5 minutes | **Cooking time:** 20 minute | **Servings:** 2

Ingredients:

- 1 teaspoon dried herbs – optional
- ½ cup raw kale leaves, shredded
- 2 small dried figs
- 3 Medjool dates
- 4 medium kiwis
- 2 big mangos, seed discarded
- 2 cup zucchini, spiralized
- ¼ cup roasted cashew

Directions:

1. On a salad bowl, place kale, then topped with zucchini noodles and sprinkle with dried herbs. Set aside.
2. In a food processor, grind the cashews to a powder. Add figs, dates, kiwis, and mangoes, then puree to a smooth consistency.
3. Pour over zucchini pasta, serve and enjoy.

Nutrition: Calories: 411, Carbs: 84.73g, Fat: 8.75g, Fiber: 11.32g, Protein: 8.45g

274. Quinoa with almonds and cranberries

Preparation time: 10 minutes | **Cooking time:** 15 minutes | **Servings:** 4

Ingredients:

- 2 cups cooked quinoa
- ⅓ teaspoon cranberries or currants
- ¼ cup sliced almonds
- 1¼ teaspoons salt
- ½ teaspoon ground cumin
- ½ teaspoon turmeric
- ¼ teaspoon ground cinnamon

- ¼ teaspoon freshly ground black pepper

Direction:

1. Toss the quinoa, cranberries, almonds, salt, cumin, turmeric, cinnamon, and pepper in a large bowl and stir to combine.
2. Enjoy alone or with roasted cauliflower.

Nutrition: Calories: 147, Carbs: 21.8g, Fat: 4.65g, Fiber: 3.39g, Protein: 5.4g

275. The Mediterranean baked chickpeas

Preparation time: 15 minutes | **Cooking time:** 15 minutes | **Servings:** 6

Ingredients:

- 1 tablespoon extra-virgin olive oil
- 2 teaspoons smoked paprika
- ¼ teaspoon ground cumin
- 4 cups halved cherry tomatoes
- 2 (15-ounce) cans chickpeas, drained and rinsed
- ½ cup plain, unsweetened, full-fat greek yogurt, for serving
- 1 cup crumbled feta for serving

Direction:

1. Preheat the oven to 425°F.
2. Heat the oil over medium heat in an oven-safe sauté pan or skillet. Cook for about 5 minutes until softened and fragrant. Stir in the paprika and cumin and cook for 2 minutes. Stir in the tomatoes and chickpeas.
3. Bring to a simmer for 5 to 10 minutes before placing in the oven.
4. Roast in the oven for 25 to 30 minutes, until bubbling and thickened. To serve, top with greek yogurt and feta.

Nutrition: Calories: 172, Carbs: 25.51g, Fat: 5.19g, Fiber: 7.11g, Protein: 7.51g

276. Falafel bites

Preparation time: 10 minutes | **Cooking time:** 15 minutes | **Servings:** 4

Ingredients:

- 1⅔ cups falafel mix
- 1¼ cups water
- Extra-virgin olive oil spray
- 1 tablespoon pickled turnips (optional)
- 2 tablespoons tzatziki sauce (optional)

Direction:

1. In a large bowl, carefully stir the falafel mix into the water. Mix well. Let stand for 15 minutes to absorb the water. Form the mixture into 1-inch balls and arrange it on a baking sheet.
2. Preheat the broiler too high.
3. Take the balls and flatten them slightly with your thumb (so they won't roll around on the baking sheet). Spray with olive oil, and then broil for 2 to 3 minutes on each side, until crispy and brown.
4. To fry the falafel, fill a pot with ½ inch of cooking oil and heat over medium-high heat to 375°f. Fry the balls for about 3 minutes, until brown and crisp. Drain on paper towels and serve with turnips, and tzatziki sauce (if using).

Nutrition: Calories: 364, Carbs: 31.8g, Fat: 21.36g, Fiber: 0g, Protein: 13.31g

277. Quick vegetable kebabs

Preparation time: 15 minutes | **Cooking time:** 20 minute | **Servings:** 6

Ingredients:

- 4 medium zucchini, cut into 1-inch-thick slices
- 4 bell peppers, cut into 2-inch squares
- 2 yellow bell peppers, cut into 2-inch squares
- 2 orange bell peppers, cut into 2-inch squares
- 2 beefsteak tomatoes, cut into quarters
- 3 tablespoons herb oil

Direction:

1. Preheat the oven or grill to medium-high or 350°F.
2. Thread zucchini, different colored bell peppers, and tomatoes onto a skewer.

Repeat until the skewer is full of vegetables, up to 2 inches away from the skewer end, and continue until all skewers are complete.

3. Put the skewers on a baking sheet and cook in the oven for 10 minutes or grill for 5 minutes on each side. The vegetables will be done when they reach your desired crunch or softness.

4. Remove the skewers from heat and drizzle with herbed oil.

Nutrition: Calories: 148, Carbs: 17.95g, Fat: 7.5g, Fiber: 4.79g, Protein: 4.3g

278. Tortellini in red pepper sauce

Preparation time: 15 minutes | **Cooking time:** 10 minutes | **Servings:** 4

Ingredients:

- 1 (16-ounce) container fresh cheese tortellini (usually green and white pasta)
- 1 (16-ounce) jar roasted red peppers, drained
- ¼ cup tahini
- 1 tablespoon red pepper oil (optional)

Description

1. Bring a large pot of water to a boil and cook the tortellini according to package directions.

2. In a blender, put the red peppers and process until smooth.

3. Once blended, add the tahini until the sauce is thickened. If the sauce gets too thick, add up to 1 tablespoon of red pepper oil (if using).

4. Once tortellini is cooked, drain and leave the pasta in a colander.

5. Add the sauce to the bottom of the empty pot and heat for 2 minutes.

6. Then, add the tortellini back into the pot and cook for 2 more minutes.

7. Serve and enjoy!

Nutrition: Calories: 489, Carbs: 63.6g, Fat: 18.12g, Fiber: 3.3G, Protein: 18.96g

279. Freekeh, chickpea, and herb salad

Preparation time: 15 minutes | **Cooking time:** 10 minutes | **Servings:** 6

Ingredients:

- 1 (15-ounce) can chickpeas, rinsed and drained
- 1 cup cooked freekeh
- 1 cup thinly sliced celery
- 1 bunch scallions, both white and green parts, finely chopped
- ½ cup chopped fresh flat-leaf parsley
- ¼ cup chopped fresh mint
- 3 tablespoons chopped celery leaves
- ½ teaspoon kosher salt
- ⅓ cup extra-virgin olive oil
- ¼ cup freshly squeezed lemon juice
- ¼ teaspoon cumin seeds

Direction:

1. Combine the chickpeas, freekeh, celery, scallions, parsley, mint, celery leaves, and salt in a large bowl and toss lightly.

2. Whisk together the olive oil, lemon juice, and cumin seeds in a small bowl. Once combined, add to the freekeh salad.

Nutrition: Calories: 302, Carbs: 35.31g, Fat: 15.06g, Fiber: 9.24g, Protein: 8.57g

280. Coleslaw Salad

Preparation Time: 5 minutes | **Cooking Time:** 10 minutes | **Servings:** 4

Ingredients:

- 1½ tsp. Dijon mustard
- 1 small head of lettuce
- ⅛ Cup extra virgin olive oil
- 1½ tsp. lemon juice
- 1 large carrot, peeled

Directions:

1. Wash lettuce well and shake to remove any extra water. Use a kitchen grater on the side with the largest holes to shred the lettuce. Transfer to a large serving dish.

2. Scrub carrot and remove the skin with a vegetable peeler.
3. Grate with a kitchen grater with the largest holes, then transfer to the serving dish.
4. In a glass dish, combine lemon juice, Dijon mustard, and olive oil until integrated.
5. Distribute over salad and toss to combine fully. Serve immediately and enjoy!

Nutrition: Calories: 74, Protein: 1g, Carbs: 3g ; Fat: 7g, Sodium: 35g, Fiber: 1g,

281. Cucumber Salad

Preparation Time: 5 minutes | **Cooking Time:** 10 minutes | **Servings:** 4
Ingredients:
- 1 large cucumber
- ½ cup chives, chopped
- 1 tsp. fresh dill
- 2 tbsp. white vinegar
- 1 cup canned coconut milk, chilled

Directions:
1. Scrub cucumber well and use a mandolin to slice to your desired thickness.
2. Remove the lid for the canned coconut milk and distribute the liquid to a lidded container for use in a different recipe.
3. Transfer to a glass dish and toss solid coconut milk, white vinegar, dill, and chives until the cucumbers are fully covered.
4. Serve immediately or ref up to 2 days in a lidded container.
5. Enjoy!

Nutrition: Calories: 37, Protein: 6g, Carbs: 3g, Fat: 0g, Sodium: 21g, Fiber: 0g

282. Croutons

Preparation Time: 10 minutes | **Cooking Time:** 10 minutes | **Servings:** 8
Ingredients:
- 2 slices gluten-free bread, stale

Directions:

1. Remove crusts from the slices of bread, then slice into small cubes.
2. In a skillet toss the bread cubes constantly for approximately 3 minutes.
3. Transfer to a plate layered with kitchen paper and serve immediately. They will also keep fresh in a lidded container or plastic bag for up to one month.
4. You can make your own homemade version w/ the recipe found in chapter 13.

Nutrition: Calories: 34, Protein: 1g, Carbs: 4g, Fat: 2g, Sodium: 37g, Fiber: 0g

283. Glazed Edamame

Preparation Time: 10 minutes | **Cooking Time:** 15 minutes | **Servings:** 4
Ingredients:
- 2 cups edamame, not-shucked and frozen
- 4 tbsp. water, separated
- ¼ tsp. iodized salt
- 2 tbsp. pure maple syrup
- 1 tsp. ginger root, minced finely
- 4 tbsp. gluten-free soy sauce**
- 2 tbsp. rice vinegar
- 4 cups of water

Directions:
1. Empty 4 cups of water in a deep pot with salt and heat until it starts to bubble.
2. Distribute edamame into the pot and boil for approximately 5 minutes.
3. Immediately remove the water with a colander and rinse under cool water.
4. In the meantime, blend maple syrup, ginger, rice vinegar, soy sauce, and the leftover 4 tablespoons of water in a glass dish until combined.
5. Transfer the edamame to the glaze and toss to coat fully.
6. Serve immediately and enjoy!

Nutrition: Calories: 156, Protein: 10g, Carbs: 17g, Fat: 6g, Sodium: 590g, Fiber: 4g

284. **Pesto Pasta Salad**

Preparation Time: 15 minutes | **Cooking Time:** 20 minutes | **Servings:** 4
Ingredients:
- ¼ tsp. black pepper
- 3½ cups arugula, separated
- 1½ cup mint leaves, separated
- ¼ tsp. iodized salt
- 7½ oz. brown rice noodles*
- ½ cup basil, chopped
- 3 Qtrs. water
- 1 tbsp. extra virgin olive oil, separated
- 2 tbsp. almond butter, unsalted
- 1 tbsp. lemon juice

Directions:
1. Empty water into a deep pot and allow it to bubble.
2. Transfer noodles to the water with 1 teaspoon of olive oil and heat for 8 minutes or until al dente.
3. In the meantime, rinse 3 cups of arugula and 1 cup of mint leaves and shake to remove any extra moisture.
4. Chop finely together and set aside.
5. Rinse the leftover ½ cup each of arugula, mint leaves, and basil, and chop into small sections, then transfer to a food blender.
6. Combine salt, lemon juice, almond butter, and black pepper into a food blender and pulse until a smooth consistency.
7. When the noodles have finished cooking, remove water with a colander, and rinse with cold water. Transfer to a serving platter.
8. Drizzle with the leftover 2 teaspoons of olive oil over the noodles.
9. Toss with the chopped mint, arugula, and pesto sauce and enjoy immediately.

Nutrition: Calories: 349, Protein: 5g, Carbs: 45g, Fat: 16g, Sodium: 301g, Fiber: 1g

285. Quinoa Salad

Preparation Time: 15 minutes | **Cooking Time:** 25 minutes | **Servings:** 4
Ingredients:
- 1 cup quinoa, uncooked
- 3 tbsp. gluten-free soy sauce*
- ½ tsp. toasted sesame oil
- ½ tsp. ginger root, grated
- 8 cups of water
- ⅓ Tsp. iodized salt
- 5 oz. baby spinach
- ⅓ Cup almonds, unsalted and sliced
- 10 oz. Carrots, grated
- ½ tbsp. lime juice
- ¼ black pepper

Directions:
1. Rinse quinoa under cold water. Distribute to a deep pot and combine salt and water with the quinoa.
2. Warm on the highest heat setting until water is bubbling. Turn the burner down to medium/low and warm for another 12 minutes or until fluid is fully reduced.
3. Meanwhile, wash ginger and carrots well. Use a kitchen grater to shred each completely.
4. Rinse spinach and shake to remove extra water. Set aside.
5. Warm ginger, & soy sauce for approximately 60 seconds.
6. Blend spinach in the pan for about 5 minutes and turn the burner off.
7. Combine quinoa, black pepper, lime juice, toasted sesame oil, carrots, and almonds to the pan and incorporate fully.
8. Serve while hot and enjoy!

Nutrition: Calories: 237, Protein: 8g, Carbs: 23g, Fat: 14g, Sodium: 673g, Fiber: 7g

286. Roasted Zucchini

Preparation Time: 20 minutes | **Cooking Time:** 20 minutes | **Servings:** 4
Ingredients:
- 2 large zucchinis
- ¼ tsp. iodized salt, separated
- ⅓ Cup extra virgin olive oil
- ¼ tsp. black pepper

Directions:

1. Set your oven to 390°F and set a flat sheet aside.
2. Scrub zucchinis thoroughly and slice the ends off. Slice into thin sections.
3. Arrange in a single layer on the flat sheet.
4. Dust the zucchini with salt and black pepper.
5. Drizzle with olive oil and heat for a total of 14 minutes.
6. Transfer to a serving dish & enjoy immediately.

Nutrition: Calories: 121, Protein: 0g, Carbs: 0g, Fat: 14g, Sodium: 146g, Fiber: 0g

287. Sautéed Zucchini

Preparation Time: 5 minutes | **Cooking Time:** 10 minutes | **Servings:** 4

Ingredients:

- 2 medium zucchinis, diagonally sliced
- ¼ tsp. black pepper
- 1 tbsp. extra virgin olive oil
- ½ tbsp. lemon juice
- 2 tbsp. parsley leaves, chopped
- ¼ tsp. iodized salt

Directions:

1. Scrub zucchinis and slice thinly on a diagonal. Set aside.
2. Empty olive oil into a skillet & warm over medium heat.
3. Toss occasionally for 6 minutes, then turn the burner off.
4. Blend black pepper, parsley, lemon zest, and salt into the skillet and toss to combine fully.
5. Serve immediately and enjoy!

Nutrition: Calories: 33, Protein: 0g, Carbs: 1g, Fat: 3g, Sodium: 147g, Fiber: 0g

288. Spinach Pasta

Preparation Time: 5 minutes | **Cooking Time:** 10 minutes | **Servings:** 4

Ingredients:

- 8 oz. spinach leaves
- ¼ tsp. black pepper
- 8 oz. brown rice pasta**
- ¼ tsp. iodized salt
- 8 cups of water
- ¼ cup Parmesan cheese, grated

Directions:

1. Empty water and salt into a deep pot and wait until it starts to bubble.
2. Distribute noodles and heat for approximately 8 minutes or until al dente.
3. Rinse spinach leaves and shake to remove excess moisture.
4. Transfer to the skillet and frequently toss for 2 minutes.
5. Remove water from the pasta with a colander and transfer to a serving dish.
6. Toss in spinach and Parmesan cheese
7. Serve while hot and enjoy!

Nutrition: Calories: 280, Protein: 8g, Carbs: 47g, Fat: 7g, Sodium: 316g, Fiber: 3g

289. Vegetable Chips

Preparation Time: 15 minutes | **Cooking Time:** 30 minutes | **Servings:** 4

Ingredients:

- 1 medium sweet potato
- 1½ medium carrots
- 1 small turnip
- ½ tsp. iodized salt
- 1 medium zucchini
- ½ tsp. black pepper
- 1 tbsp. extra virgin olive oil

Directions:

1. Set your oven to 400°F. Use baking lining to layer a flat sheet with a rim.
2. Scrub the zucchini, turnip, and carrots, and use a mandolin to slice them thinly and uniformly to be approximately ¼ inch in width. Transfer all into a glass dish.
3. Blend black pepper, olive oil, and salt, completely covering the vegetables.
4. Arrange on the prepped pan without layering. Heat for about 8-10 minutes, then turn them over.
5. Heat for approximately 8 more minutes, just before any of the sides start turning brown.
6. Wait about 5 minutes before serving and enjoy!

Nutrition: Calories: 89, Protein: 3g, Carbs: 12g Fat: 4g, Sodium: 328g, Fiber: 4g

290. Ginger Carrot Soup

Preparation Time: 10 minutes | **Cooking Time:** 20 minutes | **Servings:** 4

Ingredients:
- 12 carrots, peeled and diced
- 14 oz can coconut milk
- ½ tsp cinnamon
- 2 fresh rosemary sprigs
- 1 Tbsp. fresh ginger, chopped
- 1 ½ tsp turmeric powder
- 2 Tbsp. olive oil
- ¼ tsp pepper
- ¼ tsp salt
- 2 cups vegetable broth, Low FODMAP

Directions:
1. Preheat the oven to 400°F.
2. Place carrots on baking tray and drizzle with olive oil.
3. Roast carrots in preheated oven for 20 minutes.
4. Transfer roasted carrots in a food processor along with remaining ingredient and process until smooth.
5. Serve and enjoy.

Nutrition: Calories: 358, Total Fat: 29g, Saturated Fat: 20g, Cholesterol: 0 mg, Sodium: 0 mg, Total Carbs: 23.1g, Fiber: 5g, Sugar: 9.4g, Protein: 6.1 g

291. Tasty Ranch Potatoes

Preparation Time: 10 Minutes | **Cooking Time:** 10 Minutes | **Servings:** 2

Ingredients
- 230 grams potatoes, cut into 1-inch pieces
- 1/2 tbsp olive oil
- 1 tbsp ranch seasoning, homemade

Directions:
1. Preheat the air fryer at 375°F. Add all ingredients into the bowl and toss well.

2. Transfer potato into the air fryer basket and cook for 10 minutes.
3. Shake halfway through. Serve and enjoy.

Nutrition: Calories: 117, Total Fat: 3.6g, Saturated Fat: 0.5g, Protein: 1.9g, Carbs: 17.8g, Fiber: 2.7g, Sugar: 1.3g

292. Potato Salad

Preparation Time: 10 minutes | **Cooking Time:** 20 minutes | **Servings:** 5

Ingredients:
- 1 lb. red potatoes
- ½ Tbsp. vinegar
- 1 Tbsp. Dijon mustard
- ½ lime zest
- ½ lime juice
- 2 Tbsp. olive oil
- 2 Tbsp. fresh dill, chopped
- 2 Tbsp. chives, minced
- Pepper
- Salt

Directions:
1. Add water in a large pot and bring to boil.
2. Add potatoes in boiling water and cook until tender, about 15 minutes.
3. Drain well and set aside. In a small bowl, whisk together vinegar, mustard, lime zest, lime juice, olive oil, dill, and chives.
4. Peel potatoes and diced. Place in mixing bowl.
5. Pour vinegar mixture over potatoes and stir until well coated. Season with pepper and salt.
6. Serve and enjoy.

Nutrition: Calories: 148, Total Fat: 7.4g, Saturated Fat: 1.1g, Cholesterol: 0 mg, Sodium: 0 mg, Total Carbs: 19.7g, Fiber: 2.4 g Sugar: 1.3 g, Protein: 2.7g

293. Fluffy Blueberry Pancakes

Preparation Time: 10 minutes | **Cooking Time:** 10 minutes | **Servings:** 3
Ingredients:

- 1 cup all-purpose flour
- 1 egg
- 1 cup blueberries
- 1 1/3 cup lactose-free milk
- 1 tsp baking powder, gluten-free

Directions:
1. Mix baking powder and flour in a large bowl and set aside, whisk milk and egg together in another bowl until well combined.
2. Mix the egg mixture slowly with the flour mixture and whisk until getting a smooth consistency.
3. Make sure batter looks like thick cream. Spray pan with cooking spray and heat over low heat.
4. Pour a small ladle of batter on the hot pan and make a round pancake.
5. Immediately place 3-4 blueberries into your pancake and gently press them in.
6. Once the pancake is lightly golden brown, then turn to other side and cook for a minute.
7. Using the same step make remaining batter pancakes. Serve and enjoy.

Nutrition: Calories: 237, Total Fat: 2.1g, Saturated Fat: 0.5g, Cholesterol: 0 mg, Sodium: 0 mg, Total Carbs: 45.5g, Fiber: 2.3g, Sugar: 10.4g, Protein: 10.1g

294. Roasted Carrots

Preparation Time: 10 minutes | **Cooking Time:** 30 minutes | **Servings:** 8
Ingredients:
- 1 ½ kilograms carrots, peeled and cut into sticks
- 2 tsp dried thyme
- 1 Tbsp. balsamic vinegar
- 1 Tbsp. olive oil
- ½ tsp black pepper
- ½ tsp salt

Directions:
1. Preheat the oven to 425 °F.
2. Add all Ingredients into the large bowl and toss well.

3. Spread carrots on baking tray and roast in preheated oven for 15 minutes.
4. Turn carrots to other side and roast for 15 minutes more.
5. Serve and enjoy.

Nutrition: Calories: 86, Total Fat: 1.8g, Saturated Fat: 0.3g, Cholesterol: 0 mg, Sodium: 0 mg, Total Carbs: 17g, Fiber: 4.3g, Sugar: 8.4g, Protein: 1.4g

295. Low Fodmap Tortillas

Preparation Time: 5 minutes | **Cooking Time:** 10 minutes | **Servings:** 5
Ingredients:
- 1 tablespoon xanthan gum
- 1/2 tablespoon baking powder
- 1/2 tablespoon salt
- 2 tablespoon olive oil
- 150 ml cold water
- 150g brown rice flour
- 50g tapioca starch

Directions:
1. In a cup, combine rice meal and tapioca starch, xanthan gum, baking powder, and salt.
2. Cut the oil in the mix. Apply 100 ml of cold water. Mix a spoon of the flour.
3. Gradually add the rest of the volume.
4. The whole 50 ml, I didn't have to add. It is sticky enough if the dough is warm and sticks together.
5. You should add a small amount of additional water if the dough is too dry.
6. You should add extra flour if it is too wet.
7. Working with it should be quick. Divide the pulp into 8 gluten-free dough balls.
8. Put a slice of pastry on your table. Place a ball of dough on it.
9. Place on top another bakery slice. Roll the dough carefully with a rolling pin into a flat tortilla.
10. Taking the tortilla carefully out of the parchment paper, if it is not patient, it can break.

11. For the other balls, repeat this. Heat a bath. Heat a bowl.
12. When it is dry, put the tortilla in the cast-iron bowl.
13. No oils need to be added; the tortilla must be baked in a dry oven.
14. Bake on low, medium fire for 3-4 minutes, then turn over the tortilla. Fry 2-3 minutes longer.
15. Take off the tortilla and place it on a plate. Washcloth covered with a table.
16. For all tortillas, repeat that.

Nutrition: Calories: 96, Total Fat: 1g, Saturated Fat: 0g, Cholesterol: 0 mg, Sodium: 0 mg, Total Carbs: 20g, Fiber: 0g, Sugar: 0g, Protein: 3 g

296. Low Fodmap Vegetable Stock

Preparation Time: 10 minutes | Cooking Time: 15 minutes | Servings: 4

Ingredients:
- Bay leafs
- 15 g fresh parsley
- 5 black peppercorns
- 1/2 tablespoon of salt
- Fresh herbs, like rosemary and thyme
- 2 large carrots
- 2 leeks, the green part only
- Half a celeriac

Directions:
1. Cut all vegetables thin; the smaller they are, the better because they are more delicious.
2. If you use pepper and baking leaves in a pan, put them together with the Persil, with other fresh herbs.
3. Pour 1.5 liters (6 tablespoons) of water on top and leave the stock to cook for one hour.
4. Save the stock and salt for seasoning.
5. Taste again and, if necessary, add additional salt and pepper. Strain stock.
6. The stock can be used immediately in a recipe.
7. STORAGE TIP: leave the stock completely refreshed. Freeze for later use

in a variety of pieces. You should place your stock inside ziplock bags so that you have enough room on your freezer to freeze the bags flat on one another.
8. Freeze it in a couple of bottles.

Nutrition: Calories: 113, Total Fat: 4g, Saturated Fat: 1g, Cholesterol: 0 mg, Sodium: 872 mg, Total Carbs: 17g, Fiber: 2g, Sugar: 3g, Protein: 2 g

297. Low FODMAP Granola Bars With Peanut Prune Puree

Preparation Time: 10 minutes | Cooking Time: 15 minutes | Servings: 4

Ingredients:
- 30 gram broken flaxseed
- 35 gram almonds, chopped
- 50 gram chocolate chips
- 1 tsp ground cinnamon
- A pinch of salt
- A rectangular baking tin or baking sheet
- 100 ml maple syrup
- 3 tbsp smooth peanut prune puree
- 1 tbsp coconut oil
- 140 gram oatmeal
- 35 gram peanuts, chopped

Directions:
1. In a saucepan, blend maple soup, peanut prune puree, and cocoa oil and melt it into a smooth mixture at low heat.
2. Switch off the heat and leave it a few minutes to cool, so it's not too warm.
3. Stir in a bowl, mix a cup of oats, flaxseed, alms, almonds, cannabis, and salt. Remove the mixture of the peanut prune puree and blend together.
4. Drop the chocolate chips into the mix.
5. In a rectangular baking tray or baking sheet, put a sheet of pastry parchment and spread the mixture out until it is about 1 cm thick with a thickness of 180 grams. Place the granola bars in the refrigerator for at least four hours or overnight.

6. Cut 14 granola bars into the plate.

Nutrition: Calories: 217, Total Fat: 8g, Saturated Fat: 1g, Cholesterol: 0 mg, Sodium: 0 mg, Total Carbs: 31g, Fiber: 4g, Sugar: 19g, Protein: 6g▢

298. Low Fodmap Carrot Cake Energy Balls

Preparation Time: 10 minutes | **Cooking Time:** 15 minutes | **Servings:** 6

Ingredients:
- 1/2 tablespoon ginger
- A pinch of salt
- 35 g maple syrup
- 50 g carrot, grated
- 15 g walnuts or pecans
- 1/2 tablespoon vanilla extract
- 1/2 tablespoon cinnamon
- 45 g oats
- 60 g peanut prune puree
- 40 g flaxseed

Directions:
1. Cut the carrot into pieces. In a food processor, add all ingredients for the bliss balls and pulse them many times to mix them together.
2. You can also bring everything together in a bowl and use your hands to combine all together if you don't have a food processor.
3. Take some mixture and roll it into a ball with your hands.
4. Repeat until you've used it all.
5. In the refrigerator, placed the balls for approximately half an hour to be set.

Nutrition: Calories: 64, Total Fat: 3g, Saturated Fat: 1g, Cholesterol: 0 mg, Sodium: 2 mg, Total Carbs: 11g, Fiber: 2g, Sugar: 7g, Protein: 1g▢

299. Chocolate Zucchini Bread

Preparation Time: 10 minutes | **Cooking Time:** 35 minutes | **Servings:** 4

Ingredients:
- 150 ml maple syrup
- 80g dark chocolate chips
- 1 tablespoon of vanilla extract
- 80 ml lactose-free milk
- ¾ tablespoon baking powder
- 200-gram zucchini
- 260 grams rolled oats
- 1 tablespoon baking soda
- 2 banana's, mashed
- ½ tablespoon salt
- 1 ½ tablespoon vinegar
- ½ tablespoon cinnamon

Directions:
1. Preheat the oven to 360°F. Pre-heat the oven.
2. Grate with bread-parchment a cake or loaf tin and plate.
3. Place all the oats in the mixer and mix until the flour is in place.
4. Remove all other ingredients, except the chocolate chips, and blend in a smooth mix (it is all right if the mixture is made from small pieces of zucchini).
5. Mix the chocolate chips together.
6. Into the pot and bake 35 minutes, put the batter in it.
7. Put your chocolate zucchini bread 10 minutes after the baking time is over in the closed oven.
8. Switch off the oven and allow it to cool down.

Nutrition: Calories: 356, Total Fat: 17g, Saturated Fat: 4.1g, Cholesterol: 37 mg, Sodium: 338 mg, Total Carbs: 49g, Fiber: 2.5g, Sugar: 29g, Protein: 5.1g

300. Curry and Roasted Cauliflower

Preparation time: 10 minutes | **Cooking time:** 35 minutes | **Servings:** 4

Ingredients

For the curry:
- 1 tsp. turmeric powder
- 1 ½ C. water

- 1 tsp. Himalayan salt
- ½ tsp. garam masala
- ½ tsp. chili powder
- 2 C. floret cauliflowers
- ½ tsp. salt
- ½ C. Roma tomatoes
- 1 bell pepper/capsicum
- 1 tbsp. coriander
- 2 C. coconut milk, unsweetened
- 2 tbsp. coconut oil
- 1 tsp. ginger powder
- 1 cm fresh turmeric

For Masala:
- 6 cloves
- 1 tbsp. cumin seeds
- 1 ½ tbsp. coriander seeds
- 1 ¼ inch cinnamon stick
- ½ C. raw cashew
- Pinch cardamom powder

Directions
1. First of all, preheat the oven to 200°C. Get a large mixing bowl and add the powdered turmeric, coconut oil, a pinch of salt, and cauliflower.
2. Use your hands and mix them together properly. Now, get a baking tray lined with baking powder and pour the mix into it. Put it in the oven for 20–30 minutes.
3. Mind you, do not let the cauliflower burn. While the cauliflower is cooking in the oven, we shift our attention to the Masala. To make the Masala, blend all the masala ingredients in a food processor and make sure it is completely smooth.
4. Next, get a large pan and heat the coconut oil over gentle heat. Add ginger, and cook gently between two to three minutes. Next, add bell pepper/capsicum and tomatoes.
5. Cook until tomatoes begin to fall apart. Now add the masala mix and stir for 2–3 minutes. Keep stirring to avoid it from sticking or getting burnt. Once it is thoroughly mixed, add chili pepper, turmeric, and coconut milk, as well as water (as much as you desire).
6. Reduce the heat down to simmer and allow it to cook for 5 minutes. Season to taste. When cauliflower is done, take it away from the oven and add to the pan. Mix it thoroughly. Switch of the heat. When you decide to serve, stir through the cilantro/coriander. Serve! You can have it with brown rice or quinoa.

Nutrition: Calories :251, Fiber:19g, Protein:34g

301. Hearty Minestrone

Preparation time: 15 minutes | **Cooking time:** 20 minutes | **Servings:** 2
Ingredients
- 1 basil
- ½ C. carrot
- ½ C. sweet potato
- ¼ C. chives
- 1 tbsp. coconut oil
- ½ C. aubergine eggplant
- 1 C. vegetable stock
- ½ C. Courgette zucchini
- 1 C. fresh tomato juice, bought
- ½ C. beans
- ½ C. carrot
- Black pepper and Himalayan salt

Directions
1. Wash and dice the chives and carrot. Cube the Courgette, aubergine, and potato.
2. Next fry carrot, Courgette, aubergine, and potato in a large pot for 2 minutes.
3. Add the tomato juice, the stock, and beans. Bring it to a boil and reduce the heat to simmer for 8–10 minutes.
4. Add the basil and stir. Season to taste.

Nutrition: Calories:157, Protein:36g, Fiber:20g

302. Raw Pad Thai (With Zucchini Noodles)

Preparation time: 10 minutes | **Cooking time:** 25 minutes | **Servings:** 4

Ingredients

- 3 large carrots
- 1 floret cauliflower
- ½ packet beansprouts
- 1 C. red cabbage, shredded
- 3 Courgette zucchinis
- Coconut oil
- 1 bunch coriander/cilantro, fresh and roughly chopped

For the sauce:

- 1-inch ginger root, grated
- ¼ C. tahini
- ¼ C. tamari
- 2 tsp. lemon/lime juice
- ¼ C. almond butter
- 1 tsp. coconut sugar

Directions

1. Start with the Courgette and carrot noodles: use a mandolin or vegetable peeler to slice both, and then use a knife to slice them into thin strips.
2. Get a large bowl and add them, alongside the shredded cabbage, coriander, cauliflower, and beansprouts. For the sauce, blend the grated ginger, tahini, lime/lemon juice, tamari, almond butter, and coconut sugar. Add some water and blast till a thick sauce is formed.
3. Finally, get a bowl and mix the sauce inside. Serve with a little squeeze of lime/lemon and a spring of coriander.

Nutrition: Calories 211, Fiber 15g, Protein 25g

303. Sweet Life Bowl

Preparation time: 15 minutes | **Cooking time:** 5 minutes | **Servings:** 2

Ingredients

- 2 baby spinach
- 1 C. cherry tomatoes, sliced in half
- 4 carrots, peeled and thinly sliced
- 3 stalks celery, thinly sliced
- 3 tbsp. olive oil or coconut oil

- 2 C. brown rice /quinoa, cooked
- 1 C. chickpeas, cooked, rinsed and drained
- 1 C. curry and turmeric cauliflower, roasted
- ¼ C. pecans, toasted, chopped
- 1 bunch kale
- ½ C. fresh parsley
- Fresh pepper and sea salt, for taste

For the dressing:

- ¼ C. olive oil
- 1 tsp. Dijon mustard
- 1 tsp. maple syrup
- 2 tbsp. lemon juice, freshly squeezed
- ¼ tsp. red pepper flakes
- ½- inch fresh ginger

Directions

1. Start off by reheating the brown rice or quinoa and share into 2 different bowls. Get a large pan and heat over medium-high heat and add coconut or olive oil.
2. Stir in carrots, and celery. Sauté veggies for 3–4 minutes until they become soft and turn brownish. In the fourth minutes, add chickpeas and roasted cauliflower.
3. Add sliced kale and allow it to wilt for about a minute. Take off the pan from heat. Add tomatoes and baby spinach and stir so that the vegetable heat cooks the tomatoes and spinach.
4. Now pour the sautéed mix over the quinoa and brown rice. Sprinkle pepper and sea salt and supplement it with dried fruit.

Making Curry and Turmeric Roasted Cauliflower:

1. Preheat oven to 400°F. Get a roasting pan and oil lightly. Get a mixing bowl, add cauliflower alongside turmeric, curry powder, pepper, salt, and olive oil
2. Set the bowl on the roasting pan and roast for 20–25 minutes until the edges change to a golden brown

Making the dressing:

- In a mixing bowl, mix the mustard, maple syrup, lemon juice, red pepper flakes, and ginger.
- Gently whisk in the olive oil, the idea is to form an emulsion.
- Sprinkle the dressing over the bowls.
- Toss gently. The toppings should be fresh parsley and toasted pecans.

<u>Nutrition:</u> Calories 158, Fiber 12g, Protein 28g

Sides

304. Low-Fodmap Tomato Bruschetta

Preparation Time: 5 minutes | **Cooking Time:** 5 minutes | **Servings:** 3

Ingredients:
- 1 teaspoon of dried basil
- 1 teaspoon of balsamic reduction
- 3 medium tomatoes
- 1 teaspoon of dried chives
- 2 tablespoons of extra virgin olive oil
- A pinch of sea salt
- 2 teaspoons of balsamic vinegar
- Half a teaspoon of dried oregano

Directions:
1. To begin, rinse your tomatoes with tepid water, deseeded, then chop them.
2. Put the tomatoes into a medium sized mixing bowl, then add the vinegar, spices, reduction, and olive oil, stir to combine, then season with salt (more if needed).
3. Set aside to marinate for 30 minutes.
4. Serve with crackers or baguettes with a drizzle of balsamic reduction.

Nutrition: Calories: 130, Total Fat: 6g, Saturated Fat: 0g, Cholesterol: 0 mg, Sodium: 0 mg, Total Carbs: 19g, Fiber: 0g, Sugar: 2g, Protein: 7 g

305. Low-Fodmap Cheese Bread

Preparation Time: 12 minutes | **Cooking Time:** 30 minutes | **Servings:** 8

Ingredients:
- 2 eggs
- 1 teaspoon of sea salt
- 1 cup of lactose free milk
- 1 cup of parmesan cheese
- Half a cup of coconut oil
- 2 cups of tapioca Flour

Directions:
1. Preheat your oven to 450°F.
2. Pour the milk into a medium-sized saucepan, set over medium heat and bring to a slow boil.
3. Once bubbles start to form at the top of the milk, remove from heat.
4. Pour the tapioca flour into the milk, stir using a wooden ladle until all the flour is incorporated and no lumps are formed and the mixture starts to thicken like gelatin, then set aside to cool for a bit.
5. Beat the dough for a couple of minutes at medium speed using a standing mixer fitted with a paddle attachment.
6. Crack the egg into a small bowl and whisk until foamy, then slowly fold them into the dough, make sure to scrape down the sides of the bowl.
7. Add the cheese and beat until fully incorporated and your dough is stretchy, soft and sticky.
8. Line a baking sheet with parchment paper, then scoop some dough into it using an ice cream scoop.
9. Coat your hands or ice cream scoop with some olive oil if the dough gets too sticky to work with.
10. Place the baking sheet into the preheated oven and allow the dough to bake for 25-30 minutes.
11. Remove from the oven once the top of the bread appears dry and starts to show orange flecks of color.

Nutrition: Calories: 160, Total Fat: 13.7g, Saturated Fat: 0g, Cholesterol: 0 mg, Sodium: 0 mg, Total Carbs: 16.3g, Fiber: 0g, Sugar: 7g, Protein: 19g

306. Low-Fodmap Spring Rolls

Preparation Time: 15 minutes | **Cooking Time:** 40 minutes | **Servings:** 5

Ingredients:
Filling
- 1 carrot
- Rice paper
- Half a cup of basil
- 1 turnip
- 1 cup of cilantro
- 12 medium-sized shrimps
- Half a cup of mint
- 1 zucchini

Marinate;
- A pinch of white Pepper
- 2 teaspoons of chopped ginger
- 1 tablespoon of scallions (green part only)
- 1 teaspoon of fish sauce
- 1 tablespoon of coconut oil
- 2 teaspoons of gluten free soy sauce

Peanut Sauce;
- 2 tablespoons of wheat free soy sauce
- 2 teaspoons of fish sauce
- 2 tablespoons of freshly squeezed lime juice
- 2 teaspoons of natural cane syrup
- 1 teaspoon of dried chilli flakes
- A quarter cup of natural smooth peanut butter (sugar free)

Directions:
1. To marinate the shrimp;
2. Put all the marinade ingredients into a ziplock bag, add the shrimps (make sure they are fully covered) then refrigerate for a little over 30 minutes.
3. Put all the peanut sauce ingredients into a large mixing bowl, stir with a wooden ladle until well combined.
4. Cut up or julienne the turnip, carrot and zucchini.
5. Put the coconut oil into a large skillet and saute all the ingredients (except mint and basil leaves) for the following for 1-2 minutes (do not overcook).

6. To make the spring rolls;
7. Dip the rice paper into a large bowl of water for 3-5 seconds until it softens a bit, then remove it and a bit of all the vegetables, cilantro and shrimp, then break the mint leaves and basil by hand and put them in the rolls.
8. Fold in the sides, then gently roll the wraps and voila! Your very own Low-FODMAP spring rolls!

Nutrition: Calories: 279, Total Fat: 8g, Saturated Fat: 0g, Cholesterol: 0 mg, Sodium: 0 mg, Total Carbs: 12g, Fiber: 0g, Sugar: 2g, Protein: 24 g

307. Low-Fodmap Cucumber Bites

Preparation Time: 30 minutes | **Cooking Time:** 0 minutes | **Servings:** 20
Ingredients:
- 1 tablespoon of roasted paprika
- Half a cup of lactose-free cream cheese
- 2 cucumbers
- Half a cup of Low-FODMAP egg salad
- Half a cup of Low-FODMAP tuna salad

Directions:
1. Chop the cucumbers into round bite-sized pieces, then use a spoon to make a small groove in the middle.
2. Scoop some egg salad over a third of the cucumber slices, then the tuna salad over another third and the cream cheese over the rest, taking care not to over top them lest they start to fall off.
3. Drain and cut the roasted paprika into small pieces, then top the cream cheese with the roasted paprika and serve.

Nutrition: Calories: 159, Total Fat: 9g, Saturated Fat: 0g, Cholesterol: 0 mg, Sodium: 0 mg, Total Carbs: 4g, Fiber: 0g, Sugar: 2.1g, Protein: 11.9g

308. Low-Fodmap Salmon Cakes

Preparation Time: 10 minutes | **Cooking Time:** 40 minutes | **Servings:** 2

Ingredients:
- Pepper and salt to taste
- Half a tablespoon of coconut flour
- 2 medium carrots
- 1 lemon zest
- A handful of chives (chopped)
- A can of wild salmon
- Half a tablespoon of coconut oil

Directions:
1. Preheat your oven to 400F. Line a baking sheet with pieces of parchment paper.
2. Peel and chop the carrots, then put them into a food processor, pulse until the carrots are small and well diced up.
3. Open the can of salmons and drain it of all liquid, then set aside.
4. Add the rest of the ingredients into the food processor, along with the salmons, pulse until well combined and almost smooth.
5. Use your hand to form the mixture into palm-sized cakes, using a paper towel to pat any excess liquid.
6. Gently place the newly formed cakes onto your baking sheet and place them in the oven.
7. Bake for 40 minutes or more if you want them a bit crispy. Serve warm.

Nutrition: Calories: 226, Total Fat: 13.8g, Saturated Fat: 0g, Cholesterol: 0 mg, Sodium: 0 mg, Total Carbs: 25g, Fiber: 0, Sugar: 3g, Protein: 6.5 g

309. Feta, Pumpkin, And Chive Fritters

Preparation Time: 5 minutes | **Cooking Time:** 10 minutes | **Servings:** 4

Ingredients:
- 2 tablespoons cornstarch
- ½ to 1 teaspoon ground cumin (to taste)
- ½ teaspoon xanthan gum
- ½ cup crumbled feta 2 eggs, lightly beaten
- Pumpkin or other winter squash,
- 3 tablespoons light sour cream
- ⅓ cup fine rice flour
- Salt and freshly ground black pepper
- 2 tablespoons canola oil
- Garden Salad, optional
- ½ cup chopped chives

Directions:
1. Cook the pumpkin 8-10 minutes, until tender, in a medium saucepan of boiling water.
2. Drain and mix.
3. Reserve to be refreshing. Sift rice flour (or blend with a whisk to make sure they are properly combined), cornstarch, and xanthan gum in the large mixing bowl.
4. Attach 2 cabbage teaspoons, feta, cups, eggs, and cumin, and blend together well.
5. Add salt and pepper to taste. Burn up 1 tablespoon of oil over medium heat in a fairly large non-stick skillet.
6. Apply 2 tablespoons of heaping batter to frying and cook for 2-3 minutes.
7. Flip through the back of a spatula and flatten slightly, then cook for a further 2 minutes, or until crispy golden, and then brown.
8. Move the chips to a plate and cover them with foil to warm them if you intend on eating it right away (save them for later on in the fridge).
9. Keep in mind to cook all fritters with remaining oil and batter. Blend the sour cream together and 1 tablespoon of cabbage left.
10. If wanted, match the fritters with salad and a dollop of sour cream.

Nutrition: Calories: 294, Total Fat: 15g, Saturated Fat: 0g, Cholesterol: 0 mg, Sodium: 0 mg, Total Carbs: 28g, Fiber: 0g, Sugar: 0g, Protein: 9 g

310. Chicken Tikka Skewers

Preparation Time: 5 minutes | **Cooking Time:** 10 minutes | **Servings:** 4

Ingredients:
- ¼ teaspoon ground cumin
- ¼ teaspoon ground coriander
- 1 tablespoon garam masala
- Garden Salad
- ¾ cup Greek yogurt
- 2 teaspoons turmeric
- 1 tablespoon finely grated ginger
- Salt and freshly ground black pepper
- 2½ pounds boneless skinless chicken breast
- ¼ to ½ teaspoon chili powder (to taste)

Directions:
1. In a large bowl, mix the garam masala, cumin, chili, yogurt, ginger, coriander and turmeric, and salt and potato.
2. Incorporate the pieces of chicken and marinade until evenly coated. Cover with a wrap of plastic and cool 2 hours. Preheat broiler.
3. Load the chicken in 18 skewers.
4. Place on the broiler or baking sheet, and grill until golden, brown, and just cooked for 6 to 8 minutes on every side.
5. Serve with salad.

Nutrition: Calories: 178, Total Fat: 1g, Saturated Fat: 0g, Cholesterol: 0 mg, Sodium: 0 mg, Total Carbs: 5g, Fiber: 0g, Sugar: 0g, Protein: 13g

311. Tuna, Lemongrass, And Basil Risotto Patties

Preparation Time: 10 minutes | **Cooking Time:** 15 minutes | **Servings:** 4
Ingredients:
- ½ cup cornstarch
- Salt and freshly ground black pepper
- 2 tablespoons chopped basil
- 1⅓ cups gluten-free bread crumbs
- Canola oil
- ¾ cup arborio rice
- 2 tablespoons finely chopped lemongrass
- 2 eggs, lightly beaten, divided
- One 5-ounce can oil-packed tuna, drained

Directions:
1. In a large cup, pour the stock and bring to a boil. Incorporate the rice and let it cook until tender for 10-12 minutes.
2. Drain excess fluid. Stir in the salmon, citrus fruit, and basil while still dry and blend well together.
3. Switch to a medium bowl and keep cool until room temperature is reached.
4. Preheat the oven to 150 degrees C (300 degrees F).
5. In the cooled rice, add 1 beaten egg and 1/3 cup (40 g), salt, and pepper to taste. Shape 8 large balls into a mixture and flatten them to make pats.
6. Place the majority of the maize starch and the remainder of one cup (120 g) of bread crumbs into three small bowls. (When the mixture is not quite firm enough, add more bread crumbs.)
7. Coat the patties with maize, then beat the egg and eventually crumbs. Set the plate aside.
8. Heat oil over medium-high heat in a medium saucepan.
9. In the pot, add 4 patties, and cook on both sides for 2-3 minutes, until browned evenly. Take a baker and keep warm in the fireplace—Cook the remaining patties in the pot with a little more oil.
10. Serve with salad.

Nutrition: Calories: 54, Total Fat: 1g, Saturated Fat: 0g, Cholesterol: 59 mg, Sodium: 108 mg, Total Carbs: 1g, Fiber: 0g, Sugar: 0g, Protein: 8g

312. Cheese-And-Herb Polenta Wedges With Watercress Salad

Preparation Time: 10 minutes | **Cooking Time:** 15 minutes | **Servings:** 4
Ingredients:
- 3 tablespoons alfalfa sprouts

- ½ small cucumber, thinly sliced
- ⅓ Cup chopped marjoram
- ⅓ Cup chopped oregano
- 3 tablespoons lemon-infused olive oil
- ½ green bell pepper
- 4 cups watercress
- ½ cup grated parmesan
- 1/3 cup chopped flat-leaf parsley
- ½ red bell pepper

Directions:

1. In a medium casserole, bring the stock to a boil. Put polenta in and cook for 3 to 5 minutes over medium heat and stir continuously, making the mix very dense.
2. Add Parmesan, oil and grasses (20 g) to the mixture. Let the polenta cool down and leave it in the fridge for an hour.
3. Preheat the oven to 180°C and fill in a baking sheet of parchment paper.
4. Place the polenta on a cutting board and cut it into eight coils or rectangles.
5. Sprinkle with the remaining Parmesan onto the wedges in the baking sheet.
6. Bake the cheese for about 10 to 15 minutes until it has melted, and the wedges are somewhat white.
7. Combine cucumber, green, watercress, and red bell peppers, and lukewarm sprouts in a large bowl to make the watercress salad.
8. Drizzle and mix together with a lemon-infused oil. Serve on soft wedges of polenta.

Nutrition: Calories: 284, Total Fat: 12.6g, Saturated Fat: 6.3g, Cholesterol: 34.8 mg, Sodium: 329.9 mg, Total Carbs: 24.1g, Fiber: 3.5g, Sugar: 0.7g, Protein: 19.9g

313. Spiced Tofu Bites

Preparation Time: 10 minutes | **Cooking Time:** 25 minutes | **Servings:** 6
Ingredients:

- 14 ounces puffed tofu pieces
- Cooked rice
- ¼ teaspoon ground allspice

- 1/3 cup vegetable oil
- ¼ teaspoon paprika
- Garden Salad
- ½ teaspoon salt
- 1 teaspoon ground caraway seeds
- ½ teaspoons freshly ground black pepper

Directions:

1. In a small bowl, mix the seeds of salt, paprika, caraway pepper, and allspice, then add 2 tablespoons of the oil. Brush the mixture of spice over the tofu and pass it to a plate.
2. Cover with a lid and wait for 2 to 3 hours for the flavors to blend together.
3. In a medium-high saucepan, heat the remaining oil.
4. Fill the tofu and cook on each side for 1 to 2 minutes, until warm. Serve with rice and salad steamed.

Nutrition: Calories: 134.8, Total Fat: 7.3g, Saturated Fat: 1.1g, Cholesterol: 0 mg, Sodium: 1992.3 mg, Total Carbs: 5.9g, Fiber: 1.1g, Sugar: 1g, Protein: 14.6g

314. Chive and Onion-Infused Dip

Preparation Time: 5 minutes | **Cooking Time:** 5 minutes | **Servings:** 10
Ingredients:

- Onion chunks
- 3 tablespoons olive oil
- Mayonnaise
- Parsley, chopped
- Chives, dried
- Lemon juice

Directions:

1. Fry the onion in olive oil for 4 minutes.
2. Once fragrant, remove all of the onion chunks from the oil. Set aside to cool.
3. Now place the Ingredients in a bowl & mix well. Add more lemon juice, parsley, and chives if desired.
4. Refrigerate for 30 minutes.

In this recipe the sulfur compounds in onion that are harmful to your diet will be absent. So you can safely consume it.

Nutrition: Calories 82, Calcium 12 mg, Fat 7.8g, Satured Fat 1.2g, Iron 3 mg, Sugars 8g, Salt 0.2g, Protein 4g, Carbs 2.9g, Fiber 3g

315. Traditional Hummus

Preparation Time: 10 minutes | **Cooking Time:** 12 minutes | **Servings:** 8

Ingredients:

- 400 grams canned chickpeas, rinsed, drained and skinned
- 3 tablespoons water
- 2 tablespoons tahini
- ½ teaspoon salt
- 1 tablespoon olive oil
- 2 tablespoons lemon juice
- ½ teaspoon cumin, ground

Directions:

1. Put tahini & lemon juice in a food processor. Blend until smooth.
2. Add remaining ingredients into the tahini mixture. Blend until desired consistency is obtained.
3. Refrigerate for 30 minutes.

Nutrition: 83 calories, Calcium 25 mg, Fat 7.9g, Iron 1mg, Sugars 2g, Salt 0.2g, Proteins 2.3g, Carbs 1.9g, Fiber 0.8g

316. Sunflower Seed Butter

Preparation Time: 15 minutes | **Cooking Time:** 40 minutes | **Servings:** 26

Ingredients:

- 40 grams of raw sunflower seeds, hulled
- 1 tablespoon pure maple syrup
- 1 tablespoon coconut oil
- ¼ teaspoon salt

Directions:

1. Set the oven to 190 degrees Celsius.
2. Distribute the sunflower seeds evenly on a roasting tray lined with baking paper.
3. Bake for 20 minutes. Stir the seeds every 5 minutes throughout the cook. Set aside to cool.

4. Transfer the seeds to a food processor. Blitz the seeds for 20 minutes. Remember to stop every now and then to scrape the sides of the food processor and break down the lumps in the mixture.
5. Add the remaining Ingredients once butter is creamy and smooth—Blitz for another minute.

Nutrition: Calories 101, Calcium 13 mg, Fat 8.9g, Satured Fat 1.2g, Fiber 1.4g, Protein 3.4g, Sugars 0.9g, Carbs 3.8g

317. Pumpkin and Roast Pepper Hummus

Preparation Time: 10 minutes | **Cooking Time:** 15 minutes | **Servings:** 15

Ingredients:

- 200 grams chickpeas, rinsed and drained
- ½ teaspoon cumin, ground
- 1 red bell pepper, deseeded and sliced
- 1 ½ teaspoon paprika
- 400 grams buttercup squash, peeled and sliced
- 3 tablespoons lemon juice
- 2 tablespoons olive oil
- 4 tablespoon water

Directions:

1. Set the oven to 190 degrees Celsius.
2. Put bell pepper strips in a tray and sprinkle olive oil on top—roast for 10 minutes.
3. Place squash and water in a bowl. Set microwave on high and heat it while covered for 9 minutes.
4. Now put the remaining ingredients in a food processor. Add squash and bell pepper—season to taste.
5. Blend until smooth.

Nutrition: Calories 59, Calcium 12 mg, Fat 3.4g, Iron 4 mg, Saturated Fat 0.5g, Fiber 2.2g, Proteins 1.6g, 2.1 Sugars, Carbs 6.3g

318. Pumpkin Dip

Preparation Time: 20 minutes | **Cooking Time:** 40 minutes | **Servings:** 8

Ingredients:

- 500 grams buttercup squash, peeled and sliced
- 1 tablespoon canola oil
- 2 tablespoons lemon juice
- 2 tablespoons mayonnaise
- ½ teaspoon paprika
- 1 tablespoon fresh rosemary, chopped
- Salt and pepper

Directions:

1. Set the oven to 200 degrees Celsius.
2. Put pumpkin pieces in a tray and drizzle with oil—season to taste.
3. Roast for 30 minutes then set aside for 10 minutes to cool.
4. Transfer the roast pumpkin to a food processor. Add remaining ingredients and blend until smooth.

Nutrition: Calories 58, Calcium 11 mg, Fat 3.8g, Iron 3 mg, Satured Fat 0.5g, Sugars 2.7g, Salt 0.1g, Protein 1.3g, Fiber 2.6g Carbs 6.2

319. Smoky Red Pepper Dressing

Preparation Time: 10 minutes | **Cooking Time:** 15 minutes | **Servings:** 8

Ingredients:

- 2 red bell pepper, grilled, peeled and sliced
- 1 ½ teaspoon paprika, smoked
- 5 tablespoons olive oil
- 3 teaspoons pure maple syrup
- 2 tablespoons of rice wine vinegar

Directions:

1. Place all ingredients in a food processor.
2. Season to taste.
3. Blend until smooth.

Nutrition: Calorie 102, Calcium 7 mg, Fat 9.2g, Iron 3 mg, Satured Fat 1.3g, Fiber 1g, Protein 5g, Sugars 3.3g, Carbs 4.4g

320. Mustard Maple Sauce

Preparation Time: 5 minutes | **Cooking Time:** 5 minutes | **Servings:** 8

Ingredients:

- 60 milliliters mayonnaise
- 1/16 cayenne pepper
- 3 ½ tablespoons Dijon mustard
- 1 tablespoon white vinegar
- 3 tablespoons pure maple syrup
- Black pepper

Directions:

1. Put the ingredients together in a food processor.
2. Blend until smooth.

Nutrition: Calories 53, Calcium 9 mg, Carbs 7.3g, Fat 2.3g, Salt 3 mg, Satured Fat 2g, Sugars 4.7g, Protein 1.6g

321. Smoky Barbecue Sauce

Preparation Time: 10 minutes | **Cooking Time:** 10 minutes | **Servings:** 4

Ingredients:

- 311 grams tomato paste
- ½ tablespoon white vinegar
- 150 ml of agave syrup
- 1 teaspoon chives, dried
- 1 teaspoon black pepper
- 4 tablespoons golden syrup
- ½ teaspoon salt
- 60 milliliters apple cider vinegar
- 1/16 teaspoon cayenne pepper
- 125 milliliters water
- 2 teaspoons paprika, smoked
- 1 tablespoon Worcestershire sauce
- 2 ½ teaspoons yellow mustard powder

Directions:

1. Place all your ingredients in a saucepan & bring to a boil.
2. Reduce heat and simmer for 8 minutes.
3. Adjust flavors as desired.

Nutrition: Calories 30, Calcium 9 mg, Fat 0.5g, Iron 4 mg, Fiber 4g, Proteins 4g, Sugars 5.8g, Carbs 6.6g

322. Red Cabbage Sauerkraut

Preparation Time: 20 minutes | **Cooking Time:** 2 hour | **Servings:** 2

Ingredients:

- 850 grams red cabbage
- 1 ½ teaspoon caraway seeds
- 2 teaspoons salt

Directions:
1. Remove the outer leaves and dense core of the cabbage. Dice remaining leaves roughly. Toast with salt.
2. Leave the cabbage to sweat for 30 minutes. Add caraway seeds.
3. Place the cabbage and its juices in a jar. Compress tightly and set aside for 30 minutes.
4. Pour filtered water until 1 inch of the jar is covered. Seal with a fermentation lid.
5. Leave the cabbage to ferment until it gets a tangy taste. Refrigerate for 2 months.

Nutrition: Calories 14, Calcium 20 mg, Fat 1g, Iron 4 mg, Protein 6g, Salt 0.2g, Carbs 3.2g, Sugsars 1.6g

323.   Cranberry Sauce

Preparation Time: 20 minutes | **Cooking Time:** 40 minutes | **Servings:** 2
Ingredients:
- 150 grams cranberries, dried
- 2 teaspoons red wine
- 125 milliliters cranberry juice
- 2 teaspoons glucose syrup
- 1 ½ teaspoon corn starch
- ½ teaspoon orange zest
- 1/8 teaspoon salt
- Water

Directions:
1. Soak cranberries in boiling water while covered for 30 minutes.
2. Drain excess water and place cranberries in a food processor with the cranberry juice. Blend until relatively smooth.
3. Mix corn starch and water. Transfer mixture to a saucepan together with glucose syrup, wine, zest, and salt.
4. Heat over medium-low flame for 5 minutes. Stir occasionally.

5. Pour sauce in a bowl and refrigerate to chill.

Nutrition: Calories 51, Calcium 5 mg, Fat 0.2g, Sugars 11.2gm Urib 1 mg, Proteins 1g, Fiber 9g, Carbs 13.5g

324.   Chocolate Dipping Sauce

Preparation Time: 5 minutes | **Cooking Time:** 10 minutes | **Servings:** 6
Ingredients:
- 88 grams dark chocolate, chopped
- 1 tablespoon butter
- 63 milliliters almond milk
- 4 teaspoons glucose syrup

Directions:
1. Heat chocolate, butter, syrup over low heat.
2. Stir continuously until melted.
3. Add milk and stir well.

Nutrition: Calories 120, Calcium 23 mg, Fat 8g, Iron 18 mg, Satured Fat 3.8g, Fiber 1.6g, Proteins 1.2g, Sugar 6.8g, Carbs 10.5g

325.   Sweet Chili Sauce

Preparation Time: 15 minutes | **Cooking Time:** 45 minutes | **Servings:** 3
Ingredients:
- 250 grams mild red chili
- 375 milliliters white vinegar
- 315 ml agave syrup

Directions:
1. Chop 50 grams red chilies roughly. Place chili bits in a food processor.
2. Slice remaining chilies in half and remove the seeds.
3. Chop chilies roughly and add in the food processor together with ½ cup vinegar.
4. Blend until chilies are reduced to fine bits.
5. Put the mixture in a saucepan.
6. Add the remaining amount of vinegar and syrup.
7. Heat on low flame while stirring continuously for 5 minutes.

8. Turn up the flame to high. If the sauce is boiling, turn down the heat to medium.
9. Simmer for 25 minutes.
10. Stir occasionally.

Nutrition: Calories 43, Calciu 19 mg, Protein 2g, Iron 1mg, Carbs 11g, Fiber 1g, Sugars 9g

326. Chocolate Coconut Fudge Sauce

Preparation Time: 15 minutes | **Cooking Time:** 20 minutes | **Servings:** 16
Ingredients:

- 165 milliliters coconut cream
- 1 teaspoon vanilla extract
- 4 tablespoons Dutch cocoa powder
- 250 milliliters almond milk
- 3 tablespoons coconut oil
- 150 ml of corn syrup

Directions:

1. Put cocoa powder, milk, coconut cream, and corn syrup in a blender. Process for 30 seconds.
2. Transfer mixture into a saucepan. Simmer while occasionally stirring over medium-low heat for 15 minutes.
3. Add vanilla extract and coconut oil and stir. Simmer for 4 more minutes.
4. Refrigerate for 20 minutes.

Nutrition: Calories 95, Calcium 29 mg, Iron 5mg, Satured Fat 4.4g, Fiber 7g, Protein 6g, Sugars 6g, Carbs 12g

327. Tartar Sauce

Preparation Time: 10 minutes | **Cooking Time:** 5 minutes | **Servings:** 10
Ingredients:

- 2 tablespoons pickles, chopped
- ½ cup mayonnaise
- 1 teaspoon shallot, chopped
- 1 tablespoon white wine vinegar
- 1 tablespoon capers, chopped
- ½ teaspoon dry mustard powder

- 1 tablespoon parsley, chopped
- Black pepper

Directions:

1. Place the ingredients in a medium bowl and mix well.
2. Adjust seasoning as desired.

Nutrition: Calories 48, Calcium 4 mg, Fat 4g, Protein 2g, Satured Fat 0.8g, Salto 0.1g, Fiber 1g, Carbs 3g

328. Homemade Gravy

Preparation Time: 30 minutes | **Cooking Time:** 1 hour 40 minutes | **Servings:** 2
Ingredients:

- 240 grams carrot
- 1.5 liters water, boiling
- 120 grams green leek leaves, chopped
- 4 tablespoons corn starch
- 4 sprigs rosemary
- 5 bay leaves
- 8 chicken wings
- 5 sage leaves
- Salt and pepper
- Olive oil

Directions:

1. Slice the chicken wings and break up the bones. Place chicken meat and bones in a roasting tray together with carrots, herbs, and leek leaves.
2. Drizzle oil over the contents of the tray. Season with black pepper and salt. Toss to coat.
3. Bake for a hr. in a preheated oven at 200 degrees Celsius.
4. Next place the roasting tray over low heat and grind the contents together. Pour water into the tray. Increase the flame to high and allow to boil for 10 minutes.
5. Place corn starch in warm water. Stir well.
6. Reduce heat.
7. Add corn starch mixture to the gravy.
8. Simmer for 25 minutes—season to taste.
9. Filter the gravy using a sieve.

Nutrition: Calories 43, Calcium 40 mg, Fat 1.3g, Iron 9 mg, Satured Fat 3g, Fiber 1.5g, Proteins 8g, Sugars 1.4g, Carbs 7.6g

329. Green beans, pine nuts

Preparation time: 10 minutes | **Cooking time:** 30 minutes | **Servings:** 4

Ingredients:

- 1 pound green beans, trimmed
- 2 tablespoons extra-virgin olive oil
- ½ teaspoon kosher salt
- ¼ teaspoon red pepper flakes
- 1 tablespoon white wine vinegar
- ¼ cup pine nuts, toasted

Directions:

1. Preheat the oven to 425 °F. By using parchment paper or foil, line a baking sheet.
2. Combine the green beans, olive oil, salt, and red pepper flakes in a large bowl and mix.
3. Now spread in a single layer on a baking sheet. Roast for 10 minutes, stir, and roast for another 10 minutes, or until golden brown.
4. Mix the cooked green beans with the vinegar and top with the pine nuts.

Nutrition: Calories: 165, Carbs: 12g, Fat: 13g, Fiber: 3.58g, Protein: 4g, Sodium: 150mg, Sugars: 4.11g

330. Roasted harissa carrots

Preparation time: 10 minutes | **Cooking time:** 30 minutes | **Servings:** 4

Ingredients:

- 1 pound carrots, peeled and sliced into 1-inch-thick rounds
- 2 tablespoons extra-virgin olive oil
- 2 tablespoons harissa
- 1 teaspoon corn syrup
- 1 teaspoon ground cumin
- ½ teaspoon kosher salt
- ½ cup fresh parsley, chopped

Directions:

1. Preheat the oven to 450°f.
2. Now with parchment paper or foil, line a baking sheet.
3. In a large mixing bowl, combine the carrots, olive oil, harissa, corn syrup, cumin, and salt. Place on a baking sheet in a single layer.
4. 15 minutes in the oven for roast. Remove from the oven and stir with the parsley.

Nutrition: Calories: 140, carbs: 13.8g, Fat: 9.54g, Fiber: 4g, Protein: 1.74g, Sodium: 500mg, Sugars: 6.67g

331. Cucumbers with feta, mint, and sumac

Preparation time: 10 minutes | **Cooking time:** 30 minutes | **Servings:** 4

Ingredients:

- 1 tablespoon extra-virgin olive oil
- 1 tablespoon lemon juice
- 2 teaspoons ground sumac
- ½ teaspoon kosher salt
- 2 hothouse or English cucumbers, diced
- ¼ cup crumbled feta cheese
- 1 tablespoon fresh mint, chopped
- 1 tablespoon fresh parsley, chopped
- ⅛ teaspoon red pepper flakes

Directions:

1. Whisk the lemon juice, olive oil, salt, and sumac in a large bowl. Add the cucumber and feta cheese and toss well.
2. Place to a serving dish and garnish with parsley, mint, and red pepper flakes.

Nutrition: Calories: 85, Fat: 6g, Fiber: 0.8g, Sugars: 2.5g, Protein: 2.3g, Sodium: 359 mg, Carbohydrates: 6.3g

332. Cherry tomato bruschetta

Preparation time: 15 minutes | **Cooking time:** 0 minutes | **Servings:** 4

Ingredients:

- 8 ounces assorted cherry tomatoes, halved

- ⅓ cup fresh herbs, chopped (such as basil, parsley, tarragon, dill)
- 1 tablespoon extra-virgin olive oil
- ¼ teaspoon kosher salt
- ⅛ teaspoon freshly ground black pepper
- ¼ cup ricotta cheese
- 4 slices whole-wheat bread, toasted

Directions:
1. Combine the tomatoes, herbs, olive oil, salt, and black pepper in a medium bowl and mix gently.
2. Spread 1 tablespoon of ricotta cheese on each slice of toast. Spoon one-quarter of the tomato mixture onto each bruschetta.
3. If desired, garnish with more herbs.

Nutrition: Calories: 137, Carbs: 15.3g, Cholesterol: 7.3mg, Fat: 6.36g, Fiber: 2.4g, Protein: 5.25g, Sodium: 263 mg, Sugars: 2.7g

333. Roasted red pepper hummus

Preparation time: 10 minutes | **Cooking time:** 0 minutes | **Servings:** 4
Ingredients:
- 1 (15-ounce) can low-sodium chickpeas, drained and rinsed
- 3 ounces jarred roasted red bell peppers, drained
- 3 tablespoons tahini
- 3 tablespoons lemon juice
- ¾ teaspoon kosher salt
- ¼ teaspoon freshly ground black pepper
- 3 tablespoons extra-virgin olive oil
- ¼ teaspoon cayenne pepper (optional)
- Fresh herbs, chopped, for garnish (optional)

Directions:
1. Add chickpeas, red bell peppers, tahini, lemon juice, salt, and black pepper in a food processor.
2. Pulse 5 to 7 times and then add the olive oil and process until smooth.
3. Now add the cayenne pepper and garnish with chopped herbs, if desired.

Nutrition: Calories: 246, Carbs: 14.4g, Fat: 19.44g, Fiber: 3.77g, Protein: 5.96g, Sodium: 465.46mg, Sugars: 2.4g

334. Asparagus Pasta

Preparation time: 10 minutes | **Cooking Time:** 25 Minutes | **Servings:** 3
Ingredients:
- 8 Ounces Farfalle Pasta, Uncooked
- 1 ½ Cups Asparagus, Fresh, Trimmed & Chopped into 1 Inch Pieces
- 1 Pint Grape Tomatoes, Halved
- 2 Tablespoons Olive Oil
- Sea Salt & Black Pepper to Taste
- 2 Cups Mozzarella, Fresh & Drained
- 1/3 Cup Basil Leaves, Fresh & Torn
- 2 Tablespoons Balsamic Vinegar

Directions:
1. Start by heating the oven to 400 degrees, and then get out a stockpot. Cook your pasta per package instructions, and reserve ¼ cup of pasta water.
2. Get out a bowl, toss the tomatoes, oil, and asparagus, and season with salt and pepper. Spread this mixture on a baking sheet, and bake for fifteen minutes. Stir twice this time.
3. Remove your vegetables from the oven, and then add the cooked pasta to your baking sheet. Mix with a few tablespoons of pasta water so that your sauce becomes smoother.
4. Mix in your basil and mozzarella, drizzling with balsamic vinegar. Serve warm.

Nutrition: Calories: 638, Carbs: 68g, Fat: 27.7g, Fiber: 5.66g, Protein: 29g,

335. Eggplant Caviar

Preparation Time: 10 minutes | **Cooking Time:** 10 minutes | **Servings:** 4
Ingredients:
- 2 (1-pound) eggplants
- ½ cup finely chopped fresh parsley
- ½ cup finely diced red bell pepper

- ¼ cup freshly squeezed lemon juice
- 2 tablespoons tahini
- ⅛ teaspoon salt, plus more as needed

Directions:
1. Preheat the chic.
2. Pierce the eggplants with a fork to prevent them from bursting in the oven, and place them on a rimmed baking sheet. Broil for about 3 minutes until the skin is charred on one side.
3. Flip the eggplants and broil the other side for about 3 minutes more until charred. Remove and let cool.
4. Carefully remove the skin from the eggplants and scoop the pulp into a bowl. Using a fork or wooden pestle, mash the pulp into a smooth purée.
5. Add parsley, red bell pepper, lemon juice, tahini, and salt. Stir until well combined. Taste and then season it with more salt, as needed.
6. Refrigerate for at least 1 hour before serving. Leftover "caviar" can be kept refrigerated in an airtight container for up to 5 days or frozen for 1 month.
7. Thaw in the refrigerator overnight before using.

Nutrition: Calories: 115, Carbs: 17g, Fat: 5.4g, Fiber: 6.7g, Protein: 4.1g

336. Walnut and Red Pepper Spread

Preparation Time: 20 minutes | **Cooking Time:** 0 minutes | **Servings:** 3
Ingredients:
- 3 slices whole-wheat bread
- 1 red bell pepper
- ¼ C. Chives
- 1 cup walnuts
- 3 tablespoons Harissa, or store-bought
- 2 tablespoons pomegranate molasses or Cranberry juice
- ½ teaspoon ground coriander
- ½ teaspoon ground cumin
- ¼ cup olive oil

Directions:
1. In a food processor, combine the bread, red bell pepper, chives, and walnuts.
2. Process for a few seconds until combined but coarse. Do not overprocess. You want to retain some texture of the walnuts in this spread.
3. Add the harissa, molasses, coriander, cumin, and olive oil. Process it for a few seconds until the mixture resembles an almost smooth paste.
4. Refrigerate any leftovers in an airtight container for up to 1 week, or freeze for 2 to 3 months.

Nutrition: Calories: 706, Carbs: 38g, Fat: 59.6g, Fiber: 8.4g, Protein: 13.3g

337. Green Olive Tapenade

Preparation Time: 20 minutes | **Cooking Time:** 0 minutes | **Servings:** 3
Ingredients:
- 2 cups pitted green olives
- 1 cup coarsely chopped walnuts
- ½ cup chopped fresh parsley
- ¼ cup freshly squeezed lemon juice
- ¼ cup olive oil
- 1 teaspoon dried oregano

Directions:
1. In a food processor, combine the olives, walnuts, and parsley. Pulse about 5 times until the mixture is coarsely chopped.
2. Add the lemon juice, olive oil, and oregano.
3. Process for a few seconds more. The spread should be finely chopped but not puréed.

Nutrition: Calories: 674, Carbs: 16g, Fat: 68g, Fiber: 7.7g, Protein: 9.9g

338. Baked eggplant baba ganoush

Preparation time: 15 minutes | **Cooking time:** 1 hour | **Servings:** 4
Ingredients:

- 2 pounds (about 2 medium to large) eggplant
- 3 tablespoons tahini
- Zest of 1 lemon
- 2 tablespoons lemon juice
- ¾ teaspoon kosher salt
- ½ teaspoon ground sumac, plus more for sprinkling (optional)
- ⅓ cup fresh parsley, chopped
- 1 tablespoon extra-virgin olive oil

Directions:
1. Preheat the oven to 350°f. Place the eggplants directly on the rack and bake for 60 minutes or until the skin is wrinkly.
2. Add the tahini, lemon zest, lemon juice, salt, and sumac to a food processor. Carefully cut open the baked eggplant and scoop the flesh into the food processor. Process until the ingredients are well blended.
3. Place in a serving dish and mix in the parsley.
4. Drizzle with the olive oil and sprinkle with sumac, if desired.

Nutrition: Calories: 167, Carbs: 15.4g, Fat: 11.4g, Fiber: 6.6g, Protein: 4.6g, Sodium: 358mg

339. Roasted cherry tomato Caprese

Preparation time: 10 minutes | **Cooking time:** 30 minutes | **Servings:** 4
Ingredients:
- 2 pints (about 20 ounces) cherry tomatoes
- 6 thyme sprigs
- 2 tablespoons extra-virgin olive oil
- ½ teaspoon kosher salt
- 8 ounces fresh, unsalted mozzarella, cut into bite-size slices
- ¼ cup basil, chopped or cut into ribbons
- Loaf of crusty whole-wheat bread for serving

Directions:

1. Preheat the oven to 350°f. Employing parchment paper or foil, line a baking sheet.
2. In a large mixing bowl, combine the thyme, tomatoes, olive oil, and salt. Place in a single layer on the prepared baking sheet. Roast the tomatoes for 30 minutes or until they are bursting and juicy.
3. Place the mozzarella on a dish or in a bowl and set aside. Pour over the mozzarella the entire tomato mixture, including the liquids. Garnish with basil if desired.
4. Serve with crusty bread.

Nutrition: Calories: 267, Carbs: 8.52g, Fat: 20g, Fiber: 2g, Protein: 14.2g, Sodium: 596mg, Sugars: 4.36g

340. Easy spaghetti squash

Preparation time: 15 minutes | **Cooking time:** 25 minutes | **Servings:** 4
Ingredients:
- 1 zucchini, diced 1 red bell pepper, diced
- 1 tablespoon Italian seasoning
- 1 tomato, small & chopped fine
- 1 tablespoon parsley, fresh & chopped
- Pinch lemon pepper
- Dash sea salt, fine
- 4 ounces feta cheese, crumbled
- 3 Italian sausage links, casing removed
- 2 tablespoons olive oil
- 1 spaghetti sauce, halved lengthwise

Directions:
1. Start by heating your oven to 350°f, and get out a large baking sheet. Coat it with cooking spray, and then put your squash on it with the cut side down.
2. Bake at 350°f for forty-five minutes. It should be tender.
3. Turn the squash over, and bake for five more minutes. Scrape the strands into a larger bowl.
4. Heat a tablespoon of olive oil in a skillet, and then add in your Italian sausage.

Cook for eight minutes before removing it and placing it in a bowl.

5. In a skillett add 1tbsp of oil and throw in your Italian seasoning, red peppers, and zucchini. Cook for another five minutes. Your vegetables should be softened.
6. Mix in your feta cheese and squash, cooking until the cheese has melted.
7. Stir in your sausage, and then season with lemon pepper and salt.
8. Serve with parsley and tomato.

Nutrition: Calories: 518, Carbs: 17.22g, Fat:42g, Fiber: 4g, Protein: 19g

341. Roasted veggies

Preparation time: 5 minutes | **Cooking time:** 20 minutes | **Servings:** 6
Ingredients:
- 6 tablespoons olive oil
- 1 fennel bulb, diced
- 1 zucchini, diced
- 2 red bell peppers, diced
- 6 potatoes, large & diced
- 2 teaspoons sea salt
- ½ cup balsamic vinegar
- ¼ cup rosemary, chopped & fresh
- 2 teaspoons vegetable bouillon powder

Directions:
1. Start by heating your oven to 400°f.
2. Get out a baking dish and place your potatoes, fennel, zucchini, and fennel on a baking dish, drizzling with olive oil. Sprinkle it with salt, bouillon powder, and rosemary.
3. Mix well, and then bake at 450 °C for thirty to forty minutes. Mix your vinegar into the vegetables before serving.

Nutrition: Calories: 154, Carbs: 20g, Fat: 7.46g, Fiber: 2.8g, Protein: 2.42g

342. Roasted eggplant salad

Preparation time: 15 minutes | **Cooking time:** 40 minutes | **Servings:** 6
Ingredients:

2 tablespoons parsley, fresh & chopped
1 teaspoon thyme
2 cups cherry tomatoes, halved
Sea salt & black pepper to taste
1 teaspoon oregano
3 tablespoons olive oil
1 teaspoon basil
3 eggplants, peeled & cubed
Directions:
1. Start by heating your oven to 350°f.
2. Season your eggplant with basil, salt, pepper, oregano, thyme, and olive oil.
3. Spread it on a baking tray, and bake for a half-hour.
4. Toss with your remaining ingredients before serving.

Nutrition: Calories: 134, Carbs: 16g, Fat: 7.7g, Fiber: 7.62g, Protein: 2.9g

343. Penne with tahini sauce

Preparation time: 10 minutes | **Cooking time:** 20 minutes | **Servings:** 4
Ingredients:
- 1/3 cup water
- 1 cup yogurt, plain
- 1/8 cup lemon juice
- 3 tablespoons tahini
- ¼ cup olive oil
- 2 portobello mushrooms, large & sliced
- ½ red bell pepper, diced
- 16 ounces penne pasta
- ½ cup parsley, fresh & chopped
- Black pepper to taste

Directions:
1. Start by getting out a pot and bringing a pot of salted water to a boil. Cook your pasta al dente per package instructions.
2. Mix your lemon juice and tahini together, and then place them in a food processor. The process with water, and yogurt. It should be smooth.
3. Get out a saucepan, and place it over medium heat. Heat up your oil, and cook until soft.

4. Add in your mushroom and continue to cook until softened.

5. Add in your bell pepper, and cook until crispy.

6. Drain your pasta, then toss with your tahini sauce, top with parsley and pepper, and serve with vegetables.

Nutrition: Calories: 697, Carbs: 97g, Fat: 26g, Fiber: 6g, Proteins: 21g

344. Parmesan barley risotto

Preparation time: 15 minutes | **Cooking time:** 30 minutes | **Servings:** 6
Ingredients:

- 1 tablespoon olive oil
- 4 cups vegetable broth, low sodium
- 2 cups pearl barley, uncooked
- ½ cup dry white wine
- 1 cup parmesan cheese, grated fine & divided
- Sea salt & black pepper to taste
- Fresh chives, chopped for serving
- Lemon wedges for serving

Directions:
1. Add your broth into a saucepan and bring it to a simmer over medium-high heat.
2. Get out a stockpot and put it over medium-high heat as well. Heat up your oil. Cook for eight minutes and stir occasionally. Add in your barley and cook for two minutes more. Stir in your barley, cooking until it's toasted.
3. Pour in the wine, cooking for a minute more. Most of the liquid should have evaporated before adding in a cup of warm broth. Cook and stir for two minutes. Your liquid should be absorbed.
4. Add the remaining broth by the cup, and cook until each cup is absorbed before adding more. It should take about two minutes each time. It will take a little longer for the last cup to be absorbed.
5. Remove from heat, stir in half a cup of cheese, and top with remaining cheese chives and lemon wedges.

Nutrition: Calories: 413, Carbs: 71g, Fat: 7.2g, Fiber: 12.6g, Protein: 14g

345. Salty Cheese Fritters

Preparation Time: 5 minutes | **Cooking Time:** 15 minutes | **Servings:** 2-3
Ingredients:

- 1 egg
- 1 cup of yogurt
- 1 tbsp of oil
- 1 tsp of salt
- 2 tsp of baking powder
- 15 oz all-purpose flour
- Oil for frying

Creamy Cheese:
- ½ cup of gorgonzola cheese (or any blue cheese you have on hand)
- 1 cup of sour cream
- ¼ cup of grated cheddar
- 1 tbsp of finely chopped parsley
- ½ tsp of cayenne pepper

Directions:
1. Add the ingredients and mix it well with an electric mixer until you get a smooth dough.
2. Roll the dough to about one inch.
3. Cut it into 2.5x2.5inch pieces.
4. Preheat some of the oil at a medium temperature.
5. Fry the doughnuts for several minutes on each side.
6. Served with sour cream, kefir cream, and cheese.

Nutrition: Calories: 902, Carbs: 116g, Fat: 35g, Fiber: 4g, Protein: 28g

346. Smoked Salmon Toast

Preparation Time: 5 minutes | **Cooking Time:** 0 | **Servings:** 2
Ingredients:

- 4 slices of toast bread (you can use any bread you have)

- 2 oz smoked salmon, thinly sliced
- 2 tbsp of olive oil
- 1 tbsp of finely chopped parsley
- 4 toast-sized lettuce leaves

Directions:
1. Combine the olive oil with parsley. Spread this mixture over bread and lightly toast.
2. Arrange lettuce leaves and smoked salmon slices on top. Serve as breakfast.

Nutrition: Calories: 401, Carbs: 46g, Fat: 21g, Fiber: 12g, Protein: 16.2g

347. Chickpea Salad Pitas

Preparation Time: 15 minutes | **Cooking Time:** 0 | **Servings:** 4
Ingredients:

- 3.5 oz chickpeas, cooked
- ½ medium-sized cucumber, sliced
- ½ medium-sized red bell pepper, finely chopped
- ½ cup of feta cheese, sliced
- 1 tsp of chili pepper
- ½ tsp of salt
- ½ tsp of black pepper, ground
- 2 pita pieces of bread
- For Hummus:
- 14 oz cooked chickpeas
- 2-3 tbsp lemon juice
- 2 tbsp olive oil
- 1 tbsp of parsley, finely chopped
- 3 tbsp tahini

Directions:
1. Combine all ingredients in a bowl. Stir it well, and then set it aside for ten minutes. Cut the pitas in half and stuff with the mixture.
2. If you like, you can serve with lettuce or cherry tomatoes.

Nutrition: Calories: 482, Carbs: 58g, Fat: 21g, Fiber: 11.5, Protein: 19g

348. Zucchini pasta

Preparation time: 15 minutes | **Cooking time:** 30 minutes | **Servings:** 4
Ingredients:

- 3 tablespoons olive oil
- 3 zucchini, large & diced
- Sea salt & black pepper to taste
- ½ cup milk, 2%
- ¼ teaspoon nutmeg
- 1 tablespoon lemon juice, fresh
- ½ cup parmesan, grated
- 8 ounces uncooked farfalle pasta

Directions:
1. Get out a skillet and place it over medium heat, and then heat the oil. Start to cook and stir often so that it doesn't burn.
2. Add in your salt, pepper, and zucchini. Stir well, and cook covered for fifteen minutes.
3. During this time, you'll want to stir the mixture twice.
4. Get out a microwave-safe bowl, and heat the milk for thirty seconds. Stir in your nutmeg, and then pour it into the skillet. Cook uncovered for five minutes. Stir occasionally to keep from burning.
5. Get out a stockpot and cook your pasta per package instructions.
6. Drain the pasta, and then save two tablespoons of pasta water.
7. Stir everything together, and add in the cheese and lemon juice, and pasta water.

Nutrition: Calories: 389, Carbs: 49.5g, Fat: 15g, Fiber: 3.36g, Protein: 13.83g

349. Feta & spinach pita bake

Preparation time: 10 minutes | **Cooking time:** 20 minutes | **Servings:** 6
Ingredients:

- 2 Roma tomatoes, chopped
- 6 whole-wheat pita bread
- 1 jar sun-dried tomato pesto
- 4 mushrooms, fresh & sliced
- 1 bunch spinach, rinsed & chopped

- 2 tablespoons parmesan cheese, grated
- 3 tablespoons olive oil
- ½ cup feta cheese, crumbled
- Dash black pepper

Directions:

1. Start by heating the oven to 350 degrees, and get to your pita bread. Spread the tomato pesto on the side of each one. Put them in a baking pan with the tomato side up.

2. Top with tomatoes, spinach, mushrooms, parmesan, and feta.
3. Drizzle with olive oil and season with pepper.
4. Bake for twelve minutes, and then serve cut into quarters.

Nutrition: Calories: 310, Carbs: 26g, Fat: 19.71g, Fiber: 4.23g, Protein: 9.29g

Desserts

350. Low-Fodmap Brownies

Preparation Time: 10 minutes | **Cooking Time:** 30 minutes | **Servings:** 3
Ingredients:
- Half a cup of glucose syrup
- 1 cup of unsalted butter
- 3/4 cup of maple syrup
- 1 cup of unsweetened cocoa powder
- 3 large eggs (at room temperature)
- 2 teaspoons of pure vanilla extract
- 1 cup of gluten-free all purpose flour
- 1 teaspoon of salt
- 1 cup of Low-FODMAP chocolate chips
- Half a cup of dark chocolate (roughly chopped)

Directions:
1. Preheat your oven to 350°F. Line a baking sheet with pieces of parchment paper.
2. Put half the amount of chopped chocolate and butter into a microwave safe bowl, put into the microwave and allow to melt, stirring at 30 seconds interval, until the mixture is completely smooth.
3. Remove from the microwave, then whisk in eggs, glucose syrupo and vanilla.
4. Add the flour, cocoa powder, salt, chocolate chunks and the other half of the chopped chocolates.
5. Use a rubber spatula to carefully fold the ingredients together, then pour batter into your pre-lined baking pan.
6. Put into the oven and bake for 30 minutes or until it passes the toothpick test, if it doesn't, bake for 5-7 minutes.
7. Remove from the oven and set on a cooling rack.
8. Once cool, cut into pieces and serve.

Nutrition: Calories: 192, Total Fat: 20g, Saturated Fat: 0g, Cholesterol: 0 mg, Sodium: 0 mg, Total Carbs: 15g, Fiber: 0g, Sugar: 9g, Protein: 10g

351. Low-Fodmap Lemon Bar

Preparation Time: 10 minutes | **Cooking Time:** 50 minutes | **Servings:** 4
Ingredients:
For the crust
- ½ a cup of unsalted butter(cut into pieces)
- Half a cup of agave syrup
- 1 cup of gluten free all-purpose flour
- 2 tablespoons of water

For topping
- ¼ cup of gluten-free all-purpose flour
- 4 large eggs (lightly beaten)
- 1 cup of glucose syrup
- 4 tablespoons of freshly squeezed lemon juice

Directions:
1. Preheat your oven to 350°F.
2. Coat or grease a baking pan and set aside.
3. Put the glucose syrup and flour into a large mixing bowl, add the butter and mix by hand until crumbly, then pour in the water and mix until well combined.
4. Pour batter into greased pan and use the back of a spoon or spatula to flatten and level it.
5. Put into the oven and allow to bake for 25 minutes.
6. Put the eggs into a medium sized bowl, add the lemon juice, flour and agave syrup, stirring until smooth, then pour over baked crust.
7. Put back into the oven and bake for 25 minutes, then remove from oven and set on a cooling rack.
8. Cut into slices.
9. Serve.

Nutrition: Calories: 206, Total Fat: 15g, Saturated Fat: 0g, Cholesterol: 0 mg, Sodium: 0 mg, Total Carbs: 10g, Fiber: 0g, Sugar: 5g, Protein: 9 g

352. Low-Fodmap Butterscotch

Preparation Time: 10 minutes | **Cooking Time:** 15 minutes | **Servings:** 3
Ingredients:
- 1 teaspoon of rum or scotch
- 3 egg yolks
- 1 teaspoon of vanilla extract
- 3 tablespoons of water
- 2 tablespoons of cornstarch
- 1 cup of lactose-free full fat milk
- 1 cup of cane syrup
- Half a teaspoon of salt
- 1 cup of lactose-free whipping cream
- 40 grams of unsalted butter (at room temperature)

Directions:
1. Pour the milk into a medium sized bowl, add the whipping cream and whisk until foamy.
2. Put the eggs and cornstarch into another bowl and whisk until well combined.
3. Pour the water into a medium-sized saucepan, set over medium heat, then add the cane syrup and salt, then cook for 5 minutes without stirring. Slowly add the whipped cream mixture, whisking lightly until well incorporated, then bring to a boil.
4. Once boiled, remove half a cup of the mixture and pour into a separate bowl, then slowly add the egg yolks (to the bowl), stirring continuously so they don't scramble, then slowly pour the mixture into the saucepan, whisking lightly.
5. Set the heat on low and cook for 2 minutes or until the mixture thickens, then remove from heat.
6. Stir in vanilla, butter and scotch.
7. Allow to cool for a few minutes before serving into glasses.

8. Refrigerate overnight or for a couple of hours until it thickens. Serve with any topping of your choice.

Nutrition: Calories: 263, Total Fat: 16g, Cholesterol: 0 mg, Sodium: 0 mg, Total Carbs: 8.4g, Fiber: 0g, Sugar: 6g, Protein: 12g

353. Low-Fodmap Cookies

Preparation Time: 10 minutes | **Cooking Time:** 10 minutes | **Servings:** 7
Ingredients:
- 1 cup of glucose syrup
- A quarter teaspoon of salt
- 1 large egg
- 1 teaspoon of pure vanilla extract
- 1 cup of natural peanut butter
- Half a cup of dark chocolate chips

Directions:
1. Preheat your oven to 350°F.
2. Throw all the ingredients into a large mixing bowl and stir using a wooden spoon or ladle until well combined.
3. Line a baking sheet with pieces of parchment.
4. Cut out a tablespoon of dough and roll it into a ball, then place it on the parchment lined baking sheet and press it flat with the broad side of the spoon.
5. Repeat the process in 4 above with the rest of the dough, and put the baking sheet into the oven Bake for 10 minutes or until the edges have started to brown, then remove from the oven and let cool on the pan for a couple of minutes.

Nutrition: Calories: 0, Total Fat: 13g, Saturated Fat: 0g, Cholesterol: 0 mg, Sodium: 0 mg, Total Carbs: 28g, Fiber: 0g, Sugar: 10g, Protein: 8g

354. Low-Fodmap Cupcake

Preparation Time: 10 minutes | **Cooking Time:** 35 minutes | **Servings:** 2
Ingredients:
- A quarter teaspoon of nutmeg

- 1 cup of gluten-free all-purpose flour
- 2 teaspoons of baking powder
- Half a teaspoon of cinnamon
- 2 tablespoons of ground ginger
- A quarter cup of cold pressed rapeseed oil
- Half a cup of plant-based milk
- 1 cup of cane syrup
- 2 tablespoons of milled linseed mixed with 6 tablespoons of water

Directions:

1. Preheat your oven to 350°F. Line a few cupcake tins with pieces of parchment paper.
2. Pour all your ingredients into a blender and pulse until smooth.
3. Then pour batter into tins and put them into the oven.
4. Bake for 35 minutes or until it passes the toothpick test, then remove from the oven and set to cool on a cooling rack.

Nutrition: Calories: 197, Total Fat: 6g, Saturated Fat: 0g, Cholesterol: 0 mg, Sodium: 0 mg, Total Carbs: 33g, Fiber: 0g, Sugar: 16g, Protein: 3 g

355. Almost Classic Hummus

Preparation Time: 10 minutes | **Cooking Time:** 10 minutes | **Servings:** 2

Ingredients:

- 1/4 cup hulled pumpkin seeds
- 2 tablespoons of oil
- 1 cup canned chickpeas, rinsed well
- 3 tablespoons freshly squeezed lemon juice
- 1/2 teaspoon ground cumin
- 1/2 teaspoon sea salt
- 1 medium orange bell pepper, seeded and quartered

Directions:

1. Preheat broiler. Line a baking sheet with foil paper.
2. Place bell pepper pieces on baking sheet and broil for 8–10 minutes, or until tops begin to char.

3. Cool completely, then peel off and discard skins.
4. Add pumpkin seeds and oil to a food processor and blend to a paste consistency.
5. Add pepper pieces, chickpeas, lemon juice, cumin, and salt and blend well. Serve immediately or transfer to an airtight container and store in the refrigerator for up to 1 week.

Nutrition: Calories: 100, Total Fat: 5g, Saturated Fat: 0g, Cholesterol: 0 mg, Sodium: 103 mg, Total Carbs: 11g, Fiber: 3g, Sugar: 2g Protein: 4g

356. Carrot Dip

Preparation Time: 10 minutes | **Cooking Time:** 0 minute | **Servings:** 2

Ingredients:

- 1/4 teaspoon sesame oil
- 1 teaspoon orange juice
- 1 teaspoon pure maple syrup
- 1/4 teaspoon pure vanilla extract
- 1/4 teaspoon freshly grated gingerroot
- 1/8 teaspoon sea salt
- 1 large carrot, peeled and cut into 3 pieces

Directions:

1. Enjoy this dip with brown rice crackers, gluten-free pretzels, or raw low-FODMAP crudité (if tolerable) as a snack for two.
2. Or, if it's just for you, save the leftovers and use as a soup swirl-in, salad dressing, or sandwich spread.
3. Add all ingredients to a high-speed blender or food processor and process to a dip consistency.
4. Add water, 1 tablespoon at a time, to achieve desired thinness.

Nutrition: Calories: 86, Total Fat: 3.5g, Saturated Fat: 0g, Cholesterol: 0 mg, Sodium: 349 mg, Total Carbs: 13g, Fiber: 2g, Sugar: 4g, Protein: 0.715 g

357. Citrusy Salsa

Preparation Time: 10 minutes | **Cooking Time:** 0 minute | **Servings:** 2

Ingredients:

- 1 small lemon, peeled, seeded, and diced
- 1 small lime, peeled, seeded, and diced
- 1 small orange, peeled, seeded, and diced
- 1 small kiwi, peeled and diced
- 1 cup diced pineapple
- 1/2 teaspoon freshly grated gingerroot
- 1 tablespoon shredded unsweetened coconut

Directions:

1. Getting in your "five a day" is easy when you pile them all into one delicious salsa!
2. Serve with unsalted, gluten-free tortilla chips.
3. For a sweeter, less tart outcome, simply omit or reduce the lemon and/or lime.
4. Refrigerating this dish for a few hours will enhance its overall flavor.
5. Toss all ingredients in a medium bowl and serve.

Nutrition: Calories: 237, Total Fat: 3g, Saturated Fat: 0g, Cholesterol: 0 mg, Sodium: 10 mg, Total Carbs: 60g, Fiber: 12g, Sugar: 29g, Protein: 4 g

358. Chia Strawberry Popsicles

Preparation Time: 5 minutes | **Cooking Time:** 0 minute | **Servings:** 4

Ingredients:

- 1/2 cup water
- 1/2 cup strawberries
- 2 teaspoons chia seeds
- 1 tablespoon fresh lemon juice

Directions:

1. Add all ingredients into the blender and blend until smooth.
2. Pour blended mixture into the Popsicle molds and place in refrigerator until set.
3. Serve and enjoy.

Nutrition: Calories: 12, Total Fat: 0.5g, Saturated Fat: 0.1g, Protein: 0.4g, Carbs: 1.7g, Fiber: 0.4g, Sugar: 1g

359. Blueberry Sorbet

Preparation Time: 5 minutes | **Cooking Time:** 0 minute | **Servings:** 1

Ingredients:

- 7 oz frozen blueberries
- 1 teaspoon maple syrup
- 1 tablespoon fresh lemon juice

Directions:

1. Add all ingredients into the blender and blend until smooth.
2. Pour blended mixture into the air-tight container and place in refrigerator until firm.
3. Serve chilled and enjoy.

Nutrition: Calories: 135, Total Fat: 0.8g, Saturated Fat: 0.1g, Protein: 1.6g, Carbs: 33.5g, Fiber: 4.9g, Sugar: 24g

360. Strawberry Sorbet

Preparation Time: 5 minutes | **Cooking Time:** 0 minute | **Servings:** 4

Ingredients:

- 1/4 cup maple syrup
- 16 oz frozen strawberries, halved

Directions:

1. Add all ingredients into the blender and blend until smooth.
2. Pour blended mixture into the air-tight container and place in refrigerator until firm.
3. Serve chilled and enjoy.

Nutrition: Calories: 88, Total Fat: 0.4g, Saturated Fat: 0g, Protein: 0.8g, Carbs: 21.9g, Fiber: 2.3g, Sugar: 17.3g

361. Strawberry Gummies

Preparation Time: 5 minutes | **Cooking Time:** 15 minute | **Servings:** 2

Ingredients:

- 1/4 cup water

- ¼ cup gelatin
- 3 tablespoon maple syrup
- 2/3 cup fresh lemon juice
- 1 cup strawberries, chopped

Directions:
1. Add strawberries, water, and lemon juice into the blender and blend until pureed.
2. Pour blended mixture into the pan and heat over medium-low heat.
3. Slowly add gelatin and stir until gelatin is dissolved.
4. Once the gelatin is completely dissolved then stir in maple syrup.
5. Remove pan from heat and let it cool for 5 minutes.
6. Pour gelatin mixture into the candy mold and place in the refrigerator for 2 hours or until set.
7. Serve and enjoy.

Nutrition: Calories: 34,Total Fat: 0.2g, Saturated Fat: 0.1g, Protein: 0.5g, Carbs: 7.7g, Fiber: 0.3g, Sugar: 6.9g

362. Strawberry Ice Cream

Preparation Time: 5 minutes | **Servings:** 4 |
Cooking Time: 30 minutes

Ingredients:
- 2 small bananas, firm and frozen
- 7 oz strawberries, frozen
- 5 tbsp coconut yogurt
- 2 tbsp maple syrup
- 1 tsp vanilla extract

Directions:
1. Chop the frozen fruit into small pieces, then place the ingredients into a food processor. Blend until smooth, making sure to scrape down the sides.
2. Taste the mixture and add maple syrup or vanilla extract as desired. Serve soft or freeze for a few hours before serving. Serve with chocolate fudge sauce.

Nutrition: Calories 177, Fat 4g, Carbs 37, Protein 1.2g

363. Coconut Whipped Cream

Preparation Time: 5 minutes | **Cooking Time:** 30 minutes | **Servings:** 2

Ingredients:
- 1 (14-ounce) can coconut milk
- 1 tablespoon maple syrup
- 1 teaspoon alcohol-free vanilla extract
- 1/4 cup of corn syrup

Directions:
1. Chill can of coconut milk in refrigerator overnight. While can chills, coconut cream will separate from liquid. Once chilled, remove coconut milk from refrigerator and skim off thick white cream from top using a spoon.
2. Place cream in medium mixing bowl. Beat 1 minute or until creamy.
3. Add maple syrup, vanilla, and confectioners' sugar and mix 1 minute or until creamy.
4. To allow cream to set, refrigerate 30 minutes or longer. You can store cream in an airtight container in refrigerator up to 2 weeks.

Nutrition: Calories: 476, Fat: 42g, Protein: 4g, Sodium: 27mg, Carbs: 27.

364. Peppermint Patties

Preparation Time: 5 minutes | **Cooking Time:** 50 minutes | **Servings:** 8

Ingredients:
- 1/4 cup Caramel Sauce
- 1/4 teaspoon peppermint extract, divided
- 2 teaspoons arrowroot powder
- 1 cup Dark Chocolate Dip (see recipe in this chapter)

Directions:
1. Clear enough space in the freezer to fit a metal mini-muffin pan laid flat.
2. In a small bowl, combine Caramel Sauce with 1/8 teaspoon extract and arrowroot powder. Set aside to thicken, about 20 minutes.

3. In a small saucepan, warm Chocolate Dip. Remove from heat and stir in remaining extract.
4. Spoon 1 heaping teaspoon Chocolate Dip into each of 8 cups in a mini muffin pan. Set remaining dip aside. Carefully lay pan flat in freezer. Freeze for 10 minutes or until chocolate is completely firm.
5. Leave chocolate in the pan. Top each with 1/2 teaspoon peppermint/caramel mixture. Gently spread mixture in even circles, leaving a border of chocolate around each edge. Top evenly with another heaping teaspoon of Chocolate Dip, so all of the peppermint mixture is covered. Carefully return pan to freezer. Freeze for at least 20 minutes.
6. Remove pan from freezer, turn it over on a clean workspace, and firmly tap till all candies fall out. Transfer to an airtight container and store in refrigerator.

Nutrition: Calories: 240, Fat: 19g, Protein: 1.5g, Sodium: 3mg, Carbs: 20.

365. Kiwi Yogurt Freezer Bars

Preparation Time: 5 minutes | **Servings:** 6 |
Cooking Time: 0 Minutes

Ingredients:
- Freezing: Overnight
- 2 cups unsweetened almond milk
- 4 kiwis, peeled and chopped
- ½ cup lactose-free plain yogurt
- 4 packets stevia

Directions:
1. In a blender, combine the almond milk, kiwis, yogurt, and stevia. Process until smooth.
2. Pour the mixture into 6 ice pop molds.
3. Refrigerate overnight.

Nutrition: Calories: 59, Total Fat: 2g, Carbs: 10g, Sodium: 76mg, Protein: 2.

366. Easy Trail Mix

Preparation Time: 5 minutes | **Servings:** 4 |

Cooking Time: 0 Minutes

Ingredients:
- 1 cup dried bananas
- ½ cup raw unsalted almonds
- ¼ cup raw unsalted peanuts
- ¼ cup dried cranberries

Directions:
1. In a small bowl, mix all the ingredients.
2. Store in a resealable bag at room temperature for up to 1 month.

Nutrition: Calories: 158, Total Fat: 11g, Carbs: 13g, Sodium: 2mg, Protein: 5g

367. Caramel Sauce

Preparation Time: 5 minutes | **Cooking Time:** 10 minutes | **Servings:** 1

Ingredients:
- 1/3 cup maple syrup
- 1/3 cup filtered water
- 1 teaspoon lemon juice
- 1 tablespoon unrefined coconut oil, liquefied

Directions:
1. Grind the syrup in a coffee grinder.
2. Add lemon juice in a small saucepan over medium heat.
3. Bring just to a boil, then lower heat to a bubbling simmer. Stir constantly for 10 minutes, until sauce starts to thicken.
4. Remove from heat and stir in coconut oil.

Nutrition: Calories: 75, Fat: 3g, Protein: 0g, Sodium: 0mg, Carbs: 14g

368. Minty Melon Mélange

Preparation Time: 5 minutes | **Cooking Time:** 0 minutes | **Servings:** 4

Ingredients:
- 1 cup diced cantaloupe
- 1 cup diced honeydew melon
- 1 tablespoon chopped fresh mint leaves
- 1 tablespoon torn fresh basil leaves

Directions:

LOW FODMAP COOKBOOK - SUZANNE SCARRETT

1. Toss all ingredients together and serve.

Nutrition: Calories: 29, Fat: 0.148g, Protein: 0.625g, Sodium: 14mg, Carbs: 7.

369. Banana Coconut Nice Cream

Preparation Time: 5 minutes | **Cooking Time:** 0 minutes | **Servings:** 1

Ingredients:

- 1 ripe medium banana, frozen with skin on
- 1/4 teaspoon ground cinnamon
- 1/2 teaspoon shredded unsweetened coconut
- 1 tablespoon unsweetened almond milk

Directions:

1. Remove peel from banana.
2. Place banana and remaining ingredients in a blender or food processor and blend until smooth.
3. Enjoy immediately!

Nutrition: Calories: 117, Fat: 1g, Protein: 2g, Sodium: 9mg, Carbs: 28g

370. Salted Caramel Fondue

Preparation Time: 5 minutes | **Cooking Time:** 0 minutes | **Servings:** 1

Ingredients:

- 1/3 cup Caramel Sauce (see recipe in this chapter)
- 1/8 teaspoon pure vanilla extract
- 1/2 teaspoon sea salt
- 1/4 teaspoon arrowroot powder
- 1/2 cup Whipped Cream (see recipe in this chapter)

Directions:

1. In a small saucepan over medium-low heat, whisk Caramel Sauce with vanilla, salt, and arrowroot powder.
2. Fold in cream.
3. Transfer to a fondue pot and serve.

Nutrition: Calories: 100, Fat: 7g, Protein: 0g, Sodium: 150mg, Carbs: 9g

371. Banana Cookie Dough Nice Cream

Preparation Time: 5 minutes | **Cooking Time:** 0 minutes | **Servings:** 1

Ingredients:

- 1 ripe medium banana, frozen with skin on
- 1/4 teaspoon ground cinnamon
- 1/2 teaspoon shredded unsweetened coconut
- 1 tablespoon chocolate chip cookie dough (see Chocolate Chip Cookies recipe, Chapter 11), frozen

Directions:

1. Remove peel from banana.
2. Place banana, cinnamon, and coconut in blender and blend until smooth.
3. Cut frozen dough into chunks and stir into nice cream.
4. Enjoy immediately!

Nutrition: Calories: 109, Fat: 1g, Protein: 1g, Sodium: 1mg, Carbs: 28g

372. Broiled Spiced Orange

Preparation Time: 5 minutes | **Cooking Time:** 10 minutes | **Servings:** 1

Ingredients:

- 1 large orange
- 1/2 teaspoon freshly grated gingerroot, divided

Directions:

1. Preheat broiler. Line a baking sheet with foil.
2. Take a small slice off each end of orange. Slice orange through its middle. Set each orange half on a cutting board, exposed fruit side up. Cut around each orange segment, leaving segments intact. Sprinkle 1/4 teaspoon of ginger over each orange half. Place oranges—exposed fruit side up—onto baking sheet.

153

LOW FODMAP COOKBOOK - SUZANNE SCARRETT

3. Broil 2–4 minutes, until tops are just starting to brown. Cool for 1–2 minutes and serve warm.

Nutrition: Calories: 87, Fat: 0.23g, Protein: 2g, Sodium: 0.13mg, Carbs: 22g

373. Banana Ice Cream

Preparation Time: 5 minutes | **Cooking Time:** 0 Minutes | **Servings:** 2

Ingredients:
- 3 bananas, peeled and frozen
- 3 packets stevia
- ¼ teaspoon ground nutmeg

Directions:
1. In a blender or food processor, combine the bananas, stevia, and nutmeg.
2. Blend until smooth.

Nutrition: Calories: 106, Total Fat: <1g, Carbs: 27g, Sodium: 1mg, Protein: 1g

374. Coconut Cinnamon Popcorn

Preparation Time: 5 minutes | **Cooking Time:** 2 minutes | **Servings:** 2

Ingredients:

- 2 tablespoons coconut oil
- 1/2 tablespoon ground cinnamon
- 4 cups freshly popped natural popcorn (or 3 tablespoons popcorn kernels)

Directions:

1. Add coconut oil and cinnamon to a microwave-safe measuring cup.
2. Microwave 30 seconds or until coconut oil has melted. Stir to combine.
3. If making microwavable popcorn, carefully pour coconut and cinnamon mixture into bag, then shake well.
4. If making popcorn in a pot on the stove, once popcorn has popped, remove pot from stove and add oil mixture to popcorn as you shake pot back and forth.

Nutrition: Calories: 186, Fat: 14g, Protein: 2g, Sodium: 1mg, Carbs: 14g

375. Roasted Pumpkin Seeds

Preparation Time: 5 minutes | **Cooking Time:** 60 minutes | **Servings:** 1

Ingredients:
- 1 cup pumpkin seeds, rinsed and dried
- 1 tablespoon olive oil
- 1/2 teaspoon salt

Directions:
1. Preheat oven to 300°F. Line a rimmed baking sheet with parchment paper.
2. In a medium bowl, toss together all ingredients. Spread mixture in a single layer on baking sheet.
3. Bake 50–60 minutes, stirring every 15 minutes until seeds are crisp. Let cool completely before serving. Store at room temperature.

Nutrition: Calories: 101, Fat: 6g, Protein: 3g, Sodium: 701mg, Carbs: 8g

376. Chia Pudding

Preparation Time: 5 minutes | **Cooking Time:** 4 hours | **Servings:** 3-4

Ingredients:
- ¼ cup chia seeds
- 1 tbsp cocoa powder
- 1 tbsp peanut butter
- 1 tbsp maple syrup
- 1 can coconut milk

Directions:
1. Fill an airtight jar with all the ingredients.
2. Close the jar and shake, then remove the top and stir the ingredients.
3. Ensure that the bottom of the jar is clear.
4. Shake again and place in the fridge for a minimum of 4 hours.

Nutrition: Calories 386, Fat 10g, Carbs 73, Protein 6g

377. Sweet And Savory Popcorn

Preparation Time: 5 minutes| **Cooking Time:**5 Minutes|**Servings:** 4

Ingredients:
- ½ cup vegetable oil
- 1 cup popcorn kernels
- 2/3 cup of maple syrup
- 2 tsp salt, or to taste

Directions:
1. Blend together cranberries, butter, Greek yogurt, milk, banana, and chia seeds.
2. Add ice until the desired consistency is achieved.

Nutrition: Calories 258, Fat 16g, Carbs 24.8g, Protein 3.7g

378. Pineapple, Yogurt On Rice Cakes

Preparation Time: 5 minutes| **Cooking Time:**12 Minutes|**Servings:** 1

Ingredients:
- 2 rice cakes
- ⅓ cup fresh pineapple, sliced
- 2 tbsp Greek yogurt
- ¼ tsp chia seeds, optional
- 1 tsp oil, used to prevent the pineapple from burning

Directions:
1. Spray the pineapple slices with oil, then place them on a tray in the oven and bake for 5 minutes on each side.
2. Cut into chunky pieces.
3. Spread the yogurt over the rice cake and top with pineapple and chia seeds.

Nutrition: Calories 169, Fat 1.5g, Carbs 35.6g, Protein 3.8g

379. Prosciutto-wrapped Cantaloupe

Preparation Time: 5 minutes|**Cooking Time:** 0 Minutes|**Servings:** 4

Ingredients:

- 8 (½- to 1-inch-thick) cantaloupe wedges, rind removed
- 8 thin prosciutto slices

Directions:
1. Tap each melon wedge in a slice of prosciutto and secure it with a toothpick.
2. Chill or serve immediately.

Nutrition: Calories 73, Fat 2g, Carbs 4g, Sodium 517 mg, Protein 9g

380. Banana Almond Nice Cream

Preparation Time: 5 minutes|**Cooking Time:** 0 minutes|**Servings:** 1

Ingredients:
- 1 ripe medium banana, frozen with skin on
- 1/2 cup unsweetened almond milk
- 1 tablespoon almond butter

Directions:
1. Remove peel from banana. Place banana and remaining ingredients in a blender or food processor and blend until smooth.
2. Enjoy immediately!

Nutrition: Calories: 265, Fat: 11g, Protein: 9g, Sodium: 137mg, Carbs: 38.

381. Buttercream Lactose-free Icing

Preparation Time: 5 minutes|**Cooking Time:** 30 minutes|**Servings:** 4

Ingredients:
- 1/2 cup dairy-free margarine
- 2 cups of glucose syrup
- 1/2 teaspoon alcohol-free vanilla extract
- 1 tablespoon unsweetened almond milk
- 1/2 tablespoon lactose-free plain yogurt

Directions:
1. Using a stand mixer or an electric hand mixer with a large mixing bowl, cream margarine at low speed and gradually add glucose syrup until combined.

2. Setting speed to high, add remaining ingredients and beat until smooth and creamy. Be sure to chill 30–60 minutes in refrigerator before using.

Nutrition: Calories: 176, Fat: 9g, Protein: 0g, Sodium: 108mg, Carbs: 24.

382. Warm Lemon Tapioca Pudding

Preparation Time: 5 minutes | **Cooking Time:** 30 minutes | **Servings:** 6

Ingredients:

- 4 lemons
- 4 cups (1 liter) low-fat milk, lactose-free milk, or suitable plant-based milk
- ½ cup (100 g) pearl tapioca or sago
- ⅓ cup (75 ml) maple syrup

Directions:

1. Using a vegetable peeler, slice the zest of all 4 lemons into ¾-inch (2 cm) strips.
2. Juice the lemons until you have ½ cup juice.
3. Combine the milk and lemon zest in a medium saucepan and bring to a simmer over high heat.
4. Reduce the heat to low and simmer for 2 minutes.
5. Remove and discard the lemon zest.
6. Add the tapioca to the milk, stirring well to combine.
7. Simmer over low heat, stirring regularly, for 20 to 25 minutes, until the tapioca resembles translucent jellylike balls.
8. Remove from the heat. Add syrup and lemon juice and pour into six glass dessert dishes. Serve immediately.

Nutrition: Calories 161, Protein 5g, Fat 2g, Carbs 32g, Sodium 83 mg

383. Dark Chocolate Dip

Preparation Time: 5 minutes | **Cooking Time:** 10 minutes | **Servings:** 3

Ingredients:

- ½ cup unrefined coconut oil, liquefied
- ½ cup raw cacao powder
- 1 tablespoon pure maple syrup
- ½ cup dark chocolate chips

Directions:

1. Warm coconut oil in a small saucepan over low heat. Whisk in cacao powder and maple syrup.
2. Add chocolate chips and stir to melt.
3. Remove from heat and serve or use as a coating.

Nutrition: Calories: 250, Fat: 23g, Protein: 2g, Sodium: 3mg, Carbs: 15g

384. Chocolate Truffles

Preparation Time: 5 minutes | **Cooking Time:** 15 minutes | **Servings:** 2

Ingredients:

- 7 ounces (200 g) gluten-free vanilla cookies, finely crushed (about 2 cups)
- ⅓ cup (35 g) unsweetened cocoa powder
- ⅓ cup (80 ml) sweetened condensed milk
- 2 tablespoons rum or brandy (optional)
- 1½ cups (150 g) gluten-free chocolate sprinkles

Directions:

1. Mix together the crushed cookies and cocoa in a medium bowl.
2. Add the condensed milk and rum (if using) and mix with your hands to form a firm dough.
3. Pour the chocolate sprinkles into a shallow bowl.
4. Shape teaspoons of the truffle mixture into balls with your hands.
5. Toss in the chocolate sprinkles to coat.
6. Refrigerate until firm.

Nutrition: Calories 99, Protein 1g, Fat 2g, Carbs 20g, Sodium 29 mg

385. Sweet Potato Pudding

Preparation Time: 5 minutes | **Cooking Time:** 50 minutes | **Servings:** 4

Ingredients:

- 2 large, sweet potatoes, washed
- 1 (14.5-ounce) can coconut milk, refrigerated
- 1/2 teaspoon pure vanilla extract
- 1 tablespoon pure maple syrup
- 1/4 teaspoon ground cinnamon

Directions:

1. Preheat oven to 400°F. Poke a few holes in each sweet potato and place in a small, lined baking dish. Roast the sweet potatoes for 50 minutes. Refrigerate overnight.
2. The next day, scoop out the sweet potato flesh and add to a food processor.
3. Open the can of coconut milk and separate the liquid from the solid. Add solid to the food processor, along with the vanilla and maple syrup. (Save liquid from coconut milk for a smoothie or other use.) Blend well.
4. Scoop into pudding cups. Serve immediately, or store in coldest part of refrigerator. Sprinkle with cinnamon just before serving.

Nutrition: Calories: 182, Fat: 11g, Protein: 2g, Sodium: 51mg, Carbs: 21g

386. Chocolate–peanut Butter Balls

Preparation Time: 5 minutes | **Cooking Time:** 10 minutes | **Servings:** 4

Ingredients:

- ½ cup sugar-free natural peanut butter
- ¼ cup unsalted butter, at room temperature
- 1 cup of corn syrup
- 1 cup semi-sweet chocolate chips
- 2 tablespoons coconut oil

Directions:

1. Line a baking sheet with parchment paper and set it aside.
2. In a large bowl, stir together the peanut butter, butter, and corn sugar until well mixed.
3. Form the mixture into about 16 tablespoon-size balls.
4. In a medium saucepan over low heat, melt the chocolate chips and coconut oil for about 5 minutes, stirring constantly until melted and smooth.
5. Dip the balls in the chocolate mixture and place on the prepared sheet.
6. Freeze for 10 minutes to set the chocolate coating.

Nutrition: Calories: 165, Total Fat: 11g, Carbs: 15g, Sodium: 92mg, Protein: 2.

387. Dark Chocolate–covered Pretzels

Preparation Time: 5 minutes | **Cooking Time:** 30 minutes | **Servings:** 12

Ingredients:

- 3 ounces dark chocolate chips
- 1 tablespoon vegetable shortening
- 12 gluten-free mini pretzels

Directions:

1. Melt chocolate and shortening over a double boiler.
2. Stir until smooth and combined.
3. Remove from heat.
4. Dip each pretzel in chocolate, allowing excess to drip off.
5. Place on a cookie sheet lined with wax paper and chill in refrigerator until firm.

Nutrition: Calories: 66, Fat: 3g, Protein: 1g, Sodium: 82mg, Carbs: 9g

388. Parmesan Potato Wedges

Preparation Time: 5 minutes | **Cooking Time:** 25 Minutes | **Servings:** 4

Ingredients:

- 4 red potatoes, cut into wedges
- 2 tablespoons Oil

- ¼ cup grated Parmesan cheese
- ½ teaspoon sea salt
- ¼ teaspoon freshly ground black pepper

Directions:
1. Preheat the oven to 425°F.
2. In a small bowl, combine the potatoes, oil, Parmesan cheese, salt, and pepper and toss to coat the potatoes with the cheese and oil. Spread the potatoes in a single layer on a rimmed baking sheet.
3. Bake for about 25 minutes, or until the potatoes are tender.

Nutrition: Calories: 232, Total Fat: 9g, Carbs: 34g, Sodium: 313mg, Protein: 6g

389.   Carrot Parsnip Chips

Preparation Time: 5 minutes | **Servings:** 3

Cooking Time: 35 Minutes

Ingredients:
- 1 large parsnip, peeled and ends cut off
- 1 large carrot, peeled and ends cut off
- 2 tsp olive oil
- Pinch of salt
- 1 tsp thyme leaves

Directions:
1. Preheat the oven to 325°F.
2. Oil a baking tray lightly.
3. Peel the carrot and parsnip into long thin pieces and place onto the tray.
4. Drizzle with oil and season.
5. Cook for 35 minutes, turning the vegetables 2 times during cooking.

Nutrition: Calories 386, Fat 10g, Carbs 73g, Protein 6g

390.   Whipped Cream

Preparation Time: 5 minutes | **Cooking Time:** 15 minutes | **Servings:** 10

Ingredients:
- 1-pint heavy whipping cream

Directions:
1. Place a metal mixing bowl into the refrigerator for 10 minutes.

2. Remove bowl, add cream, and whip on medium-high speed for 3–5 minutes, or until stiff peaks form.

Nutrition: Calories: 138, Fat: 15g, Protein: 1g, Sodium: 15mg, Carbs 1g

391.   Summer Popsicle

Preparation Time: 5 minutes | **Cooking Time:** 2 minutes | Servings: 4

Ingredients:
- 4 carrots, large
- 3 oranges, large
- 1 lime, juiced
- 1 tsp orange zest
- 2 tbsp corn syrup

Directions:
1. Grate the carrots.
2. In a clean cloth, wrap the carrots and squeeze the juice into a bowl.
3. Zest an orange. Juice the oranges and lime into the bowl of carrot juice and mix the zest in.
4. Add the corn syrup. If the mixture tastes too sour, add more syrup, then pour into popsicle molds.
5. Place in the freezer overnight.
6. If using wooden sticks, place them in after 2 hours in the freezer.

Nutrition: Calories 156, Fat 0.5g, Carbs 38.9g, Protein 2.7g

392.   Banana Nut Boat

Preparation Time: 5 minutes | **Cooking Time:** 10 minutes | **Servings:** 1

Ingredients:

- 1 ripe medium banana, cut in half lengthwise
- 1 tablespoon almond butter
- 1 tablespoon shredded unsweetened coconut

Directions:

1. Place banana cut side up on a plate or shallow dish.
2. Spread on almond butter.
3. Sprinkle with coconut.

Nutrition: Calories: 217, Fat: 10g, Protein: 5g, Sodium: 76mg, Carbs: 31g

393.   Vanilla Frosting

Preparation Time: 5 minutes | **Cooking Time:** 0 minutes | **Servings:** 1

Ingredients:

- 2 cups maple syrup
- 2 tablespoons butter, softened
- 2 tablespoons lactose-free milk
- 1/2 teaspoon alcohol-free vanilla extract

Directions:

1. In a medium bowl, combine maple syrup, butter, milk, and vanilla.
2. Beat on medium speed until smooth and fluffy.
3. Place in an air-tight container in refrigerator for 3–5 days.

Nutrition: Calories 1008, Fat 24g, Protein 1g, Sodium 18 mg, Carbs 203g, Sugar 203g

394.   Candied Ginger Frosting

Preparation Time: 5 minutes | **Cooking Time:** 10 minutes | **Servings:** 2

Ingredients:

- 1/2 cup agave syrup
- 3 tablespoons butter, softened
- 3 tablespoons unrefined coconut oil, softened
- 1/4 teaspoon freshly grated ginger
- 2 tablespoons Whipped Cream (see recipe in this chapter)

Directions:

1. Add agave syrup to a coffee grinder in 1/4-cup batches and process to a powdered state.
2. Cream agave syrup, butter, oil, ginger, and whipped cream in a mixer until smooth.

Nutrition: Calories: 92, Fat: 7g, Protein: 0g, Sodium: 1mg, Carbs: 8g

395.   Fruit And Cheese Crostini

Preparation Time: 5 minutes | **Cooking Time:** 5 minutes | **Servings:** 2

Ingredients:

- 2 slices gluten-free bread, lightly toasted
- 2 tablespoons frozen cranberries, thawed
- 1" cube Camembert cheese, quartered
- 1/4 teaspoon dried thyme
- 1/2 teaspoon pure maple syrup

Directions:

1. Preheat broiler. Line a baking sheet with foil.
2. Using a round cookie cutter, cut circles out of each slice of toast.
3. Top each round with 1 tablespoon cranberries, two quarters of cheese, and sprinkle of thyme.
4. Place rounds on lined baking sheet.
5. Broil for 1–2 minutes, or until cheese melts.
6. Drizzle with maple syrup and serve immediately.

Nutrition: Calories: 100, Fat: 0.6g, Protein: 4g, Sodium: 209mg, Carbs: 20g

396.   Dark Chocolate Glaze

Preparation Time: 5 minutes | **Cooking Time:** 0 minutes | **Servings:** 3

Ingredients:

- 2 tablespoons unsweetened cocoa powder
- 3/4 cup corn syrup
- 11/2 tablespoons lactose-free milk
- 1 teaspoon alcohol-free vanilla extract

Directions:

1. In a medium bowl, whisk together cocoa powder and corn syrup.
2. Gradually add milk and vanilla. Whisk until smooth.
3. Add more milk if necessary to ensure glaze is the right consistency for dipping.
4. Refrigerate for up to 7 days.

Nutrition: Calories: 29, Fat: 0g, Protein: 0g, Sodium: 1mg, Carbs: 7g

397. Paleo Fudge

Preparation Time: 5 minutes | **Cooking Time:** 30 minutes | **Servings:** 4

Ingredients:

- 1/2 cup coconut oil
- 1/2 cup smooth peanut butter
- 1/2 cup unsweetened cocoa powder
- 1/4 cup maple syrup
- 1/2 teaspoon alcohol-free vanilla extract

Directions:

1. Allow coconut oil to come to room temperature or heat it quickly in microwave to melt.
2. Then blend coconut oil with remaining ingredients in a food processor or blender until smooth.
3. Place 10 muffin liners on a baking sheet or wide plate.
4. Fill each muffin liner 1/2" full of fudge mixture.
5. Chill 30 minutes or freeze 10 minutes.
6. When firm, remove and cut into 10 pieces. Store fudge in between pieces of wax paper at room temperature in an airtight container 1–2 weeks; store in refrigerator 2–3 weeks; store in freezer 3 months if properly wrapped (store in bags within an airtight container to prevent ice crystals and freezer burn).

Nutrition: Calories: 203, Fat: 18g, Protein: 4g, Sodium: 61mg, Carbs: 10g

398. Strawberry Tart Filling

Preparation Time: 5 minutes | **Cooking Time:** 30 minutes | **Servings:** 2

Ingredients:
- 3 cups hulled strawberries, divided
- 1 tablespoon maple syrup
- 1/2 teaspoon balsamic vinegar

Directions:
1. Purée 1 cup berries in a food processor. Slice remaining berries in half, leaving the smallest berries whole.
2. In a large bowl, mix sliced berries with purée and toss with maple syrup and vinegar.
3. Set aside to macerate (soften) for 30 minutes, stirring once or twice.

Nutrition: Calories: 47, Fat: 0g, Protein: 1g, Sodium: 1mg, Carbohydrates: 12g

399. Raspberry Curd

Preparation time: 10 minutes | **Cooking time:** 5 minutes | **Servings:** 4

Ingredients:
- 1 C. glucose syrup
- 12 oz. raspberries
- 2 egg yolks
- 2 tbsp. lemon juice
- 2 tbsp. butter

Directions
1. Put the raspberries into the Instant Pot. Add the syrup and lemon juice, stir, cover, and cook on the Manual setting for 2 minutes.
2. Release the pressure for 5 minutes, uncover the Instant Pot, strain the raspberries and discard the seeds.
3. In a bowl, mix the egg yolks with raspberries and stir well.
4. Return this to the Instant Pot, set it on Sauté mode, simmer for 2 minutes, add the butter, stir, and transfer to a container. Serve cold.

Nutrition: Calories: 110, Fat: 4g, Fiber: 0g, Carbs: 16g, Protein: 1g

400. Pear Jam

Preparation time: 10 minutes | **Cooking time:** 4 minutes | b12
Ingredients
- 8 pears, cored, and cut into quarters
- 2 apples, peeled, cored, and cut into quarters

- ¼ C. apple juice
- 1 tsp. cinnamon, ground

Directions:

1. In the Instant Pot, mix the pears with apples, cinnamon, and apple juice, stir, cover, and cook on the Manual setting for 4 minutes.
2. Release the pressure naturally, uncover the Instant Pot, blend using an immersion blender, divide the jam into jars, and keep it in a cold place until you serve it.

Nutrition: Calories: 90, Fat: 0g, Fiber: 1g, Carbs: 20g, Sugar: 20g, Protein: 0g

401.   Berry Compote

Preparation time: 10 minutes|**Cooking time:** 5 minutes|**Servings:** 8

Ingredients:

- 1 C. blueberries
- 2 C. strawberries, sliced
- 2 tbsp. lemon juice
- ¾ C. corn syrup
- 1 tbsp. cornstarch
- 1 tbsp. water

Directions:

1. In the Instant Pot, mix the blueberries with lemon juice and corn syrup, stir, cover, and cook on the Manual setting for 3 minutes.
2. Release the pressure naturally for 10 minutes and uncover the Instant Pot.
3. In a bowl, mix the cornstarch with water, stir well, and add to the Instant Pot.
4. Stir, set the Instant Pot on Sauté mode, and cook compote for 2 minutes.
5. Divide into jars and keep in the refrigerator until you serve it.

Nutrition: Calories: 260, Fat: 13g, Fiber: 3g, Carbs: 23g, Protein: 3g

402.   Key Lime Pie

Preparation time: 10 minutes|**Cooking time:** 15 minutes|**Servings:** 6

Ingredients:
For the crust:

- 1 tbsp. corn syrup
- 3 tbsp. butter, melted
- 5 graham crackers, crumbled

For the filling:

- 4 egg yolks
- 14 oz. milk, canned and condensed
- ½ C. key lime juice
- ⅓ C. sour cream
- Vegetable oil cooking spray
- 1 C. water
- 2 tbsp. key lime zest, grated

Directions:

1. In a bowl, whisk the egg yolks well. Add the milk gradually and stir again.
2. Add the lime juice, sour cream, and lime zest and stir again.
3. In another bowl, whisk the butter with the graham crackers and corn syrup, stir well, and spread on the bottom of a springform greased with some cooking spray.
4. Cover the pan with some aluminum foil and place it in the steamer basket of the Instant Pot.
5. Add the water to the Instant Pot, cover, and cook on the Manual setting for 15 minutes.
6. Release the pressure for 10 minutes, uncover the Instant Pot, take the pie out, set aside to cool down, and keep it in the refrigerator for 4 hours before slicing and serving it.

Nutrition: Calories: 400, Fat: 21g, Fiber: 0.5g, Carbs: 34g, Protein: 7g

403.   Fruit Cobbler

Preparation time: 10 minutes|**Cooking time:** 12 minutes|**Servings:** 4

Ingredients:

- 3 apples, cored and cut into chunks
- 2 pears, cored and cut into chunks
- 1½ C. hot water

- ¼ C. maple syrup
- 1 C. steel-cut oats
- 1 tsp. cinnamon, ground
- ice cream, for serving

Directions:
1. Put the apples and pears into the Instant Pot and mix with hot water, maple syrup, oats, and cinnamon.
2. Stir, cover, and cook on the Manual setting for 12 minutes.
3. Release the pressure naturally, transfer

Nutrition: Calories: 170, Fat: 4g, Carbs: 10g, Fiber: 2.4g, Protein: 3g, Sugar: 7g

404. Stuffed Peaches

Preparation time: 10 minutes | **Cooking time:** 4 minutes | **Servings:** 6
Ingredients:
- 6 peaches, pits, and flesh removed
- Salt
- ¼ C. coconut flour
- ¼ C. maple syrup
- 2 tbsp. coconut butter
- ½ tsp. cinnamon, ground
- 1 tsp. almond extract
- 1 C. water

Directions:
1. In a bowl, mix the flour with the salt, syrup, butter, cinnamon, and half of the almond extract and stir well.
2. Fill the peaches with this mix, place them in the steamer basket of the Instant Pot, add the water and the rest of the almond

extract to the Instant Pot, cover, and cook on the Steam setting for 4 minutes.
3. Release the pressure naturally, divide the stuffed peaches on serving plates, and serve warm.

Nutrition: Calories: 160, Fat: 6.7g, Carbs: 12g, Fiber: 3g, Sugar: 11g, Protein: 4g

405. Peach Compote

Preparation time: 10 minutes | **Cooking time:** 3 minutes | **Servings:** 6
Ingredients:
- 8 peaches, pitted and chopped
- 6 tbsp. agave syrup
- 1 tsp. cinnamon, ground
- 1 tsp. vanilla extract
- 1 vanilla bean, scraped
- 2 tbsp. Grape Nuts cereal

Directions:
1. Put the peaches into the Instant Pot and mix with the agave syrup, cinnamon, vanilla bean, and vanilla extract.
2. Stir well, cover the Instant Pot and cook on the Manual setting for 3 minutes.
3. Release the pressure for 10 minutes, add the cereal, stir well, transfer the compote to bowls
4. Serve.

Nutrition: Calories: 100, Fat: 2g, Carbs: 11g, Fiber: 1g, Sugar: 10g, Protein: 1

Drinks

406. Low-Fodmap Green Smoothie

Preparation Time: 5 minute | **Cooking Time:** 0 minute | **Servings:** 2

Ingredients:

- 2 cups of ice cubes
- A cup of seedless green grapes
- 2 cups of baby spinach
- 1 kiwi (peeled and cut into chunks)
- 1 big cucumber (cut into chunks)
- 2 tablespoons of water

Directions:

1. Put all the ingredients (except ice) into a blender, pulse on medium for 3-5 minutes, then increase the speed and blend until pureed and smooth.
2. Add about half the amount of ice and pulse again until frosty.
3. Add some more ice and pulse until the ice is broken into tiny little chunks, and then serve immediately.
4. You could also do the recipe without ice and put in whole ice cubes when you are ready to drink.
5. So it won't be frosty, but it will

Nutrition: Calories: 132, Total Fat: 1g, Saturated Fat: 0g, Cholesterol: 0 mg, Sodium: 0 mg, Total Carbs: 33g, Fiber: 0g, Sugar: 25g, Protein: 3g

407. Low-Fodmap Turmeric, Ginger Lemon Juice

Preparation Time: 5 minutes | **Cooking Time:** 0 minutes | **Servings:** 7

Ingredients:

- 4 cups of water
- 30 grams of fresh ginger (cut into pieces)
- 5 lemons (peeled)
- A quarter cup of maple syrup
- 30 grams of fresh turmeric root (cut into pieces)

Directions:

1. Put the ingredients (except water and maple syrup) into a juicer.
2. Preferably one at a time.
3. Once you have gotten the juice, pour it into a blender and add the rest of the ingredients, pulse on high for 30 seconds to a minute.
4. Serve over ice, or store in lidded jars for later.

Nutrition: Calories: 161, Total Fat: 7g, Saturated Fat: 0g, Cholesterol: 0 mg, Sodium: 0 mg, Total Carbs: 2g, Fiber: 0g, Sugar: 7g, Protein: 10g

408. Low-Fodmap Carrot Juice

Preparation Time: 10 minutes | **Cooking Time:** 5 minutes | **Servings:** 2

Ingredients:

- A small piece of ginger (peeled)
- 1 tablespoon of bee pollen
- 10 carrots (cut off the tops)
- 4 oranges (cut and peel)
- Ice cubes

Directions:

1. Run your carrots, oranges and ginger through a juicer.
2. Once they are all juiced, put them into a bowl and add the bee pollen, whisk until well combined. Serve over ice.

Nutrition: Calories: 202, Total Fat: 1g, Saturated Fat: 0g, Cholesterol: 0 mg, Sodium: 0 mg, Total Carbs: 47g, Fiber: 0g, Sugar: 20g, Protein: 5g

409. Low-Fodmap Tomato Juice

Preparation Time: 5 minutes | **Cooking Time:** 0 minute | **Servings:** 3
Ingredients:

- 5 grams of horseradish
- A dash of Tabasco
- 50ml of vodka (optional)
- A quarter cup of lemon juice
- 1 cup of tomato juice
- Pepper and salt to taste
- A dash of Worcestershire sauce
- Half a tablespoon of dry Sherry
- 2 grams of celery seed

Directions:

1. Pour all ingredients into a blender (if it is not enough, do it in batches), set on high and pulse for 2-3 minutes.
2. Transfer to a pitcher and serve over ice.

Nutrition: Calories: 180, Total Fat: 0.6g, Saturated Fat: 0g, Cholesterol: 0 mg, Sodium: 0 mg, Total Carbs: 11g, Fiber: 0g, Sugar: 10g, Protein: 2g

410. Low-Fodmap Lemonade

Preparation Time: 15 minutes | **Cooking Time:** 0 minute | **Servings:** 10
Ingredients:

- 8 cups of water
- 1 cup of glucose syrup
- 2 cups of freshly squeezed lemon juice

Directions:

1. Pour a cup of water into a sauce pan, add the glucose syrup and set over medium heat and allow boiling.
2. Remove from heat and allow cooling for about 30 minutes.
3. Once cooled, pour into a pitcher; add the rest of the water, and lemon juice.
4. Stir and serve over ice, or refrigerate until ready to consume.

Nutrition: Calories: 76, Total Fat: 0.2g, Saturated Fat: 0g, Sodium: 0 mg, Total Carbs: 2g, Fiber: 0g, Sugar: 4g, Protein: 0.8g

411. Cranberry Festive Water

Preparation Time: 5 minutes | **Cooking Time:** 0 minute | **Servings:** 1
Ingredients:

- 3 freeze-dried cranberries
- 1 teaspoon lemon zest, freshly grated
- 1 tablespoon lemon juice

Directions:

1. Add all ingredients to an 8-ounce glass of water and serve. Water for Optimal Digestion
2. Drinking plenty of water is essential for digestion.
3. Water helps to keep stool moist and moving! If you don't drink an adequate amount of water, your body will draw water out of the stool, leaving you at risk for constipation.
4. It is best to drink filtered tap or bottled water whenever possible to reduce your exposure to toxins.

Nutrition: Calories: 4, Total Fat: 0.06g, Saturated Fat: 0g, Cholesterol: 0 mg, Sodium: 3 mg, Total Carbs: 1g, Fiber: 0.185g, Sugar: 0.476g, Protein: 0.11g

412. Orange Ginger Festive Water

Preparation Time: 5 minutes | **Cooking Time:** 0 minute | **Servings:** 1
Ingredients:

- 2 orange slices
- 1 teaspoon freshly grated ginger
- 1 piece candied ginger for garnish

Directions:

1. Add all ingredients to an 8-ounce glass of water and serve.

Nutrition: Calories: 45, Total Fat: 0.169g, Saturated Fat: 0g, Cholesterol: 0 mg, Sodium: 5 mg, Total Carbs: 11g, Fiber: 1g, Sugar: 9g, Protein: 0.642 g

413. Berry Banana Green Smoothie

Preparation Time: 10 minutes | **Cooking Time:** 0 minute | **Servings:** 2

Ingredients:
- 1 cup rice milk
- 1 cup packed baby spinach leaves
- 1 medium firm banana
- 1/3 cup frozen strawberries
- 1/3 cup frozen blueberries
- 1/3 cup frozen raspberries

Directions:
1. Combine all ingredients in blender and run until smooth.
2. Frozen Bananas You no longer need to throw out bananas that get too ripe, too fast.
3. Simply peel and freeze in an airtight freezer bag, where they will keep for 6–8 months.
4. Frozen bananas make a great base for smoothies.

Nutrition: Calories: 194, Total Fat: 3g, Saturated Fat: 0g, Cholesterol: 0 mg, Sodium: 75 mg, Total Carbs: 40g, Fiber: 6g, Sugar: 26g Protein: 6g

414. Peanut Butter Green Smoothie

Preparation Time: 10 minutes | **Cooking Time:** 0 minute | **Servings:** 2

Ingredients:
- 2 cups kale (2 leaves)
- 1 cup rice milk
- 1 tablespoon raw cacao powder
- 1 tablespoon natural peanut butter
- 1 firm medium banana

Directions:
1. Place kale in blender with rice milk. Blend until smooth.
2. If necessary, pour mixture through strainer, then return to blender.
3. Add all other ingredients to blender and blend until smooth.

Nutrition: Calories: 205, Total Fat: 7g, Saturated Fat: 0g, Cholesterol: 0 mg, Sodium: 129 mg, Total Carbs: 31g, Fiber: 5g, Sugar: 13g, Protein: 9g

415. Turmeric Pineapple Smoothie

Preparation Time: 5 minutes | **Cooking Time:** 0 minute | **Servings:** 1

Ingredients:
- 1/3 banana
- ¾ cup almond milk
- ¼ teaspoon turmeric
- ½ cup pineapple chunks
- ¼ teaspoon ground ginger
- 2 tablespoons protein powder

Directions:
1. Add all ingredients into the blender and blend until smooth.
2. Serve and enjoy.

Nutrition: Calories: 514, Total Fat: 43.2g, Saturated Fat: 38.1g, Protein: 10.1g, Carbs: 30.5g, Fiber: 6.3g, Sugar: 19g

416. Tropical Smoothie

Preparation Time: 5 minutes | **Cooking Time:** 0 minute | **Servings:** 1

Ingredients:
- 4 strawberries
- 2/3 unripe Banana
- 6 oz pineapple juice
- 1 teaspoon collagen
- 1 tablespoon coconut oil

Directions:
1. Add all ingredients into the blender and blend until smooth.
2. Serve and enjoy.

Nutrition: Calories: 319, Total Fat: 14.2g, Saturated Fat: 11.9g, Protein: 7.8g, Carbs: 43.6g, Fiber: 3.4g, Sugar: 29g

417. Blueberry Smoothie

Preparation Time: 5 minutes | **Cooking Time:** 0 minute | **Servings:** 1

Ingredients:
- 1/3 banana
- 10 blueberries
- ½ cup spinach
- ¼ cup ice cubes
- 2 tablespoons chia seeds
- ½ cup unsweetened almond milk

Directions:
1. Add all ingredients into the blender and blend until smooth.
2. Serve and enjoy.

Nutrition: Calories: 517, Total Fat: 8.9g, Saturated Fat: 0.7g, Protein: 9.6g, Carbs: 112g, Fiber: 18.3g, Sugar: 72.4g

418. Cinnamon Carrot Milkshake

Preparation Time: 5 minutes | **Cooking Time:** 0 minute | **Servings:** 1
Ingredients:
- ¼ cup collagen
- ¼ teaspoon turmeric
- ½ cup coconut cream
- ½ teaspoon cinnamon
- 1 tablespoon maple syrup
- ¼ teaspoon ginger powder
- 1 ½ cups unsweetened coconut milk
- 2 cups carrots, peeled, chopped, and cooked

Directions:
1. Add all ingredients into the blender and blend until smooth and creamy.
2. Serve and enjoy.

Nutrition: Calories: 249, Total Fat: 17.4g, Saturated Fat: 15.7g, Protein: 3.1g, Carbs: 23.2g, Fiber: 5.2g, Sugar: 13.4g

419. Mango and Banana Smoothie

Preparation time: 5 minutes | **Cooking time:** 0 minute | **Servings:** 2
Ingredients
- 1 C. spring water
- 2 C. greens
- ½ banana, peeled
- 1 fresh mango, peeled, destoned, sliced

Directions:
1. Take a high-powered blender, switch it on, and then place all the ingredients inside, in order.
2. Cover the blender with its lid and then pulse at high speed for 1 minute or more until.

Nutrition: Calories: 134.5, Carbs:29.6g, Fat: 1g, Fiber: 4.3g, Protein:1.7,

420. Berries and Sea Moss Smoothie

Preparation time: 5 minutes | **Cooking time:** 0 minute | **Servings:** 2
Ingredients
- 1 C. coconut water
- 2 C. lettuce leaves
- 1 banana, peeled
- 1 C. berries, mixed
- 1 tbsp. sea moss
- 2 key limes, juiced

Directions:
1. Take a high-powered blender, switch it on, and then place all the ingredients inside, in order.
2. Cover the blender with its lid and then pulse at high speed for 1 minute or more until.

Nutrition: Calories: 163, Caarbs:35g, Fat: 0.9g, Fiber: 10g, Protein: 3.7g

421. Raspberry and Chard Smoothie

Preparation time: 5 minutes | **Cooking time:** 0 minute | **Servings:** 2
Ingredients:
- 2 C. coconut water
- 2 C. Swiss chards
- 2 key limes, juiced
- 2 C. fresh whole raspberries

Directions:
1. Take a high-powered blender, switch it

on, and then place all the ingredients inside, in order.

2. Cover the blender with its lid and then pulse at high speed for 1 minute or more until.

Nutrition: Calories: 137, Carbs:27g, Fat:1.4g, Fiber:13.2g, Protein: 3.4g,

422. Apple, Berries, and Kale Smoothie

Preparation time: 5 minutes | **Cooking time:** 0 minute | **Servings:** 2

Ingredients:

- 1 C. spring water
- 1 C. berries, mixed
- 2 C. kale leaves, fresh
- 1 large apple, cored

Directions:

1. Take a high-powered blender, switch it on, and then place all the ingredients inside, in order.
2. Cover the blender with its lid and then pulse at high speed for 1 minute or more until.

Nutrition: Calories: 112, Carbs:24.4g, Fat:0.7g, Fiber: 7.2g, Protein: 2g

423. Orange Banana Alkaline Smoothie

Preparation time: 10 minutes | **Cooking time:** 0 minutes | **Servings:** 2

Ingredients:

- ½ C. coconut water
- 1 C. water

- 2 medium-size bananas
- 4 oranges, peeled
- ¼ tsp. bromide plus powder
- 2 tsp. light-colored agave syrup

Directions:

1. Mash the banana and pour all ingredients into a blender.
2. Blend for 30 seconds at a time until the mixture is smooth.
3. You may dilute with water to derive the desired thickness.
4. Serve in a cup and add some ice cubes or place in a refrigerator.

Nutrition: Calories 104, Protein 14g, Sugar 8g, Fiber 10g

424. Water Melon Cucumber Smoothie

Preparation time: 10 minutes | **Cooking time:** 0 minute | **Servings:** 2

Ingredients:

- 1 C. watermelon, peeled, and chopped into bits
- 1 medium-sized cucumber, chopped into bits
- 2 tbsp. lime juice

Directions:

1. Pour all ingredients into a blender. Blend for 30 seconds at a time until the mixture is smooth.
2. You may dilute with water to derive the desired thickness.

Nutrition: Calories 125, Protein 24g, Sugar 10g, Fiber 19g

30 Day Meal Plan

Days	Breakfast	Lunch	Dinner	Dessert
1	Banana Smoothie	Antipasto On a Stick	Ginger And Spring Egg Drop Soup	Low-Fodmap Brownies
2	Berry Smoothie	Crab And Miso Soup	Turkey Burgers With Spinach	Low-Fodmap Lemon Bar
3	Breakfast Wrap	Mexican Lime Chicken	Carrot Tomato Soup	Low-Fodmap Butterscotch
4	Cinnamon Almond Crepes	Pad Thai Noodles	Lemony Feta and Sweet Potato Mash	Low-Fodmap Cookies
5	Cranberry Orange Smoothie	Parmesan Coated Wings	Salmon Cakes And Lemony Herb Aioli	Low-Fodmap Cupcake
6	French Toast	Pina Colada Bites	Chicken Avocado and Raspberry Salad	Almost Classic Hummus
7	Green Hibiscus Smoothie	Savory Chicken and Rice Muffins	Cucumber Sesame Salad	Carrot Dip
8	Hearty Oatmeal	Tuesday Tacos	Vegetable Noodle Miso Soup	Citrusy Salsa
9	Immune Boosting Smoothie	Turkey Burgers With Spinach and Feta	Eggs In Squash Rings	Chia Strawberry Popsicles
10	Peanut Butter and Banana Overnight Oats	Minestrone	Pot Beef Stew	Blueberry Sorbet
11	Scrambled Tofu	Cheesy Chicken Fritters	Chicken Ratatouille	Strawberry Sorbet
12	Sweet Potato Toast	Crispy Falafel	Low Fodmap Scampi	Strawberry Gummies
13	Turkey Sausage Patties	Chicken Alfredo Pasta Bake	Salmon With Basil-Caper Pesto	Strawberry Ice Cream
14	Egg Wraps	Rosemary Beef Stew	Orange Chicken and Broccoli Bowl	Coconut Whipped Cream
15	Tropical Fruit Salad	Shrimp With Beans	Low Fodmap Chili Mac	Peppermint Patties
16	Pineapple-Coconut Smoothie	Broccoli Fritters	Turkey Burgers	Kiwi Yogurt Freezer Bars
17	Pesto Eggs Rice Bowl	Roasted Broccoli	Sticky Pork Ribs	Easy Trail Mix
18	Flourless Banana Cinnamon Pancakes	Roasted Maple Carrots	Whole Roast Fish	Caramel Sauce

19	Flourless Vegan Banana Peanut Butter Pancakes	Sweet & Tangy Green Beans	Potato Eggplant Curry	Minty Melon Mélange
20	Peanut Butter Bowl	Easy Lemon Chicken	Thai Curry Tofu and Green Beans	Banana Coconut Nice Cream
21	Melon And Berry Compote	Flavorful Greek Chicken	Roast Beef Hash	Salted Caramel Fondue
22	Scrambled Eggs	Herb-Stuffed Pork Loin Roast	Grilled Swordfish with Tomato Olive Salsa	Banana Cookie Dough Nice Cream
23	Summer Berry Smoothie	Low Fodmap Stuffing	Turkey Shepherd's Pie	Broiled Spiced Orange
24	Melon And Yogurt Parfait	Chili Coconut Crusted Fish	Coconut Tofu Curry	Banana Ice Cream
25	Amaranth Breakfast	Spicy Chicken Drumsticks	Lamb Curry	Coconut Cinnamon Popcorn
26	Banana Toast	Paprika Calamari with Garden Salad	Parmesan Crusted Flounder	Roasted Pumpkin Seeds
27	Quinoa Tofu Scramble	Chili Salmon With Cilantro Salad	Four Cheese Baked Penne with Greens and Tomatoes	Chia Pudding
28	Bacon-Jalapeño Egg Cups	Dukkah-Crusted Snapper	Baked Rice with Olives, Feta and Pomegranate	Sweet And Savory Popcorn
29	Fish Wallpaper with Green Bean Salad	Balsamic Sesame Swordfish	Stuffed Red Peppers with Quinoa and Zucchini	Pineapple, Yogurt on Rice Cakes
30	Tomato And Basil Frittata	Lemon-Oregano Chicken Drumsticks	Cilantro Lime Rice	Prosciutto-Wrapped Cantaloupe

Conclusion

The low-FODMAP diet can benefit individuals in a number of ways. One of the main benefits is the effect on digestion, especially for those who suffer from specific disorders that impact digestion. Those on a diet often experience less gas, bloating, and abdominal pain. Relief from these symptoms leads to some other benefits.

When bloating decreases, there is a physical difference, and individuals will feel their clothes fit better, and confidence will increase. With a decrease in constipation and diarrhea, there will be less stress when going into social situations because their worry about making a run to the bathroom is minimal. This decrease in stress will have a positive effect on everyday life, from the mood to improvements in the workplace to better relationships (Paul, 2017).

Food is used to fuel our bodies. With every bite taken, the body tries to break down the food into nutrients that can be used. For these nutrients to be absorbed, the body has to use enzymes to break them down small enough to enter the bloodstream. Enzymes are what are known as catalysts. Catalysts help start changes or speed up slow changes.

During digestion, enzymes break down the bonds between molecules. Each enzyme is unique and breaks down one type of compound. An example of this is the enzyme galactose, which breaks down glucose. The tension put onto the compound by an enzyme causes it to break apart into parts that are small enough to enter the bloodstream.

From the moment you take your first bite of food, enzymes are working on breaking the food down; the enzymes in your saliva help in the breakdown of carbohydrates and proteins. As the food works its way into your digestive system, the different enzymes will work together to break down the nutrients that are needed by the body. Enzymes are a natural part of the digestive system and have many benefits. There are not many human-made enzymes that can be bought. This is why certain foods are beneficial when included in a diet.

As a whole, the low-FODMAP diet has many benefits. These extend to every area of an individual's life. By following the diet, uncomfortable digestion symptoms can be minimized or eliminated, and healthy functioning can be restored. This leads to a healthier life.

While there are benefits to a low-FODMAP diet, as with any diet, there are a few risks. The major one is nutritional deficiency, but there are other concerns. One of the biggest risks is the inappropriate use of the diet. Some will use the diet to diagnose gluten sensitivity when there are no digestive symptoms present.

When planning to start this diet, it is recommended to work with a healthcare professional, specifically a dietician, since not everyone will respond well to food restrictions. This is especially crucial for those with food allergies or restrictions due to health conditions. Some changes in the low-FODMAP diet may not mix well with allergies or dietary restrictions, and a dietician or medical professional can assist with accommodating these requirements.

Starting any diet comes with challenges that need to be worked out. One challenge is not to start changing everything in one swoop. If you are on medications or supplements, it is not ideal to start changing everything at the same time. Doing this can cause negative reactions and lead to more serious symptoms. Working with professionals gives your body the best chance of having a positive reaction to the changes being made.

Many people become frustrated and stop a diet because they do not see any immediate results. It is never good to start a change, such as a diet with the expectation of seeing improvements after a day or two, and the low-FODMAP diet is no exception. While some will feel changes sooner, those who do not may get frustrated and give up too soon.

When starting this diet to reduce IBS symptoms, it is important to set boundaries. Not everyone around you will understand the struggle you face with IBS and its symptoms. This is where boundaries are important as they will aid in the success of the diet. The benefits of eating a low-FODMAP diet will be for nothing if others can walk in and destroy all your progress. Other people will probably need time to process and respond when you tell them about your struggle because they may not understand why you are cutting different food items from your diet.

You also need to set boundaries for yourself; to benefit fully from this diet, you cannot let people dictate what you can or cannot eat. Do not be afraid to ask people around you for help and support. By talking to others and ensuring those you live with do not feel deprived of any food they enjoy, you will ensure that you not only reap the benefits of eating low-FODMAP but that those around you do too.

If you enjoyed this book, I encourage you to go to the Amazon page and leave a positive review. This way, you will help my book be seen by other people.

If you would like, you can receive also one of my cookbooks, which you will find on my site, as a gift.

To do so is very simple. Using this link, post a review of this book and send me a simple screenshot of the post you made on Amazon directly to my email:

scarrett.diet@outlook.com.

I will immediately respond by sending you the book you want.

If, on the other hand, you prefer to communicate with me directly, I invite you then to visit my site and contact me personally by mail or on suzannescarrett.com.

Have a good life and good cooking. I wish you much joy and serenity.

Made in United States
Orlando, FL
12 March 2023